D1297637

AUGUSTUS
AND THE GREEK
WORLD

Oxford University Press, Amen House, London E.C.4

GLASGOW NEW YORK TORONTO MELBOURNE WELLINGTON
BOMBAY CALCUTTA MADRAS KARACHI LAHORE DACCA
CAPE TOWN SALISBURY NAIROBI IBADAN ACCRA
KUALA LUMPUR HONG KONG

AUGUSTUS

AND THE GREEK WORLD

G. W. BOWERSOCK

OXFORD
AT THE CLARENDON PRESS
1965

MANIBUS PATRIS
ET MATRI

PREFACE

FOR its day (1890) *The Greek World under Roman Sway* by Professor Mahaffy was admirable; and Ludwig Hahn's *Rom und Romanismus im griechisch-römischen Osten*, published early in this century, made valuable contributions to the understanding of Rome and the East generally. But these books were never adequate for an appreciation of any closely defined period of Roman history, especially one so crucial as the Augustan Principate. Now they are also out of date. New evidence is still appearing, and the brilliant researches of Conrad Cichorius, Louis Robert, Michael Rostovtzeff, and Sir Ronald Syme have revealed the importance of applying new techniques to the study of Roman relations with the Greek-speaking peoples. The studies of these four men are the foundation of this book.

The principal theme of the following pages is the process of consolidation of the Graeco-Roman world under the first Princeps. The subject has been approached along lines relatively unexplored for this period. No attempt has been made to furnish a narrative account of familiar history, since the reign of Augustus is too well known. There is no examination here of the Augustan East province by province; nor have Rome's dealings with Parthia and Armenia been deemed relevant: so extensive and difficult a subject, though connected with the present one, requires independent treatment. In general, topics—however fascinating and important—which do not somehow illuminate the main theme for the period under study have perforce been omitted.

A great many scholars have helped me at various times. Above all, I am indebted to Professor Syme for encouragement and guidance; his prodigious and profound understanding of the Roman Empire has been a constant inspiration. I am also grateful to my friend and teacher, Mr. Russell Meiggs, for continuing interest. Among others in Oxford who have assisted me in matters of substance I should like particularly to thank Mr. E. W. Gray, Mrs. M. I. Henderson, Dr. B. M. Levick, and Dr. F. G. B. Millar. I have had valuable information from Athens through the courtesy of Mr. H. S. Robinson and Mr. E. Vanderpool. In America the late Professor A. D. Nock of Harvard discussed several complex topics with me. Mr. C. P. Jones has unselfishly aided me throughout. Finally, I wish to express my appreciation to the Master and Fellows of Balliol College, Oxford, as well as to the Department of the Classics at Harvard and the Master of Eliot House, for providing comfortable and congenial environments for the preparation of this work.

G. W. B.

Eliot House
December 1964

CONTENTS

ABBREVIATIONS

AE	*L'Année épigraphique*
AJP	*American Journal of Philology*
Ant. Class.	*L'Antiquité classique*
Arch. Eph.	Ἀρχαιολογικὴ Ἐφημερίς
Ath. Mitt.	*Mitteilungen des Deutschen Archäologischen Instituts, Athenische Abteilung*
BCH	*Bulletin de correspondance hellénique*
BMC	*Catalogue of Coins in the British Museum*
Broughton, *MRR*	T. R. S. Broughton, *Magistrates of the Roman Republic* (1951)
CAH	*Cambridge Ancient History*
Cichorius, *RS*	C. Cichorius, *Römische Studien* (1922)
CIG	*Corpus Inscriptionum Graecarum*
CIL	*Corpus Inscriptionum Latinarum*
CP	*Classical Philology*
CQ	*Classical Quarterly*
CR	*Classical Review*
EE	*Ephemeris Epigraphica*
E–J²	Ehrenberg and Jones, *Documents illustrating the Reigns of Augustus and Tiberius* (Second Edition, 1955).
FGH	Jacoby, *Die Fragmente der griechischen Historiker*
Grant, *FITA*	M. Grant, *From Imperium to Auctoritas* (1946)
HSCP	*Harvard Studies in Classical Philology*
Head, *HN²*	B. V. Head, *Historia Numorum* (Second Edition, 1911)
Hesp.	*Hesperia*
Hist.	*Historia*
IG	*Inscriptiones Graecae*
IGR	*Inscriptiones Graecae ad Res Romanas Pertinentes*
ILS	Dessau, *Inscriptiones Latinae Selectae*
JHS	*Journal of Hellenic Studies*
Jones, *CERP*	A. H. M. Jones, *The Cities of the Eastern Roman Provinces* (1937)
Jones, *GC*	A. H. M. Jones, *The Greek City* (1940)

JRS	*Journal of Roman Studies*
Magie, *RRAM*	D. Magie, *Roman Rule in Asia Minor* (1950)
MAMA	*Monumenta Asiae Minoris Antiqua*
OGIS	Dittenberger, *Orientis Graeci Inscriptiones Selectae*
PBSA	*Papers of the British School at Athens*
PBSR	*Papers of the British School at Rome*
PIR	*Prosopographia Imperii Romani* (*PIR*² referring to available volumes of the Second Edition)
P–W	Pauly–Wissowa–Kroll, *Real-Encyclopädie*
REA	*Revue des études anciennes*
REG	*Revue des études grecques*
Rev. Arch.	*Revue archéologique*
Rostovtzeff, *SEHHW*	M. Rostovtzeff, *Social and Economic History of the Hellenistic World* (1941)
Rostovtzeff, *SEHRE*²	M. Rostovtzeff, *Social and Economic History of the Roman Empire* (Second Edition, ed. P. M. Fraser, 1957)
SEG	*Supplementum Epigraphicum Graecum*
*SIG*³	Dittenberger, *Sylloge Inscriptionum Graecarum* (Third Edition)
TAPA	*Transactions of the American Philological Association*
Waddington	Le Bas–Waddington, *Inscriptions grecques et latines*, vol. 3
Waddington, *Recueil*²	Waddington–Babelon–Reinach, *Recueil général des monnaies grecques d'Asie Mineure* (Second Edition, 1925)

All other abbreviations, including those for excavation reports (e.g. *Corinth, Sardis*), should be clear enough without further expansion

I

THE LATE REPUBLICAN
BACKGROUND

THE last decades of the Republic were a time of oppression and revolt in the East. Historical authors, ancient and modern, unfold a tale of Roman ambition and rapacity. Prophecies of Rome's doom fell on receptive ears;[1] improvement and reform, though attempted, met with insuperable obstacles. The military exploits of Sulla, Lucullus, and Pompey dominated the age, until the Republic spent itself in violence in alien parts—at Pharsalus, Philippi, and Actium. It is not difficult to understand why the peoples of Asia massacred some eighty thousand Roman citizens in one day at the bidding of Mithridates Eupator;[2] it is less clear why such horrors were not repeated. Only a fresh approach to the subject will yield an answer: the familiar stories of strategy, campaigning, and imperialist design must be set aside for a time. Mutual interests between men of the East and West were the solid and genuine foundation of Rome's eastern empire, and Augustus was well aware of that fact.[3]

---

[1] *Orac. Sibyll.*, Book III: on the date and character of these anti-Roman documents, H. Fuchs, *Der geistige Widerstand gegen Rom in der antiken Welt* (1938), pp. 30–36. Cf. Cicero (in oratory) on the unpopularity of Rome in the provinces: *de Imp. Pomp.* 65, Difficile est dictu, Quirites, quanto in odio simus apud exteras nationes . . .; *II Verr.* 3. 207, Lugent omnes provinciae, queruntur omnes liberi populi, regna denique omnia de nostris cupiditatibus et iniuriis expostulant.

[2] Memnon, *FGH* iii. B. 434, 22. 9; Val. Max. 9. 2. *ext.* 3. Plut. *Sull.* 24. 4 gives a figure of 150,000 massacred, doubtless an exaggeration from Sulla's memoirs.

[3] See the judicious remarks of E. W. Gray in his review of Magie, *RRAM*, *JRS* 42 (1952), 123: 'One would welcome a fresh approach from an angle which M. largely ignores—a social-political study of *Asia provincia*, an examination of the relations between members of the local aristocracies in the Greek cities and the Roman governing class, the informal workings of the patronus–clientela relationship, the open conspiracy in which Greek and Roman aristocracies found a bond of sympathy and material interest. . . . In this matter there is unbroken development through Republic and Principate.'

The movement of Roman armies across the East, on their way against the forces of Pontus or against one another, brought hardship and fear to the native population; money, food, supplies, sometimes ships had to be provided,[1] and local citizens had to house an itinerant soldiery whose propensities in wartime were only too well known.[2] Meanwhile, in the intervals of relative peace, the Roman tax-collectors went about their work with a greed and inhumanity bred of the hope of personal profit. Roman pro-magistrates, however well intentioned some may have been, served in their provinces for too short a time to effect any substantial improvements in organization and administration. But a network of personal connexions between influential Greeks and eminent Romans imparted stability to the empire by providing advantages to both sides. Provincials could secure relief from oppression through diplomatic intercession, and Rome could cultivate loyalty in the provinces. This pattern of personal relationships was the secret of Roman rule in the East, no less under the Principate than the Republic.

The Principate inevitably brought certain modifications in the diplomatic system, but the principle remained the same. It was simply that under dynastic rule it was easier to see with whom connexions had to be established. Previously, during the civil struggles of the dying Republic, the shifts in allegiance among various Roman patrons had created an almost insoluble problem for many Greeks. Those who espoused the cause of patrons who lost could expect to suffer for it. The dilemma was exemplified at Rhodes after the murder of Julius Caesar, when that island remained faithful to the heirs in the face of the fugitive tyrannicides and was obliged to send to Cassius his old teacher Archelaus to plead for its survival.[3] The end of civil war and the establishment of a ruling house removed such obstructions to smooth diplomacy.

Education and culture distinguished the Greeks who were close to great Romans of the late Republic. Polybius had set the example by his intimacy with Scipio Aemilianus. The

---

[1] On all this: Rostovtzeff, *SEHHW* iii. 1561. Ships: Cic. *II Verr.* 1. 89; *pro Flacc.* 14. 33.
[2] Cf. Catullus 62, l. 24.   [3] App. *BC* 4. 65–67.

philosopher Panaetius, from an eminent and wealthy Rhodian family, was later to be found in the circle of Scipio. And Panaetius' pupil, the prolific Poseidonius, became a friend of Pompey the Great.[1] These three Greek men of letters inaugurated that gradual but inevitable cultural fusion of East and West which transformed the character of the Roman empire. They were admirers and supporters of the old Roman aristocracy; and if they perceived a decline in Roman affairs, it was precisely because of their devotion to the conservatism of the Roman upper class. Poseidonius witnessed the chaotic last century of the Republic: his sympathy was not with the Gracchi or with the slaves who revolted.[2] The growth and balance of a Graeco-Roman world depended upon ties like those between Polybius and Scipio or Poseidonius and Pompey. The same ties also brought Greeks into the civil struggles of late republican Rome; that was why, by contrast, diplomacy under the Principate seemed much easier.

Many of the first-century imperatores acquired on their campaigns cultured easterners whom they maintained in positions of trust throughout their careers. Such was the freedman of Sulla, Cornelius Epicadus, who assisted in the augural games and subsequently added the final book to his master's unfinished autobiography.[3] The confidant of Pompey was an historian, Theophanes of Mytilene.[4] Marcus Cato took back with him to Rome the chief librarian of Pergamum,[5] while L. Calpurnius Piso, the consul of 58 B.C., was accompanied during his governorship of Macedonia by a former teacher, the great Epicurean Philodemus.[6] Lucullus had as his intimate friend the founder of the Fifth Academy and teacher of Cicero and

[1] On Panaetius' family, cf. Strabo 655 and *SIG*[3] 725a. On Poseidonius: Reinhardt, *P–W* 22. 558 ff., and below, p. 5.

[2] Poseidonius on the Gracchi, esp. Diod. 34. 7. 3 and 34/35. 25. 1. On the slaves, *FGH* ii. A. 87. F. 108. Tiberius Gracchus himself is said to have fallen under Greek influence of a liberal kind: Plut. *Tib. Gracch.* 8; Cic. *Brut.* 104. And Tiberius had his own eastern clients, inherited from his father: Badian, *Foreign Clientelae* (1958), pp. 173–4. On the sources of Greek opposition to Roman rule, cf. chapter VIII below.

[3] Suet. *de Gramm.* 12.   [4] *FGH* ii. B. 188.

[5] Strabo 674; Plut. *Cat. Min.* 16.

[6] Cic. *in Pis.* 68; *Anth. Pal.* vi. 349. The inference was made by Cichorius, *RS*, pp. 295 f.; it is questioned by R. G. M. Nisbet, edition of the *in Pisonem* (1961), p. 183.

Brutus, Antiochus of Ascalon.[1] Favoured and learned Greeks of this kind could instruct a Roman in the habits and predilections of the East, prevent them from making disastrous errors, and guide them in influencing local opinions.

Beside furnishing advice, these men were valuable chroniclers of the deeds of their patrons for the Greek public; in other words, they were useful instruments of propaganda. The Greek Archias narrated the campaigns of Lucullus, and Theophanes and Poseidonius recorded the exploits of Pompey.[2] Diodotus the Stoic wanted to write a history of Julius Caesar in Greek; Empylus of Rhodes, the intimate of Brutus, produced an account of Caesar's assassination in time for Cicero to read it before he died.[3] There were also eminent Romans who had been educated under Greek professors and did not hesitate themselves to write for Greek readers about Roman affairs. Lucullus' history of the Marsic War was in Greek, though that general took care to insert a few barbarisms to show that he was really a Roman.[4] Cicero refused to do such a thing when he produced a Greek account of his own consulship.[4] It will be seen that Augustus, too, perceived the importance of providing, for the Greek public, literature concerning both Rome and himself.

But most of the cultivated Greeks who appeared regularly in the retinues of Roman luminaries did not use their good offices in the interests of particular Greek communities. Theophanes of Mytilene was an exception: he secured freedom for his city from Pompey, despite its record of stout resistance to Rome in the eighties. Mytilene was grateful to its influential citizen, and deified him.[5] But even if the other confidants and panegyrists did not secure favours for individual cities, theirs was a vital role: they offered guidance in respect to peoples they understood and made known among them the ways of

---

[1] Plut. *Lucull.* 28. 7; Cic. *Acad. Pr.* 2. 61 (where Syria is perhaps an error for Mesopotamia: Magie, *RRAM* ii. 1217).

[2] Cic. *pro Arch.* 21; cf. *ad Att.* 1. 16. 15 (Archias). *FGH* ii. B. 188 (Theophanes). Strabo 492 (Poseidonius).

[3] *FGH* ii. B. 191.

[4] Cic. *ad Att.* i. 19. 10. Rutilius Rufus also wrote a Roman history in Greek (Athenaeus 168ε), but he was living as an embittered exile in the East, at Mytilene and then at Smyrna (Dio fr. 97. 3–4).

[5] Tac. *Ann.* 6. 18. *SIG*³ 753. Head, *HN*² 563.

the conqueror. These Greeks of the late Republic carried on the task which Polybius had begun with signal success and without compromising himself overmuch. In so far as the Greek world ever came to accept the rule of Rome, these learned confidants must receive a portion of the credit.

However, the allegiance and sympathy of Greeks residing in the East were still more important than the undoubted fidelity of those who had been uprooted. There had to be Roman partisans among the Greeks themselves. Where it was possible, Rome looked again for help to the educated men of the East, rhetors and professors. Many of these, by virtue of their superior knowledge and agile minds, attained a political power that resembled a benevolent tyranny. Hence the late republican East is seen, largely from the pages of Strabo, to have produced a substantial group of influential persons who were simultaneously rhetors and politicians, not to say tyrants. Some were trustworthy, others unscrupulous; but they could not be ignored. The Maecenas of Cassius Dio is made to warn Augustus that he should not think all philosophers so politically responsible as those of whom he had already had experience: 'for infinite harm, both to communities and to individuals, is worked by certain men who use this profession only as a screen'.[1]

The names of politically active rhetors are preserved from the time of the Mithridatic Wars. The Stoic Poseidonius was one: he served as a prytanis at Rhodes and late in the year 87 B.C. went on an embassy to Rome, where he met the ageing Marius.[2] At Sardis, the distinguished Diodorus Zonas encouraged resistance against Mithridates and detached cities from his cause. A younger rhetor of the same family was a friend of Strabo and the author of historical works and verses.[3] At Antioch on the Maeander there flourished the sophist Diotrephes, called by Strabo the greatest rhetor of his time.[4] This man was the teacher of Hybreas of Mylasa, who returned from instruction at Antioch to assume at once a magistracy in his own city.[5] Hybreas was one of two rhetors at Mylasa; the other was Euthydemus, who came from a wealthy

---

[1] Dio 52. 36. 4.   [2] Strabo 316 (prytanis). Plut. *Mar.* 45.
[3] Strabo 628.   [4] Id. 630 and 659.   [5] Id. 659.

local family.[1] Hybreas' allegiance to Rome was amply displayed during the invasion of Labienus 'Parthicus', and his city received praise and favour for resistance. After Euthydemus' death, Hybreas ruled alone; he was awarded the Roman citizenship and became a high priest of Augustus.[2] At Laodicea there was another powerful rhetor who held out against Labienus. He was Zeno, whose son, Polemo, was destined to become the client king of Pontus and the head of the most influential and widely dispersed royal house in the East.[3]

Rome was fortunate in having on her side such learned and astute men as these. Yet inevitably she failed to secure the support of all the great rhetors: a few, at least, were open partisans of Mithridates, perhaps opportunists less adept than others at foretelling the future. Diodorus of Adramyttium, a philosopher of the Academy, caused the massacre of all the councillors of his city in deference to Mithridates, while another rhetor of Adramyttium spoke in the senate at Rome to defend the province of Asia against the charge of Mithridatism.[4] Two philosophers brought over the city of Athens to Mithridates in 88 B.C.[5] Metrodorus of Scepsis was another politically minded rhetor who sought advancement from the Pontic king: he passed, says Strabo, from the philosophic to the political life. He also wrote history in a new and striking style. For a time Metrodorus dispensed justice in the service of Mithridates until he succumbed to the intrigues of enemies at the court.[6]

Although professorial politicians were useful to Rome (as were some also to Mithridates), there were obviously not enough of them. Still further support for Rome lay in the

---

[1] Strabo 659.

[2] L. Robert, *REG* 72 (1959), p. 176, no. 107a. In *Hellenica* 8 (1950), 95–96, M. Robert has reported a course of his in Paris on Hybreas. A Hybreas is named on a coin as a monetary official at Mylasa: A. Akarca, *Les Monnaies grecques de Mylasa* (Paris, 1959), p. 28.

[3] Strabo 578 and 660. On Zeno's posterity, see chapter IV, p. 51 and p. 53.

[4] Strabo 614.

[5] Athenion and Aristion: on the former, Poseidonius, *FGH* ii. A. 87. F. 36; on the latter, Plut. *Sull.* 11–13, Paus. 1. 20. 5, and other references in Greenidge–Clay[2] (rev. Gray), p. 170 and p. 285 (coins). The best account is still Ferguson, *Hellenistic Athens* (1911), pp. 440–51, rejecting the view that Athenion and Aristion are the same man. Cf. below, p. 102, n. 2, and p. 103. n. 1.

[6] Strabo 609–10; Plut. *Lucull.* 22. *FGH* ii. B. 184.

aristocracies of the greater eastern cities where there could be found men who were both decently cultivated and affluent, constituting a natural extension of that class of rhetors which included the wealthy Euthydemus of Mylasa. Nor should it be forgotten that the leading citizen of Laodicea before Zeno was a certain Hieron who bequeathed more than two thousand talents to his city.[1] It was natural for Rome to favour the upper classes in view of the aristocratic character of her own government. There has never been any doubt that it was Roman policy to encourage oligarchic factions and, when possible, to establish oligarchic, or at least timocratic, constitutions.[2] When Cicero defended Flaccus in 59 B.C., he deemed worthless the testimony of the witnesses against Flaccus on the grounds of their low estate and sordid origins:[3] Rome did not deal with such Greeks, nor did they have much love for Rome. After denigrating the witnesses for the prosecution, Cicero cried out for Rome's true friends in the East, the Greeks of the upper classes with money and prestige. 'Where were those Pythodori', he asked, 'those Archedemi and Epigoni, not only known to us but nobles among their own people?'[4]

These were the persons on whom Rome relied, with whom the great imperatores forged personal links for mutual advantage. In securing bastions of Roman sentiment throughout the East, the generals at the same time enlarged their vital clientelae. The favoured natives obtained privileges for their cities and honours for themselves. The system worked, commonly for several generations in the same families. When Cicero's Flaccus or Julius Caesar himself arrived in the East, their names were already familiar there from the activities of

---

[1] Strabo 578.

[2] Livy 35. 34. 3: Inter omnes constabat, in civitatibus principes et optimum quemque Romanae societatis esse et praesenti statu gaudere, multitudinem et quorum res non ex sententia ipsorum essent, omnia novare velle. Paus. 7. 16. 9: (ὁ Μόμμιος) δημοκρατίας μὲν κατέπαυε, καθίστατο δὲ ἀπὸ τιμημάτων τὰς ἀρχάς. Also cf. Livy 34. 51. 6 (Flamininus in Thessaly) and Cic. ad Quint. Frat. 1. 1. 8. 25. Excellent are Ferguson, Hellenistic Athens (1911), pp. 427–8, and Jones, GC, pp. 170–1 on this matter. See chapter VIII below.

[3] e.g., Cic. pro Flacc. 22. 52: Trallianos Maeandrio causam publicam commisisse, homini egenti, sordido, sine honore, sine existimatione, sine censu. Cf. ibid. 4. 9.

[4] Ibid. 22. 52. Tralles is under discussion in this passage, and the exact spelling of the names after Pythodori is uncertain.

their antecedents.[1] And, on the eastern side, the fortunes of the family of Pythodorus of Tralles—a house invoked by Cicero in 59—are a marvel of ever-increasing power and influence.

Chaeremon, the father of Pythodorus, came from Nysa and was a staunch supporter of Rome at the time of Mithridates. He offered sixty thousand modii of flour as a gift to the army of C. Cassius in 88 B.C., and Mithridates himself was moved to write two letters protesting against the pro-Roman activities of Chaeremon and his son.[2] Chaeremon's son, Pythodorus, migrated to Tralles, a larger and more important city, where he became one of the leading citizens and a friend of Pompey. He possessed property valued at more than two thousand talents, which was confiscated by Caesar after Pharsalus. But the affluent Pythodorus was undaunted: he bought the land back from Caesar,[3] and his son, perhaps an adherent of Antony, produced a daughter who married into the house of Zeno of Laodicea and became queen of Pontus.[4]

Some of Caesar's aristocratic partisans can also be identified. It can safely be assumed that Priene, and in particular the family of Crates in that city, were devoted to the name of Caesar, inasmuch as Crates had secured help from Caesar's father, when he governed Asia, against the abuses of publicans.[5] And another kinsman of Caesar was remembered for a similar service at Ilium.[6] In 76 B.C. the Milesian Epicrates supplied funds for Caesar's ransom, in return for which he became a Roman citizen; his family continued in wealth and favour into the Principate.[7] Caesar also had friends at Cnidos:

[1] Cic. pro Flacc. 23. 55–56 (L. Valerius Flaccus, cos. suff. 86 B.C.); Inschrift. v. Magnesia, nos. 144–6 (also Flaccus). IGR 4. 970 = JRS 44 (1954), 67 (M) from Samos (C. Julius Caesar); Inschrift. v. Priene, no. 111 (C. Julius Caesar). OGIS 440 from Ilium (L. Julius Caesar, cos. 90 B.C.). See also IGR 4. 194.

[2] SIG³ 741. Cf. Rostovtzeff, SEHHW ii. 821.   [3] Strabo 649.

[4] Id. 555–6 and 649. The view of Mommsen that OGIS 377 revealed Antony's own daughter as the bride of the younger Pythodorus must be rejected: cf. Dessau, EE 9. 691 ff. and Magie, RRAM ii. 1130, n. 60. From the name of the great rhetor of the second century A.D., M. Antonius Polemo, it would appear that the Laodicean family into which Pythodorus married had taken the side of Antony. And one should not overlook Plutarch's contemporary, Chaeremonianus of Tralles (Plut. Quaest. Conviv. 2. 7).

[5] Inschrift. v. Priene, no. 111.   [6] OGIS 440 (L. Caesar, cos. 90).

[7] Polyaen. 8. 23. 1 (Epicrates). On Epicrates' son, C. Julius Apollonius, and Apollonius' sons, Eucrates and Epicrates: Milet i. 2, pp. 107 ff., nos. 6, 7, and

Callistus and the mythologist Theopompus.[1] It was to favour
Theopompus that Caesar granted freedom to Cnidos;[2] Theopompus also interceded with his patron on behalf of Delphi,
Rhodes, and Laodicea.[3] It was not fortuitous that the decree
which honoured Caesar's lieutenant Q. Fufius Calenus at
Delphi was engraved on the Treasury of the Cnidians. Calenus
was at Delphi in 48, and both Callistus and Theopompus were
honoured there in the same year.[4] If Caesar had heeded the
timely warning of Theopompus' son Artemidorus on the Ides
of March, he might have avoided assassination on that day.[5]

Another Caesarian partisan of no small interest was Mithridates of Pergamum, the grandson of a Galatian tetrarch.[6] He
served on embassies to Caesar on behalf of his city and distinguished himself by his loyalty at the time of the Alexandrian
War, when he came to the rescue of his besieged patron.[7]
Mithridates had his reward in the form of the tetrarchate of the
Trocmi and a kingdom in the Crimea.[8] An inscription discloses
the fact that Mithridates had been priest of Dionysus Cathe-
gemon at Pergamum: hence the miracle at Pergamum on the
day of the battle at Pharsalus can be understood, for it was from
the inmost shrine of Dionysus that the sounds of tympana and
cymbals were heard.[9] There were other miracles on the same
day at Elis, Tralles, and Syrian Antioch, for which unnamed
partisans of Caesar in those cities were no doubt responsible.[10]

15. Apollonius was connected with the first Sebasteion at Miletus (inscription no. 7).

[1] On Callistus, cf. G. Daux, *Delphes au II* et au I*er* *siècle* (1936), p. 408. On
Theopompus: G. Hirschfeld, *JHS* 7 (1886), 286 ff.

[2] Plut. *Caes.* 48. See also the treaty between Rome and Cnidos, mentioning
both Theopompus and his son Artemidorus: *Mélanges Cagnat* (1912), 53.

[3] *SIG*³ 761 C (Delphi); *IG* xii. 1. 90 (Rhodes); *BMC* iv. 801 (Laodicea).

[4] Calenus at Delphi: Caes. *BC* 3. 56. The decree: *Fouilles de Delphes* iii. 1.
318. *SIG*³ 761 A and B (Callistus), C (Theopompus). Cf. A. E. Raubitschek,
JRS 44 (1954) 74–75. [5] Plut. *Caes.* 65.

[6] See especially Hepding, *Ath. Mitt.* 34 (1909), 329 ff., and Segrè, *Athenaeum*
16 (1938), 119 ff. Also Rostovtzeff, *SEHHW* ii. 821–2.

[7] *Bell. Alex.* 26 ff.: Dio 42. 41; Jos. *BJ* 1. 187 ff., *AJ* 14. 128 ff.

[8] *Bell. Alex.* 78. 2–3; Strabo 625; App. *Mithr.* 121; Dio 42. 48. 4. See also
Cic. *de Div.* 1. 27 and 2. 79, *Philipp.* 2. 94.

[9] The inscription is republished and interpreted in this way by Segrè,
Athenaeum 16 (1938), 119 ff. The report of the Pergamum miracle in Caes. *BC* 3.
105 should be preferred to the less precise account in Dio 41. 61. 3.

[10] Caes. *BC* 3. 105 (the other miracles). For this interpretation, cf. E. W.
Gray, *JRS* 42 (1952), 123.

Antony naturally had his eastern intimates, useful in at-
tending to that portion of empire which fell to him under the
Triumvirate. Names can be recovered, as well as professions
which reflect the Hellenic tastes of the patron. Anaxenor,
a lyre-player from Magnesia, collected taxes in Asia; there
were the flute-player Xanthus and the dancer Metrodorus.[1]
A Greek rhetorician introduced Antony to the highly influential Alexas of Laodicea.[2] In Corinth Antony established
a Greek freedman as his agent.[3] But it would be wrong to
conclude that personal interest more than prudence dictated
Antony's diplomatic policy: the whole of his settlement of the
client kingdoms betrays a remarkable understanding of the
East.[4] There was nothing wrong with artistic friends.

Even where relations of patron and client cannot be worked
out in detail from available evidence, the flood of embassies in
the late Republic amply attests the importance of personal
contact between influential provincials and Romans in pre-
serving some kind of equilibrium in the East. The successful
intercession of Diodorus Pasparus with Roman magistrates in
the second century brought him high honours in his own city,
Pergamum.[5] In addition to Crates, the city of Priene saw
fit to honour several other citizens for their negotiations with
Romans: Moschion, Herodes, Zosimus, Heracleitus.[6] A certain wealthy citizen of Istros, Aristagoras, was praised for his
benefactions, which included the use of his private funds for
public purposes and numerous embassies on behalf of the city.[7]
Inscriptions from Epidaurus record repeated negotiations, and
the names of affluent envoys like Archelochus and Euanthes.[8]

---

[1] Anaxenor: Plut. *Ant.* 24; Strabo 648; *SIG*³ 766. Xanthus and Metrodorus:
Plut. *Ant.* 24.

[2] Plut. *Ant.* 72: The rhetorician was Timagenes.

[3] Plut. *Ant.* 67: Theophilus, father of Antony's freedman Hipparchus (cf.
Plut. *Ant.* 73), was ὁ ἐν Κορίνθῳ διοικητής.

[4] See chapter IV; also H. Buchheim, *Die Orientpolitik des Triumvirn M.
Antonius* (1960).

[5] *IGR* 4. 292, 293, 294. Cf. L. Robert, *Études Anat.* (1937), 45 ff.

[6] *Inschrift v. Priene*, nos. 108 (Moschion), 109 (Herodes), 112–14 (Zosimus),
117 (Heracleitus).

[7] *SIG*³ 708. Pippidi has dated this document to the second half of the first
century B.C.: *Epigraphische Beiträge zur Geschichte Histrias* (1962) 89 ff.

[8] *IG* iv². 64 (several Epidaurians); *IG* iv². 63 (Archelochus) and 66 (Euanthes).

About the same time, Iollas of Sardis was accomplishing embassies with success and holding various public offices at his own expense; not surprisingly Iollas was a priest of Rome.[1] New documents from Thasos have revealed a hitherto unknown Greek diplomat, Dionysodorus the Thasian, an intermediary with Roman magistrates on several occasions during the First Mithridatic War; he used his good offices in the interests of Assos, Lampsacus, and Rhodes, all of which honoured him in return.[2] Then there was the rich Acornion of Dionysopolis, who in the closing decade of the Republic gave himself unsparingly to embassies for his city, endured danger without trepidation, and bore much at his own expense.[3]

After Pharsalus it was natural that the traffic in embassies should be greater than ever, as countless cities and kings sought to open relations with the victor; many had to atone or to apologize for allegiance to Pompey, just as later for allegiance to Antony. Ambassadors streamed to Caesar, from south Russia, from Asia Minor, from distant kingdoms.[4] A rhetor from Mytilene, the energetic Potamo, led his city's delegation to Caesar, as he did later in an appeal to Augustus.[5] Eminent citizens from Pontic Heraclea, seeking favours, are alleged to have trailed after Caesar across the inhabited world.[6] Caesar had to be the Greeks' new patron; so Antony after him and then Augustus.

With remarkable speed and unanimity in the autumn of 48 B.C. honours were voted to Caesar throughout the Greek world.[7] These were more the outward signs of the new allegiance of the Greeks; they did not spring from a mere desire to flatter, but they exhibited adhesion to a great Roman and anticipated the bestowal of favours in compensation. Greek

---

[1] *Sardis* vii. 1, no. 27.

[2] Dunant and Pouilloux, *Recherches sur l'histoire et les cultes de Thasos* (1958), ii. nos. 170 (Assos), 171 (Lampsacus), and 172 (Rhodes).

[3] *SIG*³ 762, ll. 29–30: ἀφειδῶς ἑαυτὸν [ἐπι]διδοὺς εἰς τὰς τῆς πόλεως πρεσβήας, καὶ κινδύνους ἐπ[ι]δεχόμενος [ἀ]όκνως.

[4] See Rostovtzeff, *JRS* 7 (1917), 27 ff.

[5] *IGR* 4. 33. Suidas errs in making Potamo a sophist in Rome under Tiberius. Cf. Cichorius, *Rom und Mytilene* (1888), p. 62; also p. 35, n 5, below. It should not be forgotten that Potamo was an historian and wrote encomia of Brutus and Augustus: *FGH* ii. B. 147.   [6] Memnon, *FGH* iii. B. 434, 40. 3.

[7] A. E. Raubitschek, *JRS* 44 (1954), 65 ff.

honours will have been engineered by affluent and highly placed friends of Rome, who could use their influence either in the interest of an acknowledged patron or, in times of crisis and uncertainty, to secure a patron. And Romans were not uninterested in eastern honours. It is worth recalling the anger of Cicero when a certain Pelops of Byzantium had neglected to obtain an honorary decree for him.[1]

Graeca adulatio had an important place in the system of personal relations between Greeks and Romans. Honours commonly took the form of praise for benefaction, sometimes actually received and sometimes simply anticipated. A Roman might be called a city's benefactor, its saviour, or its founder; or, in more instances than is often realized, he might be assigned a cult.[2] But benefactor cults were nothing new in the Hellenistic world and were, in fact, merely a more extravagant form of honour than the simple title 'benefactor' or 'saviour' without imputations of divinity.[3] The cults of Roman magistrates in the East reveal little about the religion of the Greek peoples but much about diplomacy and clientela. From the time of Sulla, the word πάτρων emerges on inscriptions as a regular conjunct with εὐεργέτης and σωτήρ;[4] it is a Latin word thinly disguised as Greek, and it connotes a characteristically Roman institution.

It is left to inquire how the Greeks adapted themselves so easily to the clientela system. The explanation lies in its

---

[1] Plut. *Cic.* 24. 7.

[2] See Arist. *Rhet.* 1361ᵃ27 ff. for honours appropriate to benefactors, past or anticipated. On benefactors, saviours, &c.: Hepding, *Klio* 20 (1926), 490 f.; Charlesworth, *Harv. Theol. Rev.* 28 (1935), 8 ff.; Nock, *The Joy of Study: Papers pres. to F. C. Grant* (New York, 1951), 127 ff. For a new and substantially amplified list of cults of Roman magistrates in the East, see Appendix I below.

[3] Raubitschek, *JRS* 44 (1954), 75, like Nock (op. cit.), emphasizes that the titles εὐεργέτης and σωτήρ do not of themselves necessarily imply divine honours.

[4] The Greek word πάτρων occurs early in *SIG*³ 656 (Abdera, 166 B.C.) : when the Thracian king was threatening the Tean colony of Abdera, Teos sent envoys to Rome in her colony's behalf, and these must have brought back with them the word *patroni* to designate those Romans who agreed to support the Abderites. Cf. the patrons chosen by the Spanish envoys to Rome in 171 B.C. (Livy 43. 2. 4). The Greek word does not become common until after Sulla: e.g. *MAMA* 4. 52 (Lucullus), *IGR* 4. 970 (Julius Caesar's father, mentioned on an inscription honouring the son), *OGIS* 448 (L. Antonius), *OGIS* 452 (L. Sestius), *Arch. Class.* 10 (1958), 87 ff. (a Bibulus), *OGIS* 460 (Potitus Messalla).

peculiar similarity to the Greek institution of proxeny. In earlier centuries in the Greek-speaking world, εὐεργέτης καὶ πρόξενος was a standard honorific formula;[1] a benefactor was not only praised for what he had already done but asked to continue to render services in the future. With the spread of benefactor honours and cults, the word εὐεργέτης acquired new and extravagant conjuncts like σωτήρ or κτίστης, but the implications of the word will have remained what they had always been. In fact, a εὐεργέτης was, therefore, what the Romans called a *patronus*. The Greek concept of benefaction was consonant with patronage from the start. Hence εὐεργέτης (σωτήρ, κτίστης) καὶ πάτρων was essentially a first-century variant of εὐεργέτης καὶ πρόξενος. At least one bilingual inscription actually offers *patronus perpetuus* as a translation of εὐεργέτης instead of something like *benefici ergo*.[2] The Greek and Roman institutions fused together with marvellous ease and gave added impetus to the diplomatic activity of the late Republic.

The personal connexions between prominent Greeks and Romans are fundamental to an understanding of the Roman East. 'In this matter there is unbroken development through Republic and Principate.'[3]

---

[1] See A. Wilhelm, *Attische Urkunden* 5 (1942), 11 ff.

[2] *Patronus perpetuus*: *IG* xiv. 277 (Lilybaeum). *Benefici ergo*: *SEG* 11. 924 (Gytheum). The εὐεργέτης– (πρόξενος)–patronus equation underlies Cic., *II Verr.* 2. 154: Itaque eum non solum PATRONUM illius insulae, sed etiam SOTERA inscriptum vidi Syracusis. Cf. P. Monceaux, *Les Proxénies grecques* (1885), pp. 315–20, especially p. 316: 'C'est que la proxénie et le patronat des villes sont deux institutions très voisines ou plutôt deux faces d'une même institution.' Oliver, *The Ruling Power* (1953), p. 956, likened proxeny to Roman *amicitia*.

[3] E. W. Gray: see p. 1, n. 3, above.

II

ROMAN MAGISTRATES IN THE AUGUSTAN EAST

THE Emperor and members of his household superintended the East personally from time to time. After the constitutional foundation of the Principate, Augustus himself went to Greece, Asia, and Syria between the years 22 and 19; and his vicegerent Agrippa, who had been there before in 23, carried on the tasks of supervision from 18 to 13.[1] The earlier stages of Tiberius' mysterious retirement at Rhodes may not have been wholly unpolitical;[2] then, as Tiberius' powers ran out, the young Gaius Caesar was seen in the East. But who were the magistrates who represented the new government from year to year in particular positions of authority in the various provinces? These formed the solid core of the eastern administration, carrying out the policies of the Princeps and his family.

The men who served in eastern provinces under Augustus had in many cases considerable experience of that part of the world and had either inherited or constructed substantial eastern clientelae. A few gifted men were freshly groomed for eastern service under the newly formed Principate. The Emperor sought administrators who would know something of the regions to which they were being sent, though his favour did not fall on all who might lay claim to the requisite knowledge. Brutus, Cassius, and above all Antony had given experience of the Orient to many Romans. Some of these people survived into the Principate but never saw that part of the empire again: they might have known the provinces too well, or perhaps they were simply unreliable. But there is another and important group of Antonians who do appear on the eastern

---

[1] On Augustus' travels in the East; Bowersock, *CQ* N.S. 14 (1964) 120 f. For Agrippa: Magie, *CP* 3 (1908), 145 ff. and *RRAM* ii. 1330, n. 1.

[2] Cf. Dio 55. 9. 4.

fasti of the Augustan age; their qualifications must have included acquaintance with the East, and more.

The Sulpicii Galbae and the Valerii Messallae had republican traditions of service in the East. Scions of these
houses could have grown up expecting that they would go
there. A Sulpicius under the Emperor Tiberius took his own
life when he was prevented from entering his name in the
sortition which could have given him the proconsulship of
Asia or Africa.[1] The Sulpicii had been in the East since the
days of P. Sulpicius Galba Maximus, who served in Greece
and Macedonia in 211 and 200 B.C.[2]

The grandfather of the Emperor Sulpicius Galba was an
historian.[3] In political office he never rose higher than the
praetorship. Possibly he tried to do what was nearly impossible
under the triumvirs, to remain neutral. A greater historian, the
one-time Antonian, Asinius Pollio, took that difficult course;
but Pollio's decision to affect neutrality and become the spoils
of the victor was made only after he had held the consulship.
Galba never aimed so high. However, his son became consul in
5 B.C. and was the father of a consular and an emperor. This
man, C. Sulpicius Galba, served as proconsul of Achaea while
a praetorian and as proconsul of Asia while a consular.[4] Such
a course was appropriate for a Sulpicius Galba. The wife of the
consul of 5 B.C. also had connexions with the East: she was
none other than Mummia Achaïca, the great-granddaughter
of L. Mummius, who destroyed Corinth in 146 B.C.[5] The fasti
of Augustan Achaea show a Mummius as proconsul's legate,
perhaps Achaïca's brother.[6] The Emperor's brother, son of
Mummia and the consul of 5 B.C., was also in the East under
Augustus, though late in his reign, as proconsul of Achaea.[7]

---

[1] Tac. *Ann.* 6. 40; Suet. *Galba* 3. 4. The choice of proconsuls for senatorial
provinces, theoretically entrusted to the unprejudiced decision of the lot, was
certainly on occasion an indication of imperial favour.

[2] References in Broughton, *MRR* i. 272 and 323.

[3] Suet. *Galba* 3. 3. *SEG* 1. 169 was wrongly assigned to this man; it refers to
the consul of 5 B.C., whose praenomen is now known from the *Fasti Mag. Vici*
to have been C., not Ser. (as in *PIR*, S 722).

[4] *SEG* 1. 169 (Achaea; cf. preceding note); *SEG* 1. 391 (Asia).

[5] Suet. *Galba* 3. 3.

[6] *Inschrift. v. Olympia* no. 331; *IG* iii². 4170. Cf. Groag, *Die römischen Reichsbeamten von Achaia* (1939), p. 99.   [7] *SEG* 3. 244.

Reaching the consulship in A.D. 22, he looked forward to the proconsulship of Asia, the post which was denied him by Tiberius. It is clear that Augustus, at least, recognized the qualifications of the Sulpicii Galbae for service in the East and had reason to trust them.

There had been numerous Valerii in the East under the Republic, although the Messallae who were there must be dated to the second century. An Augustan Messalla was honoured at Magnesia at Sipylus as patron and benefactor διὰ προγόνων,[1] from which a clientela of the Valerii Messallae can be inferred.

The Augustan Messallae are a vexing house. There are four, or possibly five of them who served in the East. That is an impressive record, maintaining the traditions of the πρόγονοι and testifying to high favour. M. Valerius Messalla Corvinus, the consul of 31 B.C., was one of the three young patricians on the side of Octavian in the Sicilian War. He had previously been an Antonian, but his early conversion gave Augustus good reason to value his services. Corvinus went to the East after the fall of Alexandria and managed the affairs of Syria.[2] Two other Messallae, probably brothers, may also have been Antonians. M. Valerius Messalla, consul suffect in 32 B.C., was the recipient of honours at Pergamum;[3] a triumviral proconsulship of Asia as a praetorian would not be impossible, and there is scarcely room for him to have held that post in the twenties. The consul suffect of 29 B.C. was called Potitus Valerius Messalla. If he is identical with the M. Valerius Messalla Potitus who was honoured as a patron of Claros while quaestor,[4] his eastern quaestorship will have fallen squarely in the period of Antonian supremacy. In the case of the first of these two men, it is impossible to tell whether he was an Antonian or not, and this means his presence in Asia cannot be dated. However, the case of Potitus is clearer: possibly an Antonian, he nevertheless profited from the favour which Corvinus brought to his house and the experience which his ancestors had received in the Orient. Potitus was proconsul of Asia for two years in succession, acquiring the titles of patron and benefactor in

---

[1] *OGIS* 460 = *IGR* 4. 1338.
[2] App. *BC* 5. 102; 109–13 (Sicilian War). Dio 51. 7. 7 (Syria).
[3] *IGR* 4. 431; cf. Syme, *JRS* 45 (1955), 155.   [4] *JRS* 45 (1955), 160.

Didyma and Magnesia at Sipylus.[1] A legateship of Syria has been conjectured,[2] which is not an unlikely post for him to have held.

The quaestor honoured at Claros might have been a different and hitherto unattested man. If that is so, he will have been a brother of the consul of A.D. 5, L. Valerius Messalla Volesus, and thus Potitus' son.[3] But nothing could be said of him except that he turns up precisely where a Valerius Messalla might be expected—in the East. About Volesus' existence, however, there can be no doubt. He too went to Asia as a proconsul under Augustus, although he met with an unhappy end. He was brought to trial for extortion: the Emperor himself published an indictment, and the senate under oath voted his condemnation.[4] Cruelty and rapacity subverted imperial favour and family tradition.

Other magistrates known to the East through their πρόγονοι came from the complex house of the Calpurnii Pisones. The son of the philhellene consul of 58 B.C. and patron of Philodemus was the consul of 15, distinguished as Piso the Pontifex, who was himself a philhellene. He was the patron of a poet, Antipater of Thessalonica, as well as a governor in eastern provinces, in Pamphylia and Macedonia, and probably also in Asia and Syria.[5] Another Piso, the consul of 23 B.C., had two sons, both of whom served in the East: one was the Augur, consul in 1 B.C. and proconsul of Asia, and the other was the consul of 7 B.C. and sometime later legate of Syria.[6] On a stone from Mytilene the Augur is hailed as διὰ προγόνων εὐεργέτης; two other Augustan inscriptions from Asia honouring a Piso, who could be either the Augur or the Pontifex, have the same phrase.[7] A clientela is clear.

---

[1] *ILS* 8964, on which see A. E. Gordon, *Potitus Valerius Messalla* (1954). *AE* 1912. 135 = *Didyma* ii, no. 147; *OGIS* 460 = *IGR* 4. 1338 (Magnesia).

[2] See *JRS* 45 (1955), 160.

[3] See Syme, *JRS* 45 (1955), 156.

[4] Tac. *Ann.* 3. 68; Sen. *Contr.* 21. 22; Sen. *de Ira* 2. 5. 5.

[5] *PIR²*, C 289. The Asian proconsulship was proposed on the basis of *Anth. Pal.* x. 25 by Cichorius, *RS* 326 ff. approved by Syme in *JRS* 50 (1960), 17. The Syrian legateship: Syme, *Klio* 27 (1934), 128.

[6] *PIR²*, C 290 (*cos.* 1 B.C.), 287 (*cos.* 7 B.C.).

[7] *ILS* 8814 (Mytilene; to honour the Augur). *IGR* 4. 410 (Pergamum); *BCH* 5 (1881), 183, n. 5 (Stratoniceia).

Still other families, whose members were sent to the East under Augustus, are worth noticing for their connexions there, although their record is not so full as those of the foregoing houses. A Publius Lepidus, born into the Aemilii though perhaps adopted into another gens, governed Crete for Brutus and Cassius in 43 B.C. A kinsman of his, Paullus Aemilius Lepidus, consul in 34, was one of those patricians who turned to Caesar's heir in time for the Sicilian War. After his consulship but presumably before the censorship he held in 22, Paullus went to the East as a proconsul, possibly in Macedonia.[1] Another member of the family, Q. Aemilius Lepidus, was consul in 21, filling the place left vacant for Augustus. An anecdote in Appian would suggest that Quintus had been an Antonian to the bitter end at Actium;[2] but that is not too surprising, as Paullus' early conversion to Octavian was doubtless as beneficial to his relatives as Messalla Corvinus' similar conversion was to his. Nor is it surprising to discover that Quintus returned to the East at some point in the early Principate as proconsul of Asia.[3]

L. Marcius Censorinus, praetor urbanus in 43 B.C., joined Antony at Mutina. During the proscriptions he managed to acquire Cicero's house on the Palatine. Immediately after Philippi Antony appointed him proconsul of Macedonia and Achaea, from which he triumphed in 39 B.C., the year of his consulship.[4] Lucius himself did not attain further eminence in the provinces under Augustus, although he lived on in possession of a priesthood.[5] But his son, C. Marcius Censorinus, reached the consulship in 8 B.C. and acquired considerable experience of the East in the service of the first Princeps. He was a legate of Augustus serving in Sinope about the time of the Bosporan rebellion. As a subordinate to Agrippa, he was clearly a trusted agent of the Emperor looking after a delicate

---

[1] On Publius in Crete: App. *BC* 5. 2; Grant, *FITA*, p. 35. On his probable adoption (P. not being a praenomen of the Aemilii), cf. R. Syme, *CP* 50 (1955), 132. For Paullus: Suet. *Aug.* 16 (Sicilian War); *IG* iii. 573 (proconsulship of Asia or Macedonia; censorship not mentioned).

[2] App. *BC* 4. 49 (alluding to the consular colleague of a Lollius, presumably the consul of 21 B.C.: the colleague is called Barbula, an old cognomen of the gens Aemilia).

[3] *IGR* 4. 901 (Cibyra) = *AE* 1950. 250; Waddington 506.

[4] *PIR*, M 164.   [5] *CIL* 6.32323, l. 44.

and dangerous situation. After his consulship he was allotted the province of Asia, where he died about the year A.D. 2, in all probability while serving as proconsul.[1] A cult was established in his honour at Mylasa, the last known cult accorded by an eastern province to its Roman governor.[2]

Cicero the orator must have acquired an eastern clientela in the year of his Cilician governorship. His son Marcus, who had accompanied him at the time,[3] had another opportunity to learn about the East when he resided at Athens as a student. At Philippi the young Marcus was a partisan of Brutus, later of Cassius of Parma and Sextus Pompeius. But he soon had the foresight to ally himself with Octavian, who presented him with a priesthood.[4] A suffect consulship followed in 30 B.C. The younger Cicero then returned to the Orient to hold the two choicest of its governorships, the proconsulship of Asia and the legateship of Syria.[5] Both his knowledge and his allegiance had their rewards.

An equestrian family from Cales rose to great eminence in the eastern service of the Emperor.[6] The *novus homo*, L. Vinicius, was the first of his house to attain the consulship (suffect in 33 B.C.). He was a Caesarian tribune of the plebs in 51 B.C.,[7] after which his history is entirely dark until he emerges in the bright light of the consulship. A proconsulship of Asia perhaps fell to him in the crucial year 27 B.C.[8] Marcus Vinicius, probably Lucius' nephew, was the next member of the family to reach the consulship and to serve in the East. A *tribus Vinicia* in Corinth[9] may disclose an Achaean proconsulship for this man before he became suffect consul in 19 B.C.

---

[1] See Bowersock, *HSCP* 68 (1964), 207 ff.

[2] For the evidence, see Appendix I. Cf. Tac. *Ann.* 3. 55 on the rich nobles in the decades just after Actium: Nam etiam tum plebem socios regna colere et coli licitum; ut quisque opibus domo paratu speciosus, per nomen et clientelas inlustrior habebatur.

[3] Cic. *ad Att.* 5. 9. 3. [4] App. *BC* 4. 51; 5. 2.

[5] *PIR*, T 272. [6] Tac. *Ann.* 6. 15. [7] Cic. *ad Fam.* 8. 8. 6.

[8] H. W. Pleket, *Greek Inscriptions in the Leiden Rijksmuseum* (1958), no. 57. Mrs. Atkinson has recently suggested that not all of that inscription need be referred to 27 B.C.: *Rev. intern. des droits de l'ant.* 7 (1960), 258 ff. She therefore assumes that the Vinicius on that document is not Lucius, but Marcus. Given her hypothesis (which may be right), I should prefer Publius, consul A.D. 2; a praetorian proconsulship of Asia for Marcus is most unlikely.

[9] *AE* 1919. 2.

Subsequently he passed to the proconsulship in Asia,[1] which his uncle may have held not too many years before him. Marcus Vinicius was an intimate of the Emperor,[2] and although he was employed in the East according to that tradition which Augustus was creating for the Vinicii, his ability and fidelity were also required on the northern frontiers. Meanwhile, the son of the consul of 33, also a Lucius, was growing up in the most distinguished circles. Handsome and elegant, he was one of the suitors of Augustus' daughter, Julia.[3] That may have been his undoing, for although he became consul in 5 B.C., he was the only Vinicius in the early decades of the Principate not to have held an eastern proconsulship; in fact, he held—so far as recorded—no proconsulship at all. The scandals which shook the Augustan house soon after Lucius' consulship will explain his failure to advance thereafter. However, his kinsman P. Vinicius, son of the consul of 19, avoided danger and went from strength to strength. He commanded an army in Thrace or Macedonia a little before A.D. 1, when Velleius Paterculus served under him as a tribune.[4] After a consulship in A.D. 2 he returned to the East as proconsul of Asia.[5] Publius was a professed admirer of the poet Ovid,[6] but he managed to avoid implication in the mysterious affair which relegated Ovid to the shores of the Black Sea. Under Tiberius, P. Vinicius became celebrated as a fluent and innovatory rhetor.[7] His son Marcus maintained the family tradition, at least for a while. He married the daughter of Germanicus and was consul twice, once under Tiberius and once under Claudius.[8] Between his consulships and during the reign of the demented intervening Emperor, M. Vinicius was proconsul of Asia.[9] Messallina's poison brought his career to an end in A.D. 46,[10] thus terminating the imperial favour which had begun three generations

---

[1] *Rev. Arch.* (1935) ii. 156–8.

[2] Suet. *Aug.* 71 : lusimus *geronticos*. Surely, therefore, Marcus is the Vinicius who is Augustus' gaming partner.

[3] Ibid. 64.

[4] Vell. 2. 101 ; *AE* 1960. 378 (Callatis) in which P. Vinicius is called [ἀντι]-στρατηγός.

[5] *SEG* 12. 452 (Cnidos) ; *IG* xii. 5. 756 (Andros).

[6] Sen. *Contr.* 33. 25.   [7] Ibid. 4. 11 ; 20. 11–12.

[8] *Cos. ord.* in A.D. 30 and again in 45.

[9] *Ephesos* iii. 24.   [10] Dio 60. 27. 4.

previously. Since the beginning of the Principate there had been five consular Vinicii, of whom four appear to have been proconsuls of Asia.[1] This pattern was hardly accidental.

Some Augustan Romans became eastern specialists less because of family connexions than for the fact of their own individual qualifications. L. Volcacius Tullus was another of the very early imperial proconsuls of Asia. He knew the Orient from fighting for Caesar at Dyrrachium in 48 B.C., and a governorship of Cilicia should probably be assigned to him in 45 B.C.[2] His activities under the triumvirs have not been recorded, but it would be fair to suppose that he was in the East, perhaps in the service of Antony for a short while. He reached the consulship as *ordinarius* in 33 B.C.

Tullus was the uncle of a friend of the poet Propertius, who reveals how fond the nephew was of life in the East.[3] Propertius' friend went to Asia Minor with his father and stayed there for a long time, untouched by the poet's entreaties to return to Rome from Cyzicus, where he was living at the time. There is no word that the young Volcacius ever returned at all. In the late twenties B.C. the people of Cyzicus, in a factional dispute, flogged to death a number of Romans. It is unclear what sort of Romans these were, perhaps some citizens of Greek origin together with the families of *negotiatores* who had settled there; conceivably Volcacius himself lost his life in this outbreak.[4]

M. Titius was an Antonian partisan who deserted to Octavian before Actium in the company of his uncle Munatius Plancus.[5] He knew the East well from service as quaestor to Antony on the Parthian expedition,[6] in the year after which

---

[1] Just possibly three, if L. Vinicius is not the proconsul of the Leiden inscription. Cf. p. 19, n. 8.

[2] Caesar, *BC* 3. 52 (at Dyrrachium); Cic. *ad Att.* 14. 9. 3, as interpreted by R. Syme in *Anat. Stud. Buckler*, 321–4 (governor of Cilicia). For Tullus' Asian proconsulship: *CR* 69 (1955), 244; the Pergamene orator Volcacius Moschus must have derived his citizenship from Volcacius Tullus (R. Syme, *Hist.* 11 [1962], 152).

[3] Prop. i. 6. 19; iii. 22.

[4] Dio 54. 7. 6. Augustus took away the liberty of the Cyzicenes as a penalty for this disturbance. For the *negotiatores* at Cyzicus (and the troubles in 20): J. Hatzfeld, *Les Trafiquants italiens dans l'orient hellénique* (Paris, 1919), 114–16.

[5] Dio 50. 3. 1.   [6] Plut. *Ant.* 42.

he was responsible for the execution of Sextus Pompeius at Miletus.[1] Titius must have advanced soon to the praetorship, for while still consul designate for the year 31, he held the proconsulship of Asia in the interest of Antony.[2] His desertion did not come too late; furthermore, he gave evidence of his new loyalty by winning over the king of Paphlagonia to the cause of Caesar's heir before the final battle was joined.[3] Titius had troubled relations with the King of Cappadocia, whom the young Tiberius once defended at Rome against the complaints of the Cappadocian people (it is pretty clear that Tiberius did not care for Titius).[4] But Augustus put this former Antonian to the best use. He sent him back to the East, where the King of Judaea provided his good offices to heal the breach between Titius and Archelaus.[5] As Augustus' governor in Syria, Titius had the honour of receiving into Roman control the four children of Phraates, the Parthian monarch.[6] Titius thus spent much of his life in the East; he deserted in time for his service to be sought by Caesar's heir. And he married well; his wife was the sister of Paullus Fabius Maximus, consul in 11 B.C. and subsequently governor of Asia.[7]

Three other Romans gave notable service in the East under the Augustan Principate. One of these, the ill-fated P. Quinctilius Varus, also governed Africa and died in a celebrated disaster in Germany.[8] But it is tempting to suppose that Varus was sent by Augustus to govern Syria (c. 6–4 B.C.)[8] in view of his eastern experience as quaestor in Asia. Indeed, he may have been a part of the Emperor's entourage about 22 B.C. An inscription from Tenos calls him *quaestor Augusti*, for which

---

[1] Vell. 2. 79. 5.   [2] ILS 891.   [3] Dio 50. 13. 5.

[4] Jos. AJ 16. 270 (bad relations between Archelaus and Titius between 13 and 8 B.C.). Suet. Tib. 8 and Dio 57. 17. 3–4 record Tiberius' defence of Archelaus; the date of the trial is not clear; cf. Appendix III. Velleius, Tiberius' panegyrist, is significantly hostile to Titius.

[5] Jos., ibid.

[6] Strabo 748. L. R. Taylor, JRS 26 (1936), 161 ff., argued that Titius was twice governor of Syria, on the ground that the surrender of the hostages mentioned by Strabo occurred in 19 B.C. But surely this belongs to the same period as the reference to Titius in Jos. AJ 16. 270 (i.e. 13–8 B.C.) : Livy, Ep. 141 (10/9 B.C.) must refer to the hostages and the declaration of peace, as the standards were certainly recovered in 20. Hence, one governorship, c. 10 B.C. The ascription to Titius of the Lapis Tiburtinus is not likely: cf. p. 25, n. 1, below.

[7] IGR 4. 1716.   [8] PIR, Q 27.

the most plausible explanation is that the Emperor himself was in the East at the time.[1] Inasmuch as Varus was consul in 13 B.C., a quaestorship in the period of Augustus' eastern tour is more than likely. So Augustus himself showed the Orient to Varus. It was sensible to dispatch him to Syria when Herod was growing senile in Judaea.

M. Lollius and P. Sulpicius Quirinius were the most valued of Augustus' oriental experts. These were the men to whom the guidance of the young Gaius Caesar in the East was entrusted in turn. Secure evidence of Lollius' allegiance before Actium is lacking, although it may be suspected that an Antonian official in Crete and Cyrene was related, perhaps closely, to Marcus.[2] The father of that official must have been Pompey's legate in the Pirate War in charge of the coast of the eastern Aegean from the Hellespont to Rhodes.[3] Marcus' own father is possibly the Lollius who governed Crete and Cyrene early in the Augustan Principate.[4] Whatever the precise relations of the first-century Lollii, it would appear that M. Lollius, the consul of 21 B.C., came from an Antonian family not without experience and connexions in the East. He naturally spent much of his time there, but it is ironical that he, like Varus, also operated in Germany with disastrous results. These two men, who surely knew the East rather well, both gave their names to celebrated *clades* in Germany.

M. Lollius was Augustus' first governor of the new province of Galatia, which he organized as a praetorian.[5] That was the beginning of his eastern assignments, and it was remarkable for its importance. After his consulship in 21, Lollius fought the Bessi in support of the Thracian king Rhoemetalces at a time when he was probably consular governor of Macedonia.[6] Military prowess took him to Germany, the scene of

---

[1] *OGIS* 463; cf. *OGIS* 464 (Pergamum). He was honoured at Athens: *IG* iii. 1. 584*a*. Cf. W. John, *Hermes* 86 (1958), 254.

[2] Coins: *BMC* Cyren. ccxvi; Grant, *FITA* 55–58. *Cyrenaican Expeditions* (Manchester, 1959), p. 31.

[3] App. *Mithr.* 95; cf. Jos. *BJ* 1. 127; *AJ* 14. 29 (takes Damascus).

[4] A Palicanus on coins of Augustan Cyrene: *BMC* Cyren. ccvii. Palicanus is a cognomen of the Lollii: note the tribune of the plebs in 71 B.C. and the monetalis of 47 B.C. The father of the consul of 21 B.C. was evidently a Marcus: *AE* 1933. 85.

[5] *PIR*, L 226.   [6] Dio 54. 20. 3; *AE* 1933. 85.

the *clades*; but it was an overrated disaster.[1] Lollius did not suffer noticeably for it. When Augustus' grandson and heir, C. Caesar, went to the East, Lollius was his *comes* and *rector*.[2] He was an understandable choice, for Lollius knew the region and had demonstrated his fidelity to the Emperor. Moreover, he had probably taken a wife from the no less faithful Valerii Messallae,[3] who had connexions in Asia. But something mysterious occurred. Lollius fell from favour and was soon dead. The truth may never be known, although it is apparent that Lollius was an enemy of the exile Tiberius. Rumour went abroad that he aroused the hostility of the young Gaius against the exile. There were also reports of intrigue with oriental kings. Velleius Paterculus, the panegyrist of Tiberius, could not say whether Lollius took his own life or not,[4] and perhaps he did not.

He was succeeded in the retinue of Gaius by that other Augustan authority on the East, P. Sulpicius Quirinius, a man who had been elevated by Augustus. He was not related to the patrician family of the Sulpicii but came rather from the municipium of Lanuvium.[5] His career before his consulship in 12 B.C. is obscure. It is clear that he was a tireless general, whose military distinctions must have carried him far.[6] In the year of his consulship his colleague was an Appius Claudius, who had been adopted by the Valerii Messallae. This man was probably the brother of Quirinius' wife.[7] There can be little doubt that Quirinius of Lanuvium had made his way into high and influential circles. One of his most memorable achievements in the East as a consular cannot be securely dated, the Homonadensian War,[8] although it is clear that it belongs to the period before Gaius' eastern tour. During Tiberius' residence at Rhodes, Quirinius had followed the opposite of Lollius' policy and was to profit from it.[9] When the

---

[1] Suet. *Aug.* 23: maioris infamiae quam detrimenti. Dio 54. 20. 5; Vell. 2. 97.

[2] Vell. 2. 102. 1; Suet. *Tib.* 12.

[3] Tac *Ann.* 12. 22: cf. R. Syme, *Tacitus* ii. 748.

[4] Vell. 2. 102. 1. Cf. Suet. *Tib.* 12; Tac. *Ann.* 3. 48.

[5] Tac. *Ann.* 3. 48.

[6] A praetorian proconsulship of Crete and Cyrene may be concealed in the report that he subjugated two tribes in Libya: Florus 2. 31.

[7] Tac. *Ann.* 4. 66.

[8] Strabo 569.   [9] Suet. *Tib.* 12; Tac. *Ann.* 3. 48.

exile's detractor was eliminated, his flatterer filled the gap. The career of Quirinius in this age is obscured by the evidence of the acephalous *lapis Tiburtinus*.[1] Certainly Quirinius may have held more eastern posts than anyone can be sure of, but this particular epigraphic evidence can provide no satisfaction as to what they were. Yet it is enough to know that in A.D. 6 Quirinius was again in the East as the governor of Syria, carrying out the great census of Augustus.[2]

The younger Seneca once observed that Augustus had enrolled his entire circle of intimates from the camp of his adversaries,[3] and enough Antonians have already been adduced to give substance to such a remark. Yet it must be noted that there were still more Antonians with excellent claims to eastern service under Augustus who survived into the Principate but were never sent out. Some of these became known intimates of the Emperor at Rome; others are not heard of again. Advanced age or an early and opportune death may, in some cases, be suspected as the reason for their failure to reappear conspicuously under Augustus. But it is implausible that a whole group of potentially useful Antonians should have reached senility or died together about 27 B.C. Indeed, the survival of many can be proved. Either because they could best be watched if the Emperor saw them frequently or because their services were required in the city, they did not leave Rome.

Seneca named Sallustius, the Cocceii, and the Dellii as Antonians close to Augustus. Sallustius Crispus, born an equestrian and adopted by the historian, is said to have shared the Emperor's secrets.[4] He had no particular claims to provincial service of any kind; besides, he could aspire to a high advisory position at the imperial court. Not that he lacked contact with Greek culture: Crinagoras addressed a poem to him.[5]

---

[1] *ILS* 918. The *lapis Tiburtinus* and date of the Homonadensian War are admirably discussed by R. Syme in *Klio* 27 (1934), 131 ff. The man in the inscription may be Piso the Pontifex, consul 15 B.C. There is a fresh survey of the Quirinius problem in Sherwin-White, *Roman Society and Roman Law in the New Testament* (1963), pp. 162–71.

[2] Jos. *AJ* 17. 355; Luke ii. 2. Cf. *ILS* 2683.

[3] Sen. *de Clementia* 1. 10. 1: Sallustium et Cocceios et Deillios et totam cohortem primae admissionis ex adversariorum castris conscripsit.

[4] Tac. *Ann.* 1. 6; 3. 30.

[5] *Anth. Pal.* xvi. 40.

The Cocceii had provided two Antonian consuls, C. Balbus in 39 B.C. and M. Nerva in 36 B.C. Nerva knew the East; he had governed Asia for Antony and was honoured as imperator at Lagina in Caria.[1] When Octavian made the Cocceii patrician by virtue of the Lex Saenia in 30 B.C.[2] and welcomed to his circle the two consulars, as well as perhaps L. Cocceius Nerva, he may have been trying to still the ambitions which Antony had aroused. L. Nerva never reached the consulship, and a man who had governed Asia probably as a praetorian under Antony never went back to the East as a consular under Augustus.

The Dellii are puzzling: only one member of that family is known, the historian noted for changing sides in the civil wars.[3] Q. Dellius passed at the right moments from the camps of Dolabella to Cassius, of Cassius to Antony, and of Antony to Octavian. Such behaviour cannot have been reassuring to the last of his masters. But few men that survived into the Principate knew the East any better than Dellius. Antony had employed him on a number of confidential missions, including bringing Cleopatra to Tarsus.[4] Dellius had also accompanied Antony on his Parthian campaign and had conducted financial negotiations with the Athenians.[5] But he too never returned to the East under the Principate.

Other Antonians are discoverable who survived into the Principate but never used again such knowledge of the Orient as they acquired under the Triumvirate. They had to be satisfied with belonging to the Emperor's *cohors primae admissionis*. L. Munatius Plancus had been consul in 42 B.C.; as a partisan of Antony he had governed the great provinces of Asia and Syria.[6] His desertion to Octavian came in time, and he did his best to assure the Princeps of his loyalty by proposing

---

[1] *ILS* 8780. [2] Tac. *Ann.* 11. 25 (Lex Saenia).

[3] Sen. *Suas.* 1. 7, quoting Messalla Corvinus: desultor bellorum civilium. Dellius is not registered in *PIR*². The apparent reference to him in Sen. *de Clem.* 1. 10. 1 (quoted p. 25, n. 3) implies that he was important under Augustus. Could the MSS. be concealing *Lollios*, instead of *Deillios*, in the text of Seneca? After all, the text gives Sallustius in the singular where one person is meant; but only Quintus Dellius is known to correspond with *Deillios*. There would be several Lollii, however, just as there were three Cocceii.

[4] Plut. *Ant.* 25.

[5] Dio 49. 39. 2 f. [6] *PIR*, M 534.

the name Augustus.[1] The censorship came to him in 22 B.C., but he never governed another province. However, he may have been just too old; Plancus' nephew, M. Titius, deserted about the same time and later went out to Syria as legate of the Emperor.

Among the others who survived Actium was C. Sosius, the consul of 32 B.C., who began his term of office with a harangue against Caesar's heir.[2] Sosius had been Antony's admiral at Zacynthus, as well as his governor of Syria between 38 and 36 B.C.[3] Octavian ostentatiously spared this man as evidence of his clemency,[4] and Sosius emerged as a priest at the secular games in 17 B.C.[5] But he did not go back to the East. C. Furnius had been the Antonian governor of Asia between 36 and 35 B.C.; he was also spared after Actium.[6] In 29 B.C., he was honoured with adlection among the consulars[7] but held neither consulship nor provincial command under Augustus. However, his son, bearing the same name, was consul in the year of the secular games. Previously he had served in the province of Hither Spain.[8] Q. Didius was Antony's last governor of Syria and an obscure personage. Yet he was quite willing to serve the cause of the victor of Actium by opposing the Antonian gladiators.[9] Nothing further is heard of him. L. Pinarius Scarpus, nephew of Julius Caesar, played a similar role at Cyrene. He was the last Antonian governor in that province, and Actium convinced him of the wisdom of changing his allegiance. Scarpus manifested his new loyalty by refusing to receive Antony after Actium.[10] Nothing further is heard of him either.

There are traces of other men even more obscure whose qualifications the Emperor chose to disregard. It is possible that the Antonian consular L. Flavius lasted into the Principate. He had held his high office in absence in 33 B.C. while he was in Armenia.[11] Then there is the enigmatic L. Lollius, Antonian governor of Crete and Cyrene. He cannot be identical with his kinsman who governed the same province later

---

[1] Vell. 2. 91; Suet. *Aug.* 7.   [2] Dio 50. 2. 3.   [3] *PIR*, S 556.
[4] Dio 51. 2. 4.   [5] *ILS* 5050, l. 150.   [6] *PIR*[2], F 590.
[7] Dio 52. 42. 4. He outlived his son, consul in 17 B.C.: *PIR*[2], F 590.
[8] Dio 54. 5. 1.   [9] Id. 51. 7. 1.   [10] Id. 51. 5. 6; 9. 1.
[11] Id. 49. 44. 3.

under the name of Palicanus.[1] While M. Lollius rises ever higher in the imperial service, L. Lollius is never heard of again. It was not impossible for one member of a family to be retarded in his career while others advanced; that was also the fate of L. Vinicius, the consul suffect of 5 B.C. Perhaps the same thing happened to M. Valerius Messalla, the consul of 32 B.C. If he held—as he may well have done—a praetorian proconsulship of Asia under Antony, his career stopped utterly in the Principate. That, of course, need not suggest that he was excluded from the circle of the Emperor's intimates.

Service in the East ended for an entire family in one notable instance. Ap. Claudius Pulcher, consul of 38 B.C., was one of the patricians who appeared on the side of Octavian in the Sicilian War.[2] Like Corvinus and Lepidus, Pulcher would seem to have brought his family over to the winning side in plenty of time. But apart from the Claudius who had become a Valerius by adoption (doubtless in the 30's) and died as consul in 12 B.C., no Claudius Pulcher reached the consulship in the Augustan age. And with the possible exception of the consul of 38 in Bithynia-Pontus in 28/27 B.C.,[3] no Claudius Pulcher is known to have governed an eastern province under Caesar's heir. Yet the Claudii Pulchri had built up strong clientelae in the Orient in the late Republic. Ap. Claudius Pulcher, the consul of 79, had been proconsul in Macedonia and Thrace; one of the brothers of the turbulent tribune of 58 had governed Asia, while the other had served as proconsul in both Cilicia and Greece. The two brothers, who were the offspring of the governor of Asia, had toured as children in the East with L. Ateius Philologus.[4] Yet the brother of the consul of 38 never became consul, nor did P. Clodius' own son, in whom Antony had placed the highest hopes.[5]

Perhaps by virtue of his marriage to Livia, Augustus regarded the clientelae of the Claudii as his own. In any case, an Ap. Claudius Pulcher who became monetalis under Augustus

---

[1] See above, p. 23, nn. 2 and 4.

[2] App. *BC* 5. 98.

[3] Grant, *FITA*, pp. 255–8; cf. *PIR²*, C 984 (preferring to identify the proconsul with the brother of the consul of 38).

[4] Suet. *de Gramm.* 10.

[5] Cic. *ad Att.* 14. 13 A 2: P. Claudium, in optima spe puerum repositum.

soon sealed his fate by committing adultery with the Emperor's daughter.[1] Inasmuch as the lovers of Julia may well have been involved in a political conspiracy, it was no doubt likely that a representative of a family suppressed by Augustus would be one of them.[2]

The vicissitudes of men and families in the eastern service of Augustan Rome reveal that knowledge of the East was not the sole basis of selection. To have been an Antonian was far from ruinous. The Emperor wanted experienced men, but—more important—men with a substantial clientela, though too much experience or too large an eastern clientela could be dangerous. In those days, as Tacitus remarked, it was still permissible to cultivate friends among the provincials.[3] Many who went out to the East under Augustus were undoubtedly qualified by personal achievements and family connexions; so were some who remained behind. While realizing that a host of Antonians must inevitably be at the centre of the restored Republic, Augustus weighed each case. Certain men were suppressed; some, including Sulpicius Quirinius, were raised up by the Emperor himself. And many passed without harm from Triumvirate into Principate.

[1] *PIR*[2], C 985. Probably identical with Julia's lover: Vell. 2. 100. 5.

[2] On the political character of the Julia scandal, note the *maiestas* charge in Tac. *Ann.* 3. 24 and Dio 55. 10. 15, and the plan to assassinate Augustus alleged in Pliny, *NH* 7. 149.

[3] Tac. *Ann.* 3. 55, quoted on p. 19, n. 9.

III

GREEKS IN THE IMPERIAL SERVICE

THE great men of the late Republic were no strangers to the culture of the Greeks. Commanders in the East were disposed to abduct learned men as prisoners of war to be led to Rome, where a swift manumission awaited them. Some of these Greeks passed the remainder of their lives in lecturing to the Romans on grammar or rhetoric, while others joined the retinue of a noble household and became the confidants of eminent Romans.

Certain of the favoured Greeks were companions of the generals of republican Rome in peace and war, watched their exploits with admiring eyes, supplied advice or consolation, and composed panegyrics of their patrons. In such relationships both Greeks and Romans had much to gain. A Greek, by virtue of his very intimacy with his patron, had an unrivalled opportunity to look after the best interests of such eastern cities as he chose to support, while at the same time he earned gratitude and honour among those Greeks who experienced his patron's benefactions. His compatriots might even see fit to enrol him among the gods themselves; such were the honours accorded to Theophanes of Mytilene. As for the Roman patron, he was instructed in the ways of the Hellenes, with whom he forged a close diplomatic link. And perhaps an Archias or a Theophanes would immortalize him.

It was altogether natural that erudition and politics coincided in the relationship of Greek confidant and Roman patron. The educated men of the East regularly put their minds into the service of their cities and of their Roman patrons. Not all of these men lived and travelled with the great Romans of the day, but many, while installed in local office, remembered Roman interests on the understanding of compensatory consideration. The influence and knowledge of Greek philosophers made them important acquisitions for an imperator, either as his companions or as magistrates and dynasts of eastern cities. Conversely, those few learned politicians who were not inclined to Rome proved consistently troublesome.

Greeks who accompanied the great men of republican Rome on their journeys and campaigns were usually freedmen; several exerted enormous influence over their patrons and amassed vast wealth. In the retinue of Sulla were Cornelius Epicadus and the captive Milesian, Alexander Polyhistor; in the retinue of Pompey were the rich Demetrius of Gadara and Theophanes.

Greeks in the service of the first Princeps provide a certain continuity with the Republic: they were literate men, acting as teachers, advisers, and panegyrists to the imperial court, while not forgetting the needs of their own friends and cities. They were also the instruments of a far-reaching innovation in the administration of the empire, an innovation which was to lead in due time to the presence of eastern natives in the senate at Rome and as agents of the Emperor in their homelands. During the Republic a native holding local office often maintained an *entente cordiale* with representatives of Rome. In the developed Principate, natives *were* representatives of Rome. The transition began under Augustus, and there was no turning back. The essence of the transition, the pivotal point of the change, was the familiar fusion of erudition and politics.

In the decade after the fall of Alexandria, five or six pedagogues of Greek origin were resident in the imperial household. Among them were the teachers of Augustus himself; these men were retained by their pupil as his counsellors and friends after the defeat of his rival. Perhaps even Apollodorus of Pergamum lived to see the child Octavian wage the Civil Wars as the heir of Caesar and assume the title of Augustus. While he lived, he was a valued adviser: Octavian took him from Rome to Apollonia and may well have brought him back again to Italy at some later date. For although Apollodorus was old when he journeyed to Apollonia, he did not die until the age of eighty-two, and Strabo, a contemporary observer of the Augustan Principate, reports that Apollodorus profited greatly from the friendship of Caesar Augustus.[1] He may have died sometime in the twenties while enjoying within the imperial court the high favour of his former pupil.

Two other of Augustus' teachers were certainly there at that time. One was a native of Tarsus, the other of Alexandria. They appear to have held some kind of advisory position in the household. Both men were honest, able, and influential, destined for subsequent service in the provinces. Neither was used for the education of Marcellus or Tiberius, as were other of the court Greeks; they were too important to the Emperor himself.

Athenodorus of Tarsus, the son of Sandon, was, like Apollodorus, already an old man when Alexandria fell.[2] But he too was to be an octogenarian, and there was still much which he would do before he died. The son of Sandon was the second illustrious Stoic named Athenodorus to come to Rome from Tarsus. In the fashion of the Republic Marcus Cato had brought back from Tarsus Athenodorus Cordylion, who lived and died at his side.[3] It is not clear precisely when or how the teacher of Augustus came to Rome; he was there at least in 44 B.C., so that Octavian may be supposed to have brought him to the city in that year, much as Cato had brought Cordylion over a decade before. The son of Sandon seemed to be just as intimate with his patron as Cordylion had been with his. To impress upon the Emperor the need for more stringent security measures, he once arranged for himself to be brought into the imperial chamber in a roofed litter as if he were a woman; safely within the room, he leapt from the litter brandishing a sword and crying to Augustus, 'Are you not afraid that someone will come in like this and kill you?'[4] This was not to be the only instance of Athenodorus' vigour in old age.

---

[1] Suet. *Aug.* 89. 1 (Octavian took him from Rome to Apollonia) ; Ps.-Lucian, *Macrobioi* 23 (death at the age of eighty-two) ; Strabo 625 (profit from Augustus' friendship).

[2] Ps.-Lucian, loc. cit. The report in Eusebius (ed. Helm, p. 170) showing Athenodorus still alive in A.D. 8 must be inaccurate.

[3] Strabo 674.

[4] Dio 56. 43. 2. On the role of Athenodorus (highly conjectural) : P. Grimal, 'Auguste et Athénodore', *REA* 47 (1945), 261 ff. and 48 (1946), 62 ff.

It was precisely at the fall of Alexandria that Octavian exhibited to the world the high esteem in which he held another of his teachers, Areius the Alexandrian. When the victorious Octavian marched into Alexandria, he was observed conversing in public with Areius and giving him his hand. The Emperor pardoned the city on three accounts: its founder Alexander the Great, its great beauty and size, and his friend Areius.[1] The juxtaposition of Alexander and Areius gives some indication of Octavian's regard for his teacher. It may be noted further that Octavian announced his clemency toward the Alexandrians in a speech in Greek.[2] That was a language in which the future Princeps never achieved proficiency. He was always obliged to write whatever he had to say in Latin and then have it translated.[3] Octavian's speech to the Alexandrians may well have been delivered in a translation done by the Alexandrian Areius.

The influence of Areius not only saved the city of Alexandria, but it also saved a philosopher's life and led to the introduction of another Greek into the imperial circle. The philosopher Philostratus had been a supporter of the queen Cleopatra but a friend of Areius, through whose good offices the victor of Actium was induced to spare his life.[4] Although Philostratus was never welcomed into the court of Augustus, he was not forgotten: when he died far away on the border of Egypt and Judaea, Augustus' poet laureate composed a poem in his memory.[5]

Another friend of Areius has no attested record of offence in the triumviral period. The widely travelled Peripatetic, Xenarchus from Seleuceia on the Calycadnus, had lived in Athens and Alexandria,[6] and in the latter city he undoubtedly met Areius. When Xenarchus came to Rome, he entered into the Emperor's friendship. In high favour he lived and taught in the city till a ripe old age, enduring blindness and

---

[1] Plut. *Ant.* 80; *Praec. Rei Pub. Ger.* 18 (814 D); [Plut.] *Apophtheg.* 207 B; Dio 51. 16. 4; Julian, *Ep.* 51. 433 D. For the τόποι in regard to Alexandria, cf. *P.Oxyrh.* xxiv. 2435.

[2] Dio 51. 16. 4.   [3] Suet. *Aug.* 89. 1.

[4] Plut. *Ant.* 80. 2–3.

[5] *Anth. Pal.* vii. 645 (Crinagoras).

[6] Strabo 670.

ultimately dying of disease.[1] Xenarchus doubtless owed to Areius his friendship with Augustus.

Areius' position in the imperial household was rather analogous to that of Athenodorus. It is probable that Areius, at least, held some kind of well-defined post, inasmuch as the name of his successor has been preserved.[2] Both Areius and Athenodorus were remembered in antiquity as the authors of essays to two notable imperial women. When Livia was mourning the death of Drusus in 9 B.C., Areius provided her with a *consolatio* in her hour of grief.[3] Athenodorus is said to have written a book for Augustus' sister, Octavia; this too must have been a *consolatio* on the occasion of a son's death.[4]

While the Emperor had his own eastern teachers and advisers, he saw to it that his heirs did too. Marcellus was entrusted to the care of two men, one from Tarsus and one from Cilician Seleuceia. Nestor of Tarsus was an Academic, who, like several of his contemporary Greeks, lived to a very advanced age.[5] Indeed, Augustus was fortunate in gathering round him so many learned men remarkable for their longevity and vigour.

Nestor's colleague was Athenaeus, the authority on siege-works, who composed a treatise for Marcellus setting out to war.[6] Athenaeus must have been instructing Marcellus at the time of his departure for Spain with Augustus. Since the Seleuceian Peripatetic who was called Athenaeus was living in Rome at precisely this time, there is no difficulty in identifying him with the military instructor of Marcellus.[7] The Seleuceian was an intimate of Murena, the alleged conspirator, in

---

[1] Strabo 670. Observe the Egyptian κώμη in *P. Oxyrh.* x. 1285, l. 60 (third century A.D.), perhaps owing its name to Augustus' friend: ἐπ⟨ο⟩ικ(ίου) Ξεναρχου.

[2] Suidas s.v. Θέων: γεγονὼς ἐπὶ Αὐγούστου μετὰ Ἄρειον.

[3] Sen. *ad Marc.* 4. 5. 6. 1.

[4] Plut. *Public.* 17. 8. Cf. Cichorius, *RS* 279 ff.: 'Der Hofphilosoph Athenodorus von Tarsos'.

[5] Strabo 675. Ps.-Lucian, *Macrob.* 21 (death at the age of ninety-two): erroneous in calling him a Stoic.

[6] Cichorius, *RS* 271 ff., 'Das Werk des Athenaeus über Kriegsmaschinen', has demonstrated that the treatise was composed for Marcellus.

[7] Strabo 670.

the years before he was charged with treachery—when his kinship with Maecenas' wife brought him close to the Emperor. Athenaeus managed to survive the fall of Murena, although he fled when the conspiracy was uncovered.[1] Augustus discovered that Murena's friend was innocent, and Athenaeus was spared. He returned to Seleuceia with the opening words of Euripides' *Hecuba* appropriately on his lips.[2] But he lived only a little while longer: one night the house in which he was living collapsed and crushed him.[3]

The irreproachable Nestor, Athenaeus' colleague in the tuition of Marcellus, probably went on to instruct the young Tiberius for a short time.[4] But Tiberius' more famous teacher was another oriental, the freedman Theodorus of Gadara.[5] The parents of this man were probably brought to Rome as prisoners at the time of the Mithridatic Wars. Since one of his posterity bore the name Antonius, Theodorus may have

---

[1] Ibid. Athenaeus' association with Varro Murena the conspirator led Mrs. Atkinson (*Hist.* 9 [1960], 469) to connect the mysterious Varro who governed Syria (Jos., *BJ* 1. 398; *AJ* 15. 345) with the conspirator and to postulate an acquaintance with Athenaeus in the East. That cannot be: Athenaeus, as the author of the treatise on siege-works (cf. p. 34, n. 6), must already have been in Rome in 27, whereas Varro was in Syria later, *c.* 25 (cf. *P–W*, 2te Reihe 15. 415).

[2] Strabo quotes Euripides: ἥκω νεκρῶν κευθμῶνα καὶ σκότου πύλας λιπών. An old textual crux in this passage of Strabo (670) can now be resolved by the Vatican Palimpsest of *c.* A.D. 500 (W. Aly, *De Strabonis codice rescripto cuius reliquiae in codicibus Vaticanis Vat. Gr. 2306 et 2061 A servatae sunt* [1956], p. 112, fol. 369 II, line 38). For εἰς 'Ρώμην read ἐκ 'Ρώμης: cf. Bowersock, *CR* N.S. 14 (1964) 12 f.

[3] Strabo 670.

[4] Ps.-Lucian, *Macrob.* 21.

[5] Suidas registers two men under the name Θεόδωρος: a poet who wrote an epic to Cleopatra and a freedman Gadarene who taught Tiberius. The treacherous tutor of Antyllus (Plut. *Ant.* 81) must be identical with the author of the epic to Cleopatra; he was crucified (Plut. ibid.). A son of the Gadarene is said in Suidas to have been a senator under Hadrian, which is impossible, but the person's name is given as Antonius; it may well have belonged in the family of the Gadarene, who was perhaps an Antonian for a while. Quintilian (3. 1. 17 ff.) says that Tiberius heard Theodorus of Gadara on Rhodes: Tiberius cannot have met him on the notorious *secessus*, as Theodorus engaged in a rhetorical contest *at Rome* with Potamo of Mytilene (Suidas, loc. cit.). Potamo would have been far too old for a contest after A.D. 4, when he was probably already dead anyway. Theodorus is also mentioned in Strabo 759 and Suet. *Tib.* 57; and on an inscribed statue base from the Athenian Agora, *AJP* 80 (1959), 368. For Theodorus and his origins in the late Republic: Cichorius, *Rom und Mytilene* (1888), p. 63.

deserted to Octavian from Antony, like another Theodorus, Antony's son by Cleopatra.

Another Greek in the service of Augustus at Rome was the son of the great Theophanes and an *eques*. The Mytilenean Pompeius Macer was put in charge of organizing the imperial library.[1] It will be seen how he and his family rose still higher in the Emperor's service.

The household of Augustus could boast its own Greek poet to provide occasional verse. Such a poet had republican precedents, not to mention Antipater of Thessalonica in the retinue of Augustus' contemporary, Piso the Pontifex.[2] But inasmuch as a monarchy was taking shape in Rome, the court versifier resembled most of all a poet laureate. This was the role of another Mytilenean, Crinagoras, the son of Callippus. Crinagoras met Augustus for the first time at Tarraco in Spain in 26 B.C. as an ambassador from his city in Lesbos.[3] Some twenty years previously he had gone to Rome on a similar mission to confront Caesar the Dictator.[4] In those troubled times Crinagoras had reaped no personal profit apart from the inevitable gratitude of Mytilene for his part in a successful embassy, but in Spain he found favour with the creator of the Pax Augusta and never went home again. Resident in Rome but a companion of the Emperor on his travels,[5] Crinagoras turned out a steady stream of short poems commemorating the vicissitudes of Augustus' relatives and friends. The poet sang of the boy Marcellus returning a man from the West, of the marriage of the King of Mauretania with the offspring of the Queen of Egypt, of Antonia's last birthday before her marriage to Drusus.[6] Moreover, the poet also exercised his Muse on certain well-known events of the day: the desecration of the tomb of an eastern tyrant, who had once been a teacher in the city of Rome and a friend of many Romans though not of

---

[1] Suet. *Jul.* 56. 7.

[2] See, for example, *Anth. Pal.* vi. 241, 249, 335; ix. 93, 541, 552; x. 25; xvi. 184.

[3] *IGR* 4. 33; cf. 4. 38 (ἐν Ταρρακῶνι τῆς ᾿Ιβη[ρίας . . .]). The embassy of 26 B.C. may provide the context for *Anth. Pal.* ix. 559.

[4] *IGR* 4. 33. On the date of the embassy to Julius Caesar, see Sherk, *Greek, Roman, and Byzantine Studies* 4 (1963), 115 ff.   [5] *Anth. Pal.* ix. 224; 419.

[6] Ibid. vi. 161 (Marcellus); ix. 235 (Cleopatra Selene and Juba II); vi. 345 (Antonia's birthday).

Augustus.[1] A few lines are addressed to Philostratus, the friend of Areius who died in the East.[2] The mishap of M. Lollius in Germany is cleared of disgrace.[3] The lament of a nameless mother over the transposed fortunes of two sons is surely an allusion to the sons of Adiatorix, whose fortitude earned the admiration of the Emperor.[4]

Augustus did not shrink from employing educated Greek freedmen in his house any more than did the great men of the late Republic. Both C. Julius Marathus and C. Julius Asclepiades appear to have recorded the wonders of Augustus' birth,[5] and their gentilicia suggest ample compensation. To the freedman, M. Verrius Flaccus, was entrusted the education of Gaius and Lucius Caesar;[6] he may be presumed to be a man of Greek origin, though proof is lacking. While freedmen served the Emperor in diverse ways, the Emperor refused such intimacy with them as he accorded to certain other men. No freedman was privileged to dine with him, with the sole exception of that expert traitor, Menas, after he had been declared free-born.[7]

As the Principate took shape, the Augustan circle of Greeks did not remain quite the same. Death removed the trusted Areius, but his place was filled by another Alexandrian, the Stoic Theon.[8] While evidence for this man is far less abundant than it is for his predecessor, he appears to have been favoured almost as highly. That would be implied by his position alone, but there are two other valuable items on record. His name was C. Julius Theon, which means that the citizenship was granted to him either by Caesar or Caesar's heir. The latter is more likely, for a papyrus has revealed that Augustus presented Theon with large estates in Egypt out of his royal land.[9]

---

[1] Ibid. ix. 81 (Nicias of Cos).   [2] Ibid. vii. 645.

[3] Ibid. vii. 741. Cichorius, *RS*, pp. 312–13, is right in referring this to Lollius. Varus' disaster is out of the question because of its late date.

[4] *Anth. Pal.* vii. 638. See Bowersock, *Hermes* 92 (1964) 255 f.

[5] Suet. *Aug.* 94 (cf. 79) on Marathus; Suet. *Aug.* 94 (Asclepiades).

[6] Id. *de Gramm.* 17.   [7] Id. *Aug.* 74.

[8] Suid. s.v. Θέων.

[9] *P. Oxyrh.* xii. 1434. Theon made his land over to Isis, but subsequently requested that C. Julius Aquila, the prefect of Egypt, turn it over to his son Theon. On Theon and his family, see especially H. A. Musurillo, *Acts of the Pagan Martyrs*, p. 103.

The citizenship and the succession to Areius can be connected plausibly with the imperial favour revealed in a substantial land grant.

The sons of Areius, Nicanor and Dionysius, went on to assist Augustus with his Greek studies after their father's death; in particular they were probably responsible for drafting Latin texts into Greek for promulgation among the Greek-speaking peoples.[1] In Augustan Athens there appeared a C. Julius Nicanor: as his father's name was Areius and his origins were Alexandrian, it is more than likely that he was the philosopher's son looking after Augustan interests in Greece.[2]

Supervision of the imperial libraries passed from the hands of the eminent knight Pompeius Macer into the care of C. Julius Hyginus, a freedman.[3] He was a Spaniard according to some, but others said he was an Alexandrian brought to Rome by Julius Caesar. Augustus already employed several Alexandrians, and he may have added still another.

Macer's translation to a new post was a matter of some importance. He was not the only Greek who left the domestic service of the Emperor for employment elsewhere. Augustus appears quite deliberately to have sent out those Greeks who had proved themselves in his service at Rome to serve as his agents in organizing and administering the Greek-speaking portions of his empire. Inevitably from the nature of the Greek circle in the Roman court, these agents were men of considerable literacy and diplomatic experience; several were philosophers and therefore acquainted with the political arts. This policy of using Greeks as imperial agents in Greek nations determined the character of the Principate for the generations to follow.

Pompeius Macer was sent to Asia, whence he had come. There he held the equestrian office of procurator.[4] The retinue of Macer may have included two literary celebrities: the poet Ovid and Nemesis, the aptly named object of Tibullus' affections.[5] Macer's employment among Greeks did not cease with

---

[1] Suet. *Aug.* 89. 1.   [2] See chapter VII, p. 96, n. 5, below.
[3] Suet. *de Gramm.* 20.
[4] Strabo 618; cf. *JRS* 51 (1961), 116–17, n. 42.
[5] Ovid, *Pont.* ii. 10. 21; Tibullus II. 6.

his term in Asia. He appears to have moved on, at some later date, to a post in Sicily. At least he acted as a guide for Ovid when the poet visited the island some time before his banishment.[1]

Athenodorus may also have seen something of Sicily as a representative of Augustus.[2] The evidence is obscure on this point. But there can be no doubt of a far more vital mission of Athenodorus. He was sent back to his native city of Tarsus, which was both economically and strategically important and boasting the most stimulating intellectual life in the Near East. The Emperor bestowed upon his teacher and friend a special *imperium* by which he was to remove the Antonian tyrant there and to reorganize the constitution of the city.[3] Here was Augustus interfering—not for the first nor for the last time— wilfully and manifestly in the affairs of a free city, but he could not afford to leave Tarsus to an untrustworthy and demagogic Antonian. It was a wise move to use one of the city's most distinguished citizens to make the necessary adjustments. Although he was an old man, Athenodorus lacked neither energy nor repartee; coarse insults could not keep him from accomplishing his task. The tyrant Boëthus and his men were driven from the city, whereupon Athenodorus took his place as the political leader of Tarsus.[4]

Another Tarsian was still at Rome; this was Nestor, the Academic and the teacher of Marcellus. When Athenodorus died, the affairs of the free city of Tarsus could still not be left quite to themselves. Nestor was dispatched there, an able successor to his aged fellow citizen.[5] Thus the teacher of Augustus' heirs followed the teacher of Augustus himself in managing the political life of the city in which both pedagogues had been born.

The Alexandrian Areius, like his colleagues at Rome, was

---

[1] Ibid. ii. 10. 21 ff. Perhaps Macer was acting in a purely private capacity: *P–W* 21. 2. 2276 f.

[2] [Plut.] *Apophtheg.* 207 B, on which see Cichorius, *RS*, pp. 280 ff. The text reads Theodorus, for which Cichorius prefers Athenodorus. One is left to wonder when or why Athenodorus was in Petra: Strabo 779.

[3] Id. 674–5.

[4] Ibid. Athenodorus dealt wittily with his opponents, who were commenting: ἔργα νέων, βουλαὶ δὲ μέσων, πορδαὶ δὲ γερόντων. Cf. Ps.-Lucian, *Macrob.* 21.

[5] Strabo 675.

destined for service in the Greek-speaking provinces. He was
sent to Sicily to serve as imperial procurator in succession to
a Greek whom he had known at the court at Rome.[1] His predecessor may have been the Gadarene Theodorus or perhaps
the Tarsian Athenodorus before his return to the East;[2] exact
identification in this case is of no great consequence. A Greek
succeeded a Greek. In time Areius was offered another post
abroad, significantly in the land of his birth. Augustus proposed to make him ἐπίτροπος of Egypt, but Areius declined
this office.[3] If Areius' reason for refusing is obscure, Augustus'
policy in asking is not.

It would be satisfying to know more exactly the appointment which was offered to Areius, because there may be
parallels in the history of Augustan Egypt. Other Greek agents,
who did not refuse the Emperor's offer, can be discovered
there. Eros, a Greek freedman with a taste for quail, is
described as ὁ τὰ ἐν Αἰγύπτῳ διοικῶν.[4] A regular official called
διοικητής does not emerge in imperial Egypt until the second
century A.D.,[5] nor is he included in Strabo's account of the
administration of that province under Augustus. Eros was perhaps the ἴδιος λόγος.[6]

C. Julius Theon, who had received large estates in Egypt
from the Emperor, was high priest of Alexandria and all
Egypt; not many years later the incumbent of this office can
be shown to be identical with the ἴδιος λόγος.[7] Perhaps Theon
too was both magistrates in one. Similarly C. Julius Asclepiades, who can easily be the Augustan panegyrist and authority
on Egypt, was also ἀρχιερεύς,[8] therefore probably ἴδιος λόγος
as well.

---

[1] [Plut.] *Apophtheg.* 207 B.

[2] See p. 39, n. 2; Theodorus, *pace* Cichorius, is plausible.

[3] Julian, *Epist. ad Themist.* 343 f. (Hertlein).

[4] [Plut.] *Apophtheg.* 207 B: Augustus is said to have nailed the man to a ship's
mast for having eaten a quail which had been undefeated in combat. Cf.
Suet.–Donat. *Vita Verg.* 34.

[5] Bell, *CAH* x. 289. Cf. P. M. Meyer, 'Διοίκησις und ἴδιος λόγος', *Festschrift f.
Hirschfeld* (1903), 131 ff. esp. 135–48. There is one isolated διοικητής from the
first century (under Nero), but clearly he is a person of much lower rank than
the official familiar from the second century: *P. Fouad* i (1939), no. 21.

[6] Cf. Hirschfeld, *Verwalt.* 359, n. 2.

[7] *P–W* 9. 900–1.

[8] *P. Rainer* 172; *PIR²*, A 1199.

Now it is clear that Areius was offered an ἐπιτροπή of Egypt.[1] In the age to which this evidence for Areius belongs, the office of the ἴδιος λόγος in that province was regularly described as ἡ τοῦ ἰδίου λόγου ἐπιτροπή and the official himself was designated ὁ ἐπίτροπος Αἰγύπτου ἰδίου λόγου.[2] The Emperor Julian alluded to Areius' rejected office as τὸ κράτιστον τέλος:[3] the papyri reveal the terminology ὁ κράτιστος πρὸς τῷ ἰδίῳ λόγῳ and ὁ κράτιστος ἀρχιερεύς for its conjunct.[4] Accordingly it may safely be conjectured that Augustus proposed to make Areius an ἴδιος λόγος. It becomes even more probable that the other Greek agents in Egypt also held that office. In particular, C. Julius Theon, as Areius' successor at Rome, was doubtless given the same opportunity in his homeland as Areius himself. Theon evidently accepted.

Among the possible ἴδιοι λόγοι of Augustan Egypt, two were dispatched from the educated imperial circle of Greeks at Rome, and a third was apparently a favoured freedman; there would have been a fourth, had he not refused his appointment.[5]

It is clear that Augustus was well aware of the value of intelligent and loyal Greeks both in his court at Rome and in the Greek-speaking portions of the empire. The names of many of the Greeks in his service testify to the Emperor's bestowal of the Roman citizenship, and it is only fair to conjecture that men known to posterity merely as Athenodorus or Areius received no less an honour.[6] An even closer assimilation of Greeks to the Roman imperial system lay still in the future; but Q. Pompeius Macer, son of the Augustan procurator of Asia and grandson of the freedman Theophanes, was a forerunner of what was to come. He was a senator.[7]

---

[1] Julian, loc. cit.   [2] P–W 9, loc. cit.   [3] Julian, loc. cit.
[4] P–W 9, loc. cit.

[5] Two other ἴδιοι λόγοι are known from the Augustan period: Q. Attius Fronto in A.D. 12–13 (P. Oxyrh. ix. 1188) and C. Seppius Rufus in A.D. 14–16 (P. Oxyrh. iv. 721; 835). The nomen of the latter is Oscan.

[6] It is worth remembering that Julius Caesar bestowed the citizenship on all physicians and teachers of the liberal arts at Rome (Suet. Jul. 42. 1).

[7] Praetor in A.D. 15: Tac. Ann. 1. 72; 6. 18; ILS 9349. On Tacitus' mistake in the generations involved: Syme, Tacitus ii. 748–9 and Bowersock, JRS 51 (1961), 116–17, n. 42.

IV

KINGS AND DYNASTS

THE administration of the East required men who knew the East and its peoples. Certain Romans, with extensive service in that part of the Mediterranean, inevitably became instruments of the Augustan government, unless they had incurred suspicion of hostility or treachery. Certain Greeks passed from intimacy with the Emperor into his service among the nations from which they had come.

Not all the Greek-speaking nations and principalities were included in the provinces of official Roman magistrates, but they could not on that account be neglected. Pompey had perceived the economic and strategic importance of Roman influence where outright subjection was lacking. Kings and dynasts were a useful means of control, especially in the more remote and barbaric regions, provided that the political sentiments of those rulers could be assured. For native dynasts understood their people and their country better than the average Roman republican governor his province. Moreover, upon such natives devolved the costly and burdensome work of organizing the territory over which they ruled. The Roman treasury was spared further expense. In a generation or two a king would have sufficiently civilized his regions so that they could then be incorporated as a Roman province with minimum difficulty. Nor was the native going to lose anything from dependence on Rome. His position against rivals and enemies, inside and outside his kingdom, was secured. As a faithful client, he could look forward to territorial expansion as a reward for his loyalty. Although the client princes of the late Republic had no knowledge of it at the time, the favours which they enjoyed were to find their natural outcome in the emergence of their posterity in the senate of Rome.

Antony understood the convenience of Pompey's system. And the kings and princes whom Antony sanctioned or elevated

realized that their rule would be stabilized and perhaps enlarged by allegiance to Rome's general. A settlement of the
East was impossible without advantages on both sides. But
a lasting settlement was difficult in any case because of the
difficulties in maintaining devotion to one party or one man.
If a republican or triumviral imperator were regarded as the
representative of Rome, then allegiance to that man meant
allegiance to Rome. The theory was admirable, but useless
when Rome was rent by civil strife. A man whom Antony had
raised up in an Eastern city or principality had good reason to
fear Antony's conqueror, for favour from one man could entail
hostility or ruin at the hands of his victorious enemy. Abstract
fidelity to Rome in such an age was not only insufficient: it was
impossible. The princes who sought Rome's favour during the
civil wars could only do so by pledging themselves to the man
of the moment. To be sure, in the early years of the Triumvirate they could regard themselves as attached to a single
party which included both Octavian and Antony, but the
breach between the two triumvirs forced a choice. Antony was
present in the East, and there, naturally enough, he was the
favoured man.

With the fall of Alexandria, Octavian found himself the
heir to an empire. Both within it and at its borders in the East
were the men whom Antony had elevated to power or supported in a power they already held. A few of these, observing
before the final blow that they were espousing a losing cause,
deserted to the camp of Octavian. The brigand lord of Gordioucome in Mysia and the King of Paphlagonia continued to
be held in honour by virtue of their treachery at Actium.[1] The
King of Galatia may have secured his position for the future
by covert intrigue before the battle was joined.[2] But desertions
play an insignificant role in the policy of Octavian toward the
kings and dynasts of the East. Antony's conqueror might have
been expected to uproot the eastern Antonians from high
position, to honour the deserters, and to raise up new client
rulers, if he did not intend directly to annex a region stripped

---

[1] Strabo 574 (Cleon of Gordioucome); Dio 50. 13. 5 (Philadelphus of
Paphlagonia).
[2] Dio 50. 13. 8. Cf. Plut. *Ant.* 63. 3.

of its king. But Octavian was too shrewd. He knew that un-
relenting Antonians could not be tolerated in his empire;
they would be sources of discontent and turbulence. And some
Antonian favourites would have to fall together with the man
who favoured them simply in proof of the victor's newly won
authority. However, there was an abundance of petty prince-
lings who could easily be sacrificed without disrupting the
major arrangements of Antony. Octavian recognized that the
system of client kingship rested upon a foundation of mutual
advantage, and to a Roman just entering upon the possession
of a vast empire that system was indispensable for maintaining
an equilibrium in the periphery of the eastern provinces. In
the larger kingdoms Antony's arrangements were eminently
satisfactory. If Octavian was willing to overlook their past and
favour them as his own clients, the kings and tyrants had much
to gain from transferring their allegiance and nothing to lose;
they would shine the more resplendently for not having betrayed their previous patron at a time of crisis. It was clear
how to perpetuate Antony's eastern settlement, and in broad
outline that is what Octavian chose to do.

First, however, a conqueror must uncover and remove his
enemy's supporters: conquerors are expected to do that, if
they are not to be thought weak and lacking in initiative.
A succession of local dynasts would suffice for Octavian's victims. A few had to be eliminated anyway because they were
courageous enough to remain loyal to a man defeated and dead.

On the southern shore of the Black Sea two tyrants fell, one
at Amisus and another at Heraclea Pontica. Antony had given
Amisus over to kings; in 30 B.C. a tyrant, Strato by name, was
deposed by Octavian. Strato will have been one of Antony's
men and perhaps a member of another Antonian dynasty, the
Tarcondimotids of Hierapolis-Castabala.[1] At Heraclea Pontica, where Julius Caesar had planted a Roman colony, Antony
had put Adiatorix in charge of the Heracleot division of the
city. But Adiatorix, seeing an opportunity for the East in the
civil wars of Rome, recalled the Mithridatic massacre; shortly
before Actium, he rose up against the Romans of Heraclea and

---

[1] Strabo 547. Note a IIvir at Pisidian Antioch, C. Julius Straton, regis
Tarcondimoti Philopatoris f.: *JRS* 2 (1912), 108.

slaughtered them. On no account could Octavian spare so murderous a traitor. Adiatorix and his elder son were exhibited in a triumph at Rome and condemned to die. But Galatian heroism altered fate: Adiatorix' younger son offered himself in place of his brother and so died with his father. The Emperor was amazed: men of such mettle could not be wasted. Adiatorix' elder son, Dyteutus, the man who nearly died, was soon given a priestly tyranny in Pontus.[1]

On the island of Cos the tyrant Nicias was finally overthrown with the elevation of Octavian. Nicias belonged to the grand republican tradition of well-educated dynasts, like Zeno of Laodicea and Hybreas of Mylasa, who knew the value of Roman friends. Politics and literacy mingled successfully in that age. Nicias' career was more spectacular than most. He had been taken to Rome in 62 B.C. by Pompey in the company of Lucretius' patron, C. Memmius, and as a teacher in the city had enjoyed the friendship of men of no less stature than Cicero, Brutus, Cassius, and Dolabella.[2] He evidently incurred the wrath of Pompey and was compelled to leave Rome,[3] but after Pharsalus a man whom Pompey had punished could look forward to a new era of favour. The literate and well-connected Nicias stood on the right side of the tyrannicides and of the Antonians, with the result that he attained to a moderate tyranny in Cos with the support of Antony. His rule lasted for at least eight years.[4] But Nicias had neglected to include the youthful heir of Caesar among his Roman friends; indeed, Octavius had been a small child when Nicias was at Rome. Besides, the tyrant's friendship with Antony could not, in the end, have won him the enthusiastic support of the Coan people. In the year before Actium an Antonian admiral issued an order to cut down the sacred cypress trees of Asclepius on Cos to build ships.[5] Therefore Nicias could hope for little

---

[1] Strabo 543, 558–9. The subject of *Anth. Pal.* vii. 638 (Crinagoras): see Bowersock, *Hermes* 92 (1964), 255f.

[2] Suet. *de Gramm.* 14 (Memmius, Cicero, Dolabella). On his connexion with Brutus and Cassius: F. Munzer, *Röm. Adelsp.*, p. 357, n. 2, nos. 12–13.

[3] He carried a note *de stupro* from Memmius to Pompey's wife, the daughter of Metellus Scipio, who betrayed him (Suet. *de Gramm.* 14).

[4] The evidence is numismatic: *BMC* Caria 213.

[5] Dio 51. 8. 3. On the sacred cypresses: Val. Max. 1. 1. 19.

favour in 30 B.C. either from the people of his island or from Octavian. His chances would only have been better if he had ruled a larger and more important region. The dynast of Cos was uprooted, but the island's tribute was reduced in return for a painting of Venus.[1] Nicias went to the grave soon afterward, although not even there was he secure. The body of the man whom Cos once had honoured as a son of the people was torn from the tomb and desecrated.[2]

Certain minor dynasties of the East exhibit a remarkable similarity in their history at this time. Each was ruled by an Antonian, and each was deprived of its ruler by Antony's rival. These were to be in areas which would pay the price of supporting the wrong side, for Octavian had seen the least risk in sacrificing the minor princes. But he miscalculated; it was not long before he appreciated Antony's sagacity in providing dynasts for these places. In three instances Augustus was obliged to re-establish the Antonian houses he had overthrown; in a fourth he installed an Antonian prince whom he had removed from power elsewhere. And in a fifth he provided his own tyrant.

One of these dynasties was centred in Hierapolis-Castabala in Level Cilicia. Tarcondimotus Philantonius was king in the triumviral period and gave his life while fighting for Antony at Actium.[3] His son, Tarcondimotus Philopator, acceded to the throne, but his reign was brief. Octavian deposed him in 30 B.C.[4] Yet ten years later Caesar Augustus reverted to the arrangement of Antony. The Tarcondimotids were reinstated at Hierapolis-Castabala, and Philopator received all his father's kingdom with the exception of certain coastal districts which were assigned to the Cappadocian king.[5] In the next year Philopator caused Anazarbus to adopt a new name as an

---

[1] Strabo 657. Augustus dedicated the painting in the shrine of Julius Caesar and possibly uttered some Greek verses on the occasion; the piece was imperfect and replaced by Nero (Pliny, *NH* 35. 91).

[2] *Anth. Pal.* ix. 81 (Crinagoras), revealing that Nicias is dead in 30 B.C. He is called 'son of the people' on inscriptions: Paton and Hicks, *Inscriptions of Cos* (Oxford, 1891), nos. 76–80. Four unpublished: *P-W* 17. 334. On Nicias, see the excellent account of R. Syme, *JRS* 51 (1961), 25–28.

[3] Plut. *Ant.* 61. 1. Cf. Dio 51. 2. 2. The name Philantonius is attested on coins: Head, *HN²* 735. Cf. Jones, *CERP*, pp. 436–7, nos. 18–21.

[4] Dio 51. 2. 2.   [5] Dio 54. 9. 2.

expression of his indebtedness to the Princeps; henceforth it was to be known as Caesarea-by-Anazarbus.[1] The client dynasty of Tarcondimotus Philopator spanned the remainder of the Augustan Principate and was doubtless a comfort in the period of the Homonadensian war.

The Tarcondimotids were further confirmed in their dependence upon the Roman emperor at an unknown date by a grant of citizenship.[2] Augustus knew the usefulness of the citizenship as a means of binding his client kings closer to himself; Tarcondimotus was hardly the only one upon whom he bestowed it, although there is irony in the son of a Philantonius with the name C. Julius.

In the kingdom of Emesa in Syria, Antony had watched after the interests of the house of Iamblichus. Alarmed by reports and threats of treachery in the last desperate hours before Actium, Antony had the king put to death and granted the succession to Iamblichus' brother, Alexander, whose fidelity was assured by the manner of his elevation. But his reign was swiftly terminated by the victorious Octavian.[3] Emesa was presumably incorporated into the province of Syria. However, a decade later, in the year of the Tarcondimotid restoration, Augustus re-established the house of Iamblichus at Emesa. The ancestral dominion was assigned to Iamblichus, son of the Antonian of the same name.[4] That was a wise choice: a father's murder on Antony's order was not quickly forgotten. Iamblichus' debt to the Emperor was enlarged by the gift of citizenship. Some of his posterity were to bear conjointly the names of a Pompeian potentate and the first Princeps, C. Julius Samsigeramus.[5]

Antony had allowed an inferior poet, Boëthus, to manage the affairs of Tarsus. Octavian left the man in control of the

---

[1] Head, *HN*[2] 716–17. Cf. Pliny, *NH* 5. 93.

[2] *Jahresh. Oest. Inst.* 18 (1915), Beiblatt, p. 58: βασιλὶς 'Ιουλία νεωτέρα (Anazarbus).

[3] Dio 50. 13. 7 (murder of the elder Iamblichus); Dio 51. 2. 2 (Octavian's deposition of Alexander). H. Buchheim, *Die Orientpolitik des Triumvirn M. Antonius* (1960), p. 22, infers that there had been 'keine sehr guten Beziehungen'.

[4] Dio 54. 9. 2.

[5] *IGR* 3. 1023 (C. Julius Samsigeramus). His son, C. Julius Sohaemus: *ILS* 8958.

city for a few years, but he was apparently not satisfactory.[1]
Early in the Principate, Athenodorus the Tarsian was dispatched from Rome with special powers given him by the
Emperor to settle the affairs of Tarsus.[2] In effect, Athenodorus
replaced Boëthus as lord of the city and guided its opinion into
support of the Emperor. Nestor, another Augustan Tarsian,
was sent back to succeed Athenodorus after his death.[3] Augustus found it too dangerous to leave a loyal Antonian in control
of Tarsus, but the city needed someone to run it. Accordingly
a client tyrant was displaced by a member of the imperial
court invested with special powers. Athenodorus and Nestor
symbolize the close link in policy between the support of client
princes and the employment of natives directly in the imperial service.

Caesar had installed Lycomedes the priest as dynast of
Pontic Comana, and Antony had left him there.[4] Octavian
made a change. He deposed Lycomedes and assigned his
principality to the traitorous robber, Cleon of Gordioucome,
honoured for his timely desertion from Antony. But Cleon
was an impious glutton, no fit man for the priesthood of
Comana; his contravention of a local taboo was alleged to
have brought him a swift death.[5] He was succeeded by the
Galatian Dyteutus, the elder son of Adiatorix.[6] Thus the
Augustan dynast of the priest-state of Pontic Comana was none
other than the son of an Antonian partisan who had murdered
the Roman colonists of Heraclea Pontica. Yet Dyteutus owed
his position to Augustus and, so far as is known, was faithful.

Olba in Rough Cilicia had fallen into the hands of pirates,
but the old priestly dynasty of Olban Teucrids survived none
the less. Aba, the favourite of Antony and Cleopatra, was the
daughter of a robber baron, but she and her father had been
sufficiently discreet to ensure her marriage into the ancient

[1] Strabo 674: Βοήθου, κακοῦ μὲν ποιητοῦ κακοῦ δὲ πολίτου.
[2] Ibid. Cf. above, p. 39. [3] Strabo 675.
[4] Id. 558. Cf. Dio 51. 2. 3.
[5] Strabo 574–5 (Cleon). To be sure, Strabo was not without prejudice in regard to the priests of Comana: a relative of his had been one earlier in the
century (Strabo 557). Dio 51. 2. 3 says that a certain Medeius succeeded
Lycomedes. Medeius must be identical with Cleon: Jones, CERP, p. 427, n. 43.
[6] Strabo 558–9.

house of Teucer. The victorious Octavian saw fit to dissolve the tyranny of Aba, an inconsequential Antonian.[1] She was not a great loss, nor can Octavian's displeasure have been much more than nominal. He subsequently entrusted Olba to the rule of Teucrid priests who were Aba's own descendants.[2] They were obviously the best qualified to govern that remote little principality.

Almost in spite of himself, the heir of Caesar was unable to do away with the petty tyrannies of Hierapolis-Castabala, Emesa, Tarsus, Pontic Comana, and Olba. In one instance he allowed a tyranny to continue, controlled by the offspring of a lady he deposed; in two instances a hiatus of ten years convinced him of the need to reinstate the tyrannies. He found himself obliged to rely in four principalities upon dynastic houses which had once enjoyed the favour of Antony. The removal of dynasts after Actium was only a small part of the eastern arrangements of Octavian. Augustus realized that it ought to have been even smaller.

As it was, Octavian had left several petty tyrannies undisturbed. One was that of Cleon, the brigand chieftain, who had betrayed Antony before Actium and received the priesthood of Pontic Comana among the rewards he had so little time to enjoy. His own territory in Mysia was enlarged, and he was presented with the priesthood of Zeus Abrettene.[3] A traitor once might be a traitor twice, as Octavian intimated to Herod of Judaea;[4] but that worry never led to the dishonour of a man who went over to the winning side. Cleon acknowledged his closeness to the Emperor by giving Gordioucome the new name of Juliopolis.[5] Perhaps the Emperor, on his part, had augmented Cleon's name through a bestowal of the citizenship.

To the east of Juliopolis, in Caranitis and Amaseia, two other petty Antonian dynasties were left intact, though granted

---

[1] Strabo 672: ἔπειθ' ἡ μὲν κατελύθη, τοῖς δ' ἀπὸ τοῦ γένους διέμεινεν ἡ ἀρχή. Jones, CERP, p. 209, has misunderstood what happened: 'Antony confirmed Aba in the principality, but on her death it reverted to the old line.'

[2] Strabo 672 (quoted in the foregoing note).   [3] Id. 574.

[4] Josephus, BJ i. 391: ἄξιος γὰρ εἰ πολλῶν ἄρχειν οὕτω φιλίας προϊστάμενος. πειρῶ δὲ καὶ τοῖς εὐτυχεστέροις διαμένειν πιστός, ὡς ἔγωγε λαμπροτάτας ὑπὲρ τοῦ σοῦ φρονήματος ἐλπίδας ἔχω.   [5] Strabo 574.

no additional honours. Caranitis was in the hands of the Galatian Ateporix, while Amaseia was ruled by kings un-named.[1] However, when these dynasties died out, they were not perpetuated. In 3 B.C. Caranitis was annexed and its capital, Carana, renamed Sebastopolis.[2] In the following year, Amaseia regained its status as a city and was incorporated in the Pontic province.[3] It mattered little how these regions were governed provided that they caused no trouble to the rest of Pontus.

The petty tyrannies reveal the modest attempts of a victor to expel his rival's partisans, but they also reveal a remarkable satisfaction with the arrangements he inherited. The final Augustan settlement of the minor dynasts is distinguished by its similarities to the Antonian, not only in the distribution of dynasties but in the dynastic houses themselves. The history of the larger client kingdoms provides even more conclusive evidence of Augustus' satisfaction with the triumviral pat-tern. The greater kings were too important and too useful to be sacrificed to Antony's conqueror, as a few smaller rulers had been.

Augustus maintained precisely six of the major kings who had ruled under Antony. Of these, five had been active An-tonian partisans. Octavian deposed only two of the greater triumviral kings, and one of them was a man whose un-reliability had given Antony himself good reason to depose him.

A cluster of major client kings occupied the north-east corner of the empire. Their histories are interwoven. In the kingdom of the Bosporus on the northern shore of the Black Sea lay the source of food for Asia Minor and a protection against the barbarian hordes farther north. If that region were ill disposed toward Rome, a severe economic crisis for the north-eastern provinces would inevitably ensue. A devastating in-vasion might follow. In Caesar's day the Bosporan kingdom had passed into the power of Asander, a former general of Pharnaces and the conqueror of the Caesarian Mithridates of

---

[1] Strabo 560 (Caranitis), 561 (Amaseia).

[2] See Anderson, *Anat. Studies pres. to Ramsay* (1923), p. 8.

[3] Head, *HN²* 496. Cf. also Anderson, loc. cit., and Jones, *CERP*, p. 170.

Pergamum. Asander ruled as king for some twenty-five years.[1] He abstained from the civil wars of the Romans and was left undisturbed both by Antony and by his successful rival. Asander enlarged his kingdom to the north and strengthened his barriers against the Scythians.[2]

Meanwhile, Antony had raised up kings in Pontus, Paphlagonia, Galatia, and Cappadocia. In 39 B.C. the son of Pharnaces was given the kingdom of Pontus, but two years later death or a dissatisfied Antony removed him from the throne, which passed to the son of Zeno, the celebrated rhetor and dynast of Laodicea.[3] Literacy, power, and influence with Rome characterized the house of Polemo, the new king of Pontus. The man belonged to the finest tradition of eastern politicians. Subsequently Polemo's kingdom was enlarged when Antony presented him with Armenia Minor. Octavian deprived Polemo of that accretion, not to punish him for his past but rather to bestow it upon another Antonian, the former king of Media who lacked a kingdom.[4]

In 40 B.C. Antony had honoured a certain Castor with the kingdoms of Paphlagonia and Galatia, but Castor died in 37.[5] The two kingdoms were separated. Paphlagonia passed to Castor's son, Deiotarus Philadelphus, who deserted to Octavian before Actium.[6] Antony bestowed Galatia upon Amyntas, secretary to the former King Deiotarus; part or possibly all of Pamphylia was included in Amyntas' portion. So was

[1] Dio 42. 46. 4 (Pharnaces' general). Id. 42. 48. 4; Strabo 625 (killed Mithridates of Pergamum). The coins of Asander show that he ruled for at least twenty-nine years and that he had assumed the title of king by the fourth year of rule: cf. *PIR*[2] A 1197. A coin of Dynamis, his wife, to whom he bequeathed his kingdom, dates from 17/16 B.C., whence it is inferred that Asander was already dead in that year. He thus will have come to power *c.* 47. Pseudo-Lucian, *Macrobioi* 17, records that Augustus bestowed the title of king upon Asander, but this has to be rejected in view of the numismatic evidence.

[2] Strabo 495 (his power extended to the Tanais), 311 (barriers against the Scythians).

[3] App. *BC* 5. 75 (Darius, son of Pharnaces); Dio 49. 25. 4 (Polemo already king in 36 B.C.); Strabo 578 (Zeno), 660 (Zeno's resistance to Labienus Parthicus). Cf. Buchheim, *Die Orientpolitik des Antonius*, pp. 50–52.

[4] Dio 49. 33. 2 and 44. 3 (gift of Armenia Minor to Polemo). In 20 B.C. Augustus gave Armenia Minor to Archelaus of Cappadocia, because the Mede, who had previously ruled that kingdom, was dead: Dio 54. 9. 2.

[5] Id. 48. 33. 5.

[6] Id. 50. 13. 5; Plut. *Ant.* 61. 1; Strabo 562; Head, *HN*[2] 509.

Rough Cilicia.[1] In adjacent Cappadocia Antony set up Archelaus, son of the temptress Glaphyra, as king and a few years later killed Archelaus' only rival for the throne.[2] All these arrangements passed without change into the Augustan empire. Neither Octavian nor the kings had much to lose from a preservation of the *status quo* on condition of a transference of allegiance.

Client kings might look after themselves for a while but not for ever. Death would overtake each of them. In 25 B.C. Amyntas was killed by the Homonadensians, and Galatia ceased to be a client kingdom.[3] Here, as elsewhere, the kings had unknowingly prepared their regions for incorporation into the empire. Galatia was now ready for organization as a new province and need not be entrusted to an untried king. Central Asia Minor was thereby committed irrevocably to Rome. At Pisidian Antioch, Amyntas' death meant an end of power for the affluent dynasty of priests in the service of Mēn Arkaios.[4] Roman colonists assumed the reins of government there, but not because it was Augustus' policy to dissolve priestly tyrannies—a policy he never had; the colonists, strategically situated in Pisidia, would naturally rule themselves, and they needed land, which the priests had held. The unmanageable territory of Rough Cilicia was omitted from the new province and transferred to the realm of Archelaus.[5]

In 6 B.C. another of the north-eastern kings died, Deiotarus Philadelphus of Paphlagonia. There, as in Galatia, the work of the kings was done, and incorporation was at hand. Paphlagonia was added to the province of Galatia.[6]

After the death of Asander, trouble arose in the Bosporan

---

[1] Dio 49. 32. 3; Strabo 671 (Rough Cilicia). Amyntas coined at Side: *BMC* Galat. xvii; Head, *HN*² 747.

[2] Dio 49. 32. 3; App. *BC* 5. 7; Strabo 540; Val. Max. 9. 15. *ext.* 2. Cf. Buchheim, op. cit., p. 56.

[3] Strabo 567; Dio 53. 26. 3; Strabo 569 (Homonadensians).

[4] Id. 577. Miss B. M. Levick, 'Roman Colonies in Southern Asia Minor' (unpublished Oxford D.Phil. thesis, 1958), pp. 113–15, thinks that the administration of the Mēn temple was handed over to colonial officials. Not necessarily: cf. the observations of T. R. S. Broughton on temple estates in Asia Minor, *Studies in Honour of A. C. Johnson* (Princeton, 1951), 236 ff.

[5] Dio 54. 9. 2.

[6] Strabo 562. The Paphlagonian era began in 6 B.C.: Head, *HN*² 506–7 and *IGR* 3. 137 (Oath of Gangra).

kingdom. An obscure man with the name Scribonius stirred up revolt, strengthening his position by marrying Asander's widow, Dynamis.[1] Agrippa, in the East at that time, attempted to put one of the client kings to good use; he ordered Polemo to proceed against the rebel. Polemo was singularly ineffective, but the presence of Agrippa in the Black Sea sufficed to remind the Bosporan peoples of their folly. They murdered Scribonius themselves.[2] Although Polemo had himself done little to suppress the revolt, he had the virtues of intelligence, fidelity, and knowledge of the region, for which Augustus presented him with the Bosporan kingdom. Polemo knew his duty toward Rome; moreover, he doubtless hankered to preserve the large kingdom which now was his. He went to war against a contender for the Bosporan throne, a certain Aspurgus, whose supporters were styled Aspurgiani. But Polemo was cut down in the year 8 b.c.[3] The damage to Rome was not very great, however. Aspurgus proved himself a reliable husband to Dynamis; he was later to receive the citizenship from Tiberius Caesar.[4]

Polemo died in the Bosporan kingdom, and his original kingdom in the Pontus passed into the hands of his widow. He had married into the wealthy family of Pythodorus of Tralles, which had enjoyed the friendship and favour of several of the great Romans of the first century.[5] The brother of his wife was perhaps the envoy from Tralles who sought the Emperor in Spain after an earthquake in 26 b.c.[6] The foremost house of Laodicea was united in Pontus with the foremost house of Tralles. In time to come, offspring of that distinguished marriage would accede to the royal house of Thrace, the kingship of Armenia, and the priestly dynasty of Olba, while Pythodoris herself, the client Queen of Pontus, married Archelaus, King of Cappadocia.[7] The network of Antony's appointments in the

---

[1] Dio 54. 24. 4.   [2] Id. 54. 24. 5.
[3] Strabo 495 (Aspurgiani), 556 (Polemo's death). Cf. *CAH* x. 269.
[4] *IGR* I. 880, cf. 879.
[5] Strabo 649 (house of Pythodorus); cf. Cic. *pro Flacc.* 22. 52. *OGIS* 377 (Antonia, grandmother of Pythodoris' son). Cf. Chapter I above, p. 8.
[6] Agathias 2. 17.
[7] Antonia Tryphaena, wife of King Cotys in Thrace: *IGR* 4. 144; Strabo 556. Zeno, king of Armenia: Tac. *Ann.* 2. 56; Strabo 556. Olba: Dio 60. 8. 2; Head, *HN*² 726–7 (Marcus Antonius Polemo). Pythodoris' marriage to Archelaus: Strabo 556.

north-eastern kingdoms grew tighter after his death by an evolution which Augustus had made possible. It was the studied policy of the first Princeps to unite his client dynasts by the mutual bonds of intermarriage.[1]

It was to be a long time before Archelaus of Cappadocia would die, thereby precipitating the annexation of his kingdom. His was not an untroubled reign. In the first decade of Augustus' Principate the people of Cappadocia levelled accusations at their king, who obtained the aid of the young Tiberius in pleading his case in the court of the Princeps.[2] Archelaus will have been acquitted, his discontented subjects somehow satisfied. Nor did Archelaus keep quiet after his trial: at one point his instability compelled Augustus to install a guardian over the realm. And he was on bad terms with a governor of Syria whose enmity he may have incurred through his cultivation of Tiberius. However, the client system can claim the end of Archelaus' hostility to M. Titius as one of the early proofs of its efficacy. Herod, King of Judaea, whose son had married a daughter of Archelaus, undertook to reconcile the Cappadocian monarch with the Syrian governor and succeeded.[3] This was a moment of strength for the Cappadocian–Judaean axis, just before the treachery of a petty dynast from Sparta and the death of Herod himself destroyed it. And although Archelaus could hardly have known at the time, his reconciliation with Titius adumbrated his slight to Tiberius, exiled at Rhodes; for Tiberius was no friend of Titius.[4] When the exile ultimately became emperor, Archelaus was shown how unwise he was to have forsaken his former advocate.[5]

Herod of Judaea was ultimately Antony's man. In 40 he had received the title of king with the manifest good will of *both* triumvirs; as a protégé of Julius Caesar, he belonged naturally to the Caesarian party in so far as it was represented jointly by Octavian and Antony.[6] But when the split inevitably

---

[1] Suet. *Aug.* 48: Reges socios etiam inter semet ipsos necessitudinibus mutuis iunxit, promptissimus affinitatis cuiusque atque amicitiae conciliator et fautor.

[2] Suet. *Tib.* 8; Dio 57. 17. 3–4.

[3] Jos. *AJ* 16. 270.

[4] Tiberius' panegyrist, Velleius, treats him harshly: ii. 79. 6.

[5] Tac. *Ann.* 2. 42; Dio 57. 17. 3–4.

[6] See Buchheim, *Die Orientpolitik des Antonius*, p. 66.

came between those two men, Herod—like so many others—
had to choose, and he chose Antony. But he had been in
Arabia when Actium was fought, so that it was relatively simple
to transfer his allegiance to Octavian if Octavian would have
him. Herod established his new loyalty in opposing the Antonian gladiators.[1] If inference can be made from his dealings
with other kingdoms, the victor of Actium would have wanted
to support Herod anyway; it was comforting to see how well
Herod understood the folly of loyalty to the dead. Nor indeed
was he troubled by turning his back on the living: he put away
his first wife, for she was only a common woman, and perhaps
he also eliminated his elderly rival, Hyrcanus, though he was
too civilized to admit the deed outright.[2] Octavian planned
Herod's future on the island of Rhodes in 30 B.C.; Herod's
loyalty to Antony till the last was a credit to him. He deserved
to rule over many peoples after showing such loyalty to a friend.
Herod and Octavian both understood client kingship.[3]

The King of Judaea was an admirer of the Hellenes. The
Greek world was full of his benefactions. Cos, Rhodes, Pergamum, Athens, Sparta, Augustus' own Nicopolis had known
Herod's generosity.[4] In Judaea itself there arose monuments
testifying to the greatness of Herod's patron. City after city
erected temples to the Emperor; an old city was transformed,
endowed with a tower in honour of Augustus' stepson, and
renamed Caesarea. A new city arose in Samaria with the
meaningful name Sebaste.[5]

Such culture did not go without its reward. Octavian had
left Zenodorus to rule over the land east of the Jordan and
leased to him Abilene in the north, but Zenodorus was a failure
as a ruler.[6] His realm was given over to Herod in two stages.
Zenodorus had furnished aid to the Ituraean bandits in the

---

[1] Jos. *BJ* 1. 392; *AJ* 15. 195.
[2] Id. *BJ* 1. 432 ff.; *AJ* 15. 164 ff.
[3] Id. *BJ* 1. 387–92; *AJ* 15. 187–93. It is appropriate that Herod's sons
stayed in Rome with a certain Pollio (id. *AJ* 15. 343), perhaps the notorious
Vedius Pollio, friend of Augustus: see R. Syme, *JRS* 51 (1961), 30 *addendum*.
[4] Jos. *BJ* 1. 423–5. He even settled a debt which some Chians owed to
Augustus' procurators: *AJ* 16. 26.
[5] Id. *BJ* 1. 403; *AJ* 15. 292 ff.
[6] Id. *BJ* 1. 398 ff.; *AJ* 15. 344 ff. Strabo 756.

mountains south-east of Chalcis, and when he died Herod
acquired at last his entire kingdom.[1]

The ties which bound Augustus and Herod were soon to
break apart. No client king could be left wholly to his own
devices. The household of Herod was stricken by ambition,
jealousy, and murder, and at Rome was the Emperor, to
whom flowed all complaints. Herod travelled to Rome to ac-
cuse his own son before the Emperor, who was called upon
a few years later to sanction the wilful assassination of Herod's
son by his father.[2] The tumult in the house of Herod shook the
kingdom of Cappadocia, whose king was connected with
Herod through the marriage of his daughter to a son of the
Jew. The dynast of Sparta, whom the heir of Caesar had
elevated from a disreputable obscurity, journeyed to the Near
East and turned all things to his own gain.[3] This much was
bad enough: the client kings, established to relieve the Emperor of worry and expense, had plunged the East into commotion.

What was worse was Herod's invasion of Arabia. Syllaeus,
a treacherous general of the Nabataean king, had lent support
to rebels in Trachonitis, which had passed into Herod's kingdom from the portion of Zenodorus.[4] Obodas of Arabia was
recently dead, and Syllaeus was ambitious. Herod retaliated,
not without the approval of certain Roman officials in Syria,
but Syllaeus went to Rome to explain his position to Augustus.
The Emperor was enraged. He wrote to Herod that he had
long treated him as a friend but henceforth would treat him
as a subject.[5] The diplomatic Damascene, Nicolaus, managed
to effect a reconciliation with Augustus; Syllaeus was condemned to die as a token of that reconciliation. He was alleged to have caused the disasters of Aelius Gallus' expedition
into Arabia Felix twenty years earlier.[6]

Yet the kingdom of Judaea saw no change from blood and
chaos. In 4 B.C. Herod died, and Augustus was compelled to
weigh the arguments of Archelaus and Antipas, rival claimants

---

[1] Jos. *BJ* 1. 399–400; *AJ* 15. 345–60. Dio 54. 9. 3.
[2] Jos. *BJ* 1. 536–7. Cf. Macrob. *Sat.* 9. 4. 11.
[3] Id. *BJ* 1. 513 ff.; *AJ* 16. 301 ff.   [4] Id. *AJ* 16. 290.
[5] Id. *AJ* 16. 271 ff.   [6] Strabo 782; not known to Josephus.

to the throne. A partition resulted, which did not suffice.[1] Archelaus the ethnarch was brutal and murderous; he had to be removed, and he was removed far away—to Vienne in Narbonese Gaul.[2] Further distributions of the Judaean principalities were not necessitated. Octavian had chosen the simple solution in retaining Antony's king in Judaea, but the house of Herod brought with it perhaps more trouble than it was worth. In A.D. 6 the procuratorial province of Judaea was created.[3]

The home of Syllaeus was one of the two major kingdoms, which (unlike Egypt) nevertheless survived as kingdoms, where Octavian did not preserve the Antonian ruler. Malchus, King of the Nabataean Arabs during the Triumvirate, was an unreliable man anyhow. Ventidius had fined him in 40 B.C. for supporting the Parthians, and Antony himself had deprived him of part of his kingdom.[4] Furthermore, if Herod was to be retained in Judaea, Malchus would have to be replaced in Arabia, for Herod and Malchus were acknowledged foes. Octavian placed Obodas II, from an old Arabian royal family, on the throne of the Nabataeans.[5]

In Commagene, between Cappadocia and Syria to the west of the Euphrates, Octavian displaced another of Antony's men. For a certain Mithridates lent support to Antony at Actium, but the King of Commagene who was executed at the order of Octavian in 29 B.C. was called Antiochus.[6] Manifestly the Antonian nominee had been deposed, making way for Octavian's chosen successor, whose brief career was another reminder to the youthful victor of the wisdom of his enemy's settlement. Internal dynastic rivalries were a constant threat to the client system: Antiochus tried to secure his own power by forcibly preventing a hearing at Rome for an embassy from his dissentient brother. An envoy was murdered. With

[1] Jos. *BJ* 2. 93 ff.; *AJ* 17. 317 ff.

[2] Id. *BJ* 2. 111; *AJ* 17. 344.

[3] Id. *BJ* 2. 117 (territory of Archelaus under the knight Coponius); *AJ* 18. 2. Dio 55. 27. 6.

[4] Id. 48. 41. 5 (fine); 49. 32. 5 (deprived of territory by Antony). Plut. *Ant.* 61 (Antonian in 31).

[5] Jos. *BJ* 1. 365 ff. *AJ* 15. 110 ff. (war between Herod and Malchus). Id. *BJ* 1. 487; *AJ* 16. 220 (Obodas).

[6] Plut. *Ant.* 61 (Mithridates II). Dio 52. 43. 1 (Antiochus II).

markable swiftness Octavian struck down the man he must
have elevated two years earlier. Antiochus was tried before the
senate and condemned.[1] The name of the man who succeeded
the executed monarch has not been recorded, but he too murdered a royal rival. Accordingly, in 20 B.C. Augustus deposed
his second failure in Commagene and put upon the throne
a son of the very one whose murder had occasioned the latest
deposition.[2]

At the western and eastern extremities of the client orbit,
the history was either chaotic at the time or confounded in the
subsequent tradition. Armenia lay outside the world of Greek
culture and hence strictly outside this inquiry; yet Augustus
hoped for a dynasty there as elsewhere to favour the interest of
Rome. But his hopes, temporarily aroused, were shattered.
The missions of Tiberius and Gaius ultimately bore no fruit,
and when Augustus died, the natives had four times declared
their unwillingness to endure a client king.[3] Indeed, the fact
was that, apart from the reign of Tigranes II, Armenia under
Augustus was not a client kingdom at all.

In Thrace, far to the west, an Augustan dynasty emerges
from the tantalizing obscurity of the ancient evidence. The
first Princeps left to his successor latent hostilities which were
to lead inevitably to annexation; but, while he lived, this
westernmost of the Greek kingdoms was superficially as successful as the easternmost was a failure. It would occasion no
surprise to discover that Augustus adopted without change an
Antonian settlement of Thrace. Certainty on this point is out of
reach.[4] However, Antony's supporters before Actium included
representatives of each of the two royal houses of Thrace. In
42 B.C. the Sapaean line was domiciled in Macedonia, but
under Augustus it was installed at Bizye, the royal citadel of
the Odrysian branch. The union of these two houses was
secured through a marriage whose date is plausibly triumviral.
Before it was too late in 31 B.C., Antony's Sapaean partisan,
Rhoemetalces, deserted to Octavian. The Sapaeans, linked by
marriage with the Odrysians, were confirmed in their rule
by the customary grant of the Roman citizenship. Cotys, an

---

[1] Dio 52. 43. 1. [2] Id. 54. 9. 3. [3] *CAH* x. 260–5; 273–9.
[4] See Appendix II.

Odrysian, ruled at the opening of the Principate, but at his death a Sapaean was made regent for his children. The Odrysians may have seized this opportunity to rebel against a house which had been based not long before in Macedonia but was not secure in its power at Bizye. Marcus Primus fought the Odrysians in the period in which Cotys died, and after that there was never again an Odrysian king of Thrace.[1]

At first the Sapaeans reaped all the profit from the new arrangement. Primus was only the first of the Romans to defend their Thracian clients. M. Lollius subjugated the Bessi to aid Rhoemetalces, uncle and guardian of Cotys' children, and L. Tarius Rufus thrust the Sarmatians across the Danube for the same reason.[2] A few years later a priest of Dionysus from the Bessi initiated the Bellum Thracicum, in which a son of Cotys was killed and his uncle fled to the Chersonese. But L. Piso the Pontifex brought victory, and Rhoemetalces and his brother, Rhescuporis, were charged to keep the peace for Rome.[3] The balance now inclined the other way, and the clients succoured their patrons in the Pannonian Rebellion.[4]

The seeds of discord were sown by Augustus when the old king Rhoemetalces died. Thrace was partitioned between his son, Cotys, and his brother and former collaborator, Rhescuporis.[5] A link with other dynasties was ensured by the marriage of Cotys to the daughter of Polemo and Pythodoris of Pontus.[6] But the elder partner was only waiting for Augustus' death before invading his nephew's realm and murdering him.[7]

In the Peloponnese to the south, Augustus had established a local dynast of his own. A pirate's son called Eurycles had given vigorous support to the winning cause at Actium, and his reward was the citizenship and control of Sparta.[8] A devoted partisan in that city might have been no less desirable than those petty tyrants whom Augustus supported elsewhere. But

---

[1] Dio 54. 3. 2. Cf. Appendix II.
[2] Id. 54. 20. 3 (Lollius and Tarius). For Λούκιος Γάϊος read Λούκιος Τάριος on the strength of *AE* 1936. 18, confirming Ritterling's conjecture in *P-W* 12. 1229.
[3] Dio 54. 34. 5–7.
[4] Id. 55. 30. 3, 6; Vell. 2. 112. 4.
[5] Tac. *Ann.* 2. 64.
[6] Strabo 556; *IGR* 4. 144.
[7] Tac. *Ann.* 2. 65; 3. 38.
[8] Plut. *Ant.* 67. On the career of Eurycles, see *JRS* 51 (1961), 112–18.

the choice of Eurycles was a disaster and the chaotic end of his rule illustrated simultaneously almost all the dangers of the client system. Eurycles travelled to Judaea and Cappadocia for his own financial gain; he visited the client kings of those nations and by treachery undermined the security of both. Augustus had taken care to strengthen the ties between the monarchs of his empire, and he cannot have been pleased to see his work sabotaged by a petty tyrant from the Peloponnese. Meanwhile, Eurycles returned enriched to his own city: there and throughout the province of Achaea he stirred up civil disturbance. Twice his opponents in Sparta brought him to trial before the Emperor himself, who was ultimately compelled to drive his nominee into banishment.[1]

It is ironic that a contribution of Augustus' own to the circle of client rulers should have failed so miserably; but it is typical that the traces of this failure should nearly have disappeared from historical record. Were it not for a report in Josephus and an anecdote in Plutarch,[2] no one would know how Eurycles confounded two kingdoms and provoked tumult in Greece. He was rehabilitated posthumously; a cult was established in his honour, and his son resumed the dynasty.[3]

In north-western Africa, another ruler established by Augustus turned out, however, to be a success in a surprising way. This was King Juba II of Mauretania, who deserves mention in this context—despite the westerly location of his realm—for being one of the most eminent philhellenes of the Augustan age. As a child he had been exhibited in Caesar's quadruple triumph in 46;[4] but his life was spared and he received his education in Italy.[5] To Octavian he was a loyal partisan, participating in campaigns and accompanying him on journeys. His reward was the Roman citizenship and, at first, restoration to the Numidian kingdom of his father, but after

---

[1] Jos. *BJ* 1. 513 ff.; *AJ* 16. 301 ff.

[2] Id. *BJ* 1. 531; *AJ* 16. 310. [Plut.] *Reg. et Imp. Apophtheg.* 207 F.

[3] *AE* 1929, 99 (11. 19–20). Cf. article cited on p. 59, n. 8. A statue-base from Corinth with the top line of an inscription C. IULIO C. F. has been identified with Eurycles' son or (better) grandson: *Hesp.* 31 (1962), 116. Sir Ronald Syme (in conversation) has advised caution; the man might be Caesar the Dictator, founder of Roman Corinth, or some other Julius.

[4] Plut. *Caes.* 55; App. *BC* 2. 101.

[5] Dio 51. 15. 6.

the Cantabrian War he was displaced westward to Mauretania, where he settled on the coast at Iol, renamed Caesarea
in honour of the Princeps.[1] His first bride was Cleopatra
Selene, the offspring of Antony and Cleopatra, and their
marriage was commemorated by Augustus' poet Crinagoras.[2]
At Iol-Caesarea, Juba presided over what was virtually an
Hellenistic court; endowed with a taste for theatre and works
of art, he wrote voluminously and eruditely in the Greek
language.[3] Later in life he married into the Cappadocian royal
family.[4] Augustus' encouragement of such a client monarch
in the western part of the empire is not without significance for
his attitude toward Greek culture.

To sum up, in spite of the dangers inherent in the client
system, Augustus, like Antony, needed it and knew that he
needed it. This is apparent from the extent to which he maintained Antony's arrangements. It is equally apparent from his
considered policy of linking the dynastic houses to one another
by marriage. Moreover, time and again the rulers themselves
are seen in possession of the Roman citizenship: where specific
evidence is lacking—as also in the case of Greeks in the imperial service—that honour must surely be assumed. It was
a reward for fidelity in the past or a guarantee for the future;
often it was both. Purpose and pattern are the hallmarks of
Augustus' policy toward the client kings of the Greek world.

[1] Ibid., together with Dio 53. 26. 2 and Strabo 831; also *PIR* I. 48. It is
noteworthy that Juba held two duovirates in Spain, at Gades and New Car-
thage. On his reputation at Athens (and generally), cf. W. Thieling, *Der
Hellenismus in Kleinafrika* (1911), p. 20.

[2] *Anth. Pal.* ix. 235.

[3] Cf. Chapter X below, p. 138. See also *Athen.* 8. 343e (an actor) and Pliny,
NH 13. 92 (hanging tables of citrus-wood).

[4] His second wife was Glaphyra, daughter of King Archelaus: Jos., *BJ* 2.
115; *AJ* 17. 350.

V

EASTERN COLONIES

THE colonial policies of Julius Caesar and Augustus in the East must be examined conjointly before the Augustan colonies can be understood. Doubt has long prevailed as to the correct dating of most of the eastern foundations,[1] so that it is currently possible on one reckoning to marvel at the large number of Augustus' colonies in the East and on another to declare that Augustus sent few colonies there altogether. Then there are the intermediate positions according to which the colonies are distributed between Caesar, Antony, and Augustus, with some holding the view that the plan which was carried out was Caesar's. In fact, that age which embraces together the civil wars, Triumvirate, and nascent Principate is the right unit for a study of colonial policy. It was an age of common dilemmas. The precise attribution of a colony to one or another imperator makes little difference. It is otiose to speculate about the plans of Caesar. Who can tell? If there had been no plans, Antony or Augustus would not have done much differently.

However, for convenience in analysis, some acceptable view of the colonial foundations must be discovered. Caesar's colonies in old Greece are undisputed, namely Buthrotum, Dyme, and Corinth.[2] But the Asian foundations cause trouble. The date of the deduction to Heraclea Pontica can be fixed with certainty to the period before Actium, since shortly before that battle Adiatorix annihilated the resident Romans.[3] Strabo's account

---

[1] For a full discussion of divergent hypotheses, see especially F. Vittinghoff, 'Römische Kolonisation und Bürgerrechtspolitik unter Caesar und Augustus' (1952), published originally in *Abhandl. Akad. Wiss. Mainz*, 14 (1951).

[2] Buthrotum: Strabo 324. Augustus sent new colonists there after Actium: Head, *HN²* 320, Grant *FITA* 269 ff. Dyme: Strabo 387; 665. Pompey had settled pirates there: App. *Mithr.* 96. Corinth: Strabo 381. Cf. Grant *FITA* 266.

[3] Strabo 542–3.

of the fate of Heraclea is such as to imply a pre-Antonian deduction, thus a Caesarian date. Possibly the Romans at Heraclea formed only a settlement and not a genuine colony, inasmuch as there is no evidence for a colony apart from Strabo. But that is not very surprising, as there were no colonists left after the massacre. Sinope is another colony whose date is reasonably secure. The era of the colonial coinage of Sinope is dated from 46/45 B.C. throughout the following century.[1]

For Apamea Myrleia a *terminus post quem* of 45 B.C. has been established;[2] it is unlikely to be a colony of Augustus, since the *Res Gestae* omits any mention of a colony in Bithynia. Further precision is impossible, although the name, Colonia Julia Concordia, suggests a date in the late forties. Apamea must have been one of several foundations of that period bearing the name Concordia, whose splendour was enhanced by the senate's decree for a temple at Rome in 44 B.C.[3] If Apamea was an Antonian colony, it appears nevertheless to have been supplied with additional colonists by Augustus: a colonial coin with the legend CIC and a portrait of Augustus surely originated in Apamea.[4]

Parium is the most difficult of all the pre-Augustan Asian colonies about which to say anything definite. Second-century coins of that colony bear a portrait of Julius Caesar;[5] it would be natural to assume that he was the founder. The occurrence of C(olonia) G(emella or -emina) I(ulia) P(ariana) on coins from Augustus onwards need mean nothing more than an increment in veteran colonists, perhaps from a different legion

---

[1] Id. 546. Coins with the legend C(olonia) I(ulia) F(elix): Waddington, *Receuil* I² p. 201* f. The colony appears to have been organized separately along-side the Greek community: cf. Strabo's remark, loc. cit.: νυνὶ δὲ καὶ 'Ρωμαίων ἀποικίαν δέδεκται, καὶ μέρος τῆς πόλεως καὶ τῆς χώρας ἐκείνων ἐστί. Cf. Adiatorix receiving from Antony the μέρος ὃ κατεῖχον οἱ 'Ηρακλειῶται (Strabo 543). Cf. also *Rev. Arch.* 3 (1916), 338, no. 5, and *IGR* 3. 94. On this, see Magie, *RRAM* ii. 1267–8.

[2] Terminus given by a coin of C. Vibius Pansa: see the discussion and citations in Magie, *RRAM* ii. 1270, n. 40.

[3] The name of the colony appears, for example, in *ILS* 314; the Concordia temple at Rome is mentioned in Dio 44. 4. 5.

[4] Grant *FITA* 255 f.

[5] Grant, *FITA* 248. Vittinghoff, p. 130, n. 7, argues that Caesar's portrait proves nothing; cf. Grant, *Emerita* 20 (1952), 4, n. 3.

from that of the first colonists, sometime in the Augustan Principate.[1]

There was also at least one non-colonial settlement of Roman citizens under Julius Caesar, and that was at Lampsacus. When Sextus Pompeius took the city by treachery, it contained many Italians ἐξ ἐποικίσεως Γαΐου Καίσαρος.[2] Lampsacus is never thereafter attested as a colonia, although the colonial population there was not extirpated as it was at Heraclea. Appian appears to have chosen his word ἐποίκισις with care in place of ἀποικία, his usual word for colony.

Two other non-colonial settlements appeared along the northern coast of Asia Minor. They are first attested under Augustus, but perhaps the settlements were coincidental with the Caesarian colonial foundations in those regions. The cities concerned were Cyzicus and Amisus. The first of these was the city of which a friend of Propertius was so enamoured; yet the Cyzicenes temporarily lost their liberty for flogging certain of the Romans in their midst. The other city, far to the east, reveals on an inscription οἱ συμπολιτευόμενοι Ῥωμαῖοι.[3]

[1] BMC Mysia 102 f.; Grant FITA 248. See the following note.

[2] App. BC 5. 137. Coins bearing the legend C(olonia) G(emina, -emella) I(ulia) with Caesar's portrait are discussed by Grant FITA 246. There is no need to assign those to Lampsacus as a supposedly sister colony of Parium. The coins will belong to Parium itself. (See the remarks in the text on Parium.) The title Gemina or Gemella does not require a sister foundation; it merely implies a single unit made out of two components. Cf. Caes. BC 3. 4. 1 on Legio Gemella, one legion made out of two; the VII Galbiana became part of the VII Gemina (Birley, JRS 18 [1928], 56 ff.). Cf. Pliny, NH 3. 22 (Emporia); also NH 3. 12 (Castra Gemina). In regard to Parium, Broughton, AJP 62 (1941), 107, suggests that G(emina, -emella) alludes to a combination of Caesarian and Augustan colonists there, i.e. two deductions. Vittinghoff, p. 88, n. 1, discusses various interpretations of the expressions Gemina and Gemella. It should perhaps be noted that Lystra, which is called Julia Felix Gemina Lustra in CIL iii. 6786 (cf. BMC Lycaonia, p. 10, n. 1), honoured Antioch as τὴν λαμπροτάτην Ἀντιοχέων κολωνίαν . . . τὴν ἀδελφήν: J. R. S. Sterrett, The Wolfe Expedition to Asia Minor (Papers Amer. School Class. Stud. Athens, vol. iii) (Boston, 1888), pp. 218–19, n. 352. But Levick, 'Roman Colonies' (unpublished Oxford D.Phil. thesis, 1958), p. 59, has shown that ἀδελφή has only honorific significance, nothing more.

[3] Dio 54. 7. 6; 57. 24. 6; Prop. iii. 22 (Cyzicus). IGR 4. 314 (Amisus) mentions Ῥωμαῖοι συμπολιτευόμενοι. Other non-colonial settlements of uncertain date are discoverable elsewhere: Magie, RRAM ii. 1615–16. There was evidently one in the Augustan period at Attaleia: SEG vi. 646. Similarly, probably, at Tralles: Agathias 2. 17, where ἀποικία is literally impossible, but plausible as a non-colonial settlement. On this, cf. Broughton, TAPA 66 (1935), 21 f.

With a pre-Augustan date for the foregoing colonies and settlements, the work of Augustus is relatively plain. In Greece, certainty prevails in regard to Patrae, Dyrrachium, and Dium.[1] Byllis may also be an Augustan foundation;[2] Cassandreia was colonized by Brutus, and Philippi by Antony, but both were clearly refounded by Augustus.[3] Pella was probably another Augustan foundation, although Grant regards that colony as Antonian.[4] Pliny's designations of Actium and Megara as colonies are erroneous.[5]

In Asia Minor, Augustus planted a colony at Alexandria in the Troad and a nest of colonies in Pisidia.[6] Of the Pisidian group, Antioch, Olbasa, Comama, Cremna, Parlais, and Lystra are indisputably Augustan. The colonies at Ninica and Germa have been variously dated to Augustus, Nero, and Domitian; yet they belong most plausibly to the network of south central Asia Minor: each is called Colonia Julia Augusta Felix. Some of the earliest coinage of Ninica shows an eagle between two military standards, as on the coins of Olbasa and Antioch.[7] The same colony also used the type of the founder ploughing, which appears in Asia Minor only on the coins of Caesar and Augustus.[8]

Augustus planted one colony on Crete and two in Syria. The colony at Cnossus is omitted from the Res Gestae, presumably because it was not a military foundation.[9] However,

---

Broughton has missed *BCH* 11 (1887), 67, which suggests a non-colonial settlement at Isaura: Ἰσαυρέων ἡ βουλὴ καὶ ὁ δῆμος οἵ τε συμπολιτευόμενοι Ῥωμαῖοι.

[1] Strabo 387; Paus. 7. 18. 7 (Patrae). Dio 51.4.6 (Dyrrachium). Pliny, *NH* 4. 35 (Dium). [2] Pliny, *NH* 4. 35; *CIL* iii. 600. See Jones, *GC*, p. 61.

[3] Cassandreia: *Zeitschr. f. Numism.* 36 (1926), 139; Vittinghoff, p. 127, n. 6. Cf. Grant, *FITA* 272 (against an Augustan refoundation). Philippi: *Zeitschr. f. Numism.* 39 (1929), 261. 1: A(ntoni) I(ussu) C(olonia) V(ictrix) P(hilippensium); Dio 51. 4. 6 (30 B.C.); Grant, *FITA* 275: *IVSSV AVG.*

[4] Grant, *FITA* 281.

[5] Pliny, *NH* 4. 5 (Actium), 23 (Megara). Cf. Jones, *GC* 312, n. 80.

[6] Pliny, *NH* 5. 124 (Alexandria Troas). On the Pisidian colonies, *Res Gestae* 28; above all, see now Levick, 'Roman Colonies' (unpublished Oxford D.Phil. thesis, 1958).

[7] Magie, *RRAM* ii. 1328, n. 46, comparing issues of Ninica with those of Antioch and Olbasa. Jones, *CERP* 123 and 211, dated these colonies to the reign of Domitian, Levick, op. cit., p. 51, to Nero. On the location of Germa, cf. L. Robert, *L'Annuaire du Collège de France* (1961–2), p. 313.

[8] T. R. S. Broughton, *AJP* 62 (1941), 107.

[9] Dio 49. 14. 5; Vell. ii. 81. 2. Head, *HN²* 463.

the two in Syria are recalled on that document. No one has ever doubted that Berytus was an Augustan colony,[1] but the date of the colony at Heliopolis has been called into question because, unlike Berytus, it minted no coins until the reign of Septimius Severus.[2] Yet it bears the same name as Berytus, Colonia Iulia Augusta Felix. An inscription from Heliopolis honours the king of Emesa under Nero, C. Julius Sohaemus, as *patronus coloniae*. The colonia must be Heliopolis, not—as Jones thought—Berytus incorporating Heliopolis in a vast territorium.[3] A recently published inscription has been reported to confirm that Heliopolis was a colony of Augustus.[4]

Such were the colonies of Caesar, Antony, and Augustus. The reasons for these foundations are far more important than their precise dates. If Caesar did not send a colony to Apamea Myrleia, Antony or Augustus could be expected to have done so, not because they were carrying out the plans of Caesar but simply because it was a sensible thing to do. There were men to be disposed of: the problem was how to dispose of them most efficiently on available land. If a colony happened to cause the neighbouring natives to adopt certain Roman customs or learn a little Latin, no Roman emperor would object. But that was hardly the reason for colonial foundations, at least in the East. There were not enough of them. Anyway, most of the natives went on being as Greek (or as native) as they ever had been; if they ended up a few centuries later by calling themselves 'Ρωμαῖοι that did not mean that they were thoroughly romanized, but rather that they were Greeks under a different name.[5] Ultimately, the natives did not absorb the colonists' Latin. It was the colonists who absorbed the natives' Greek.[6]

---

[1] Strabo 756: Agrippa settled veterans there; *CIL* iii. 161 ff. Colonized by veterans of V Mac. and VIII Aug.: Goodfellow, *Roman Citizenship* (Diss. Bryn Mawr, 1935), p. 86.

[2] See Jones, *GC*, p. 465, n. 86, assuming a Severan date for the colony. Not so, Sherwin-White, *The Roman Citizenship* (1939), p. 174, opting for Augustus.

[3] *ILS* 8958. Jones, op. cit., loc. cit.

[4] *Bull. Musée Beyrouth* 16 (1961), 111–12.

[5] The development is traced by J. Palm, *Rom, Römertum und Imperium in der griechischen Literatur der Kaiserzeit* (Lund, 1959).

[6] See especially Levick on the decline of Latin at Pisidian Antioch: pp. 171–91. Also at Comama (pp. 199–202), Cremna (pp. 202–8), Lystra (pp. 208–11),

Effective disposal of men and families on available land was the primary purpose of colonization in the age of Caesar and Augustus. The colonists derived from one or more of three groups: the urban population of Rome, the dispossessed Italians, and veterans. It was Caesar alone at this time who concerned himself with relieving the overcrowded condition of the city of Rome. Buthrotum was colonized with emigrants from Rome, doubtless of the lower classes, and Strabo says explicitly that the Caesarian colonists at Corinth came from the city and consisted largely of freedmen.[1] The dictator could hardly have had romanization in mind when he sent so many Greeks back to their old environment. The *Graeculi* of Rome could not have been regarded as importers of the Roman way of life in the country from which they had emerged. Caesar's colony at Dyme may also have been composed of emigrants from Rome.[2] The first Princeps founded no colonies for such people— which is worth emphasizing. Augustus was concerned chiefly with the disposal of veterans.

When veterans were planted in Italy both by Caesar and by Augustus, Italians were, on occasion, inevitably dispossessed of land so that certain of the choicest plots might go to the more deserving and faithful soldiers. It was probably such dispossessed that Appian meant by the Italian settlers at Lampsacus; the colonists at Heraclea may have been of the same kind. At any rate, Adiatorix must have regarded them as singularly easy victims, therefore perhaps not veterans. Augustus too was obliged to resettle those Italians whom he had dispossessed for his own veterans. Two of his eastern colonies, indeed the only two which were patently not veteran colonies, were filled by the dispossessed, namely Dyrrachium and Cnossus.[3] But colonies consisting of Italians, who were altogether inexperienced in war, were weak and served no other

---

and Olbasa (pp. 212–15). Parlais was never much romanized: p. 216. On the persistence of Hellenism in the East, note the admirable lecture of N. H. Baynes, 'Hellenistic Civilisation and East Rome', in *Byzantine Studies* (1955), pp. 1 ff.

[1] Buthrotum: Strabo 324. Cf. Vittinghoff, p. 85, a colony for 'Umsiedler der Hauptstadt'. Corinth: Strabo 381.

[2] Ibid. 387; 665. Cf. Vittinghoff, p. 86.

[3] See p. 65, n. 1 and n. 9. However, other colonies also accommodated dispossessed persons, notably Philippi: cf. Dio 51. 4. 6.

function than to settle the homeless. Augustus was too shrewd
to send out many colonies of that kind; he did not even care to
acknowledge them in the ostentatious and magniloquent *Res
Gestae*. Dio Cassius reveals that the remainder of the Italian
dispossessed, for whom Augustus had to make some arrangements, were dispersed amid the veteran colonies.[1]

Caesar was feeling his way in the technique of eastern
colonization. He realized that colonies could be much more
than merely a means of relieving his obligations to masses of
Roman citizens. Corinth was a manifest stimulus to the stag-
nant economy of Greece. An imposing chain of colonies and
settlements along the southern coast of the Propontis and the
Black Sea represents effective garrisoning of those regions; on
the present system of dating Caesar may be held responsible
for the Romans at Lampsacus, Parium, Cyzicus, Heraclea,
Sinope, and Amisus. Antony soon strengthened the chain with
a link at Apamea Myrleia. Possibly Caesar had envisaged that
colony; even if he had not, it was a sensible and natural move
for another commander. The series of Black Sea colonies cannot have been fortuitous. They constituted a quasi-military
investment of a crucial area hitherto lacking detachments of
legionaries. Caesar's scheme had its weaknesses, for not all the
Romans there were veterans. Some were inexperienced Italians,
ill prepared for defence.

Augustus was interested, above all, in the veteran colony: in
that lay strength. He perceived the inadequacy of non-veteran
settlements in strategic positions and therefore with two exceptions incorporated the Italian dispossessed in veteran settlements. The colony chain of Caesar on the Black Sea was
imitated—it makes little difference whether consciously or
not—by the chain of Augustan colonies along the coast of
Mauretania. Those were veteran colonies, protecting com-
munications on the north African coast.[2]

Augustus, like Caesar, knew that a colony could serve to
revive the East's flagging economy. In economic importance

---

[1] Dio 51. 4. 6.
[2] S. Gsell, *Histoire ancienne de l'Afrique du Nord* (Paris, 1928), viii. 199–205. On
veteran colonies, see generally J. C. Mann, *The Settlement of Veterans in the Roman
Empire* (unpublished London Ph.D. thesis, 1956).

Patrae matched Corinth;[1] Alexandria Troas was a focus for the traffic of Thrace, Bithynia, and Asia. But it is well to observe that both Patrae and Alexandria were colonized by veterans. The new Corinthians had been freedmen from Rome. Augustus took no chances.

Proponents of romanization as a colonial policy point to the organization of the colonists. Colonial institutions are initially Roman in character, but it would be very surprising indeed if they were not. Gellius refers to colonies *quasi effigies parvae simulacraque* of Rome.[2] The colony at Pisidian Antioch was divided into *vici* which bore the names of districts at Rome.[3] Moreover, each colony boasted its duoviri and aediles. Yet when a Roman commander settled Roman citizens, he could hardly be expected to organize them otherwise than on Roman constitutional lines. Evidence for deliberately trying to influence the customs and speech of natives, at least in the East, is still to seek. In the colonies at Heraclea and Sinope the colonists were rigorously distinguished from the natives and had their own separate polity.[4] Integration seemed utterly out of the question.

The colonies are satisfactorily explained in terms of the disposal of men and families. It has appeared that Augustus concerned himself primarily with veteran colonies precisely because they constituted at once *ad hoc* garrisons. This is not to deny that he understood the economic role of certain foundations. Augustus, like Caesar, realized that a colony could be made to perform several functions at the same time. The first Princeps did not worry about removing segments, especially Greek segments, of Rome's urban population, as the dictator did; but both men knew that it was not enough merely to settle the veterans and the dispossessed wherever there happened to be available land.

Literary texts and colonial inscriptions show that the role of colonies as *ad hoc* garrisons was well known to the Romans.

[1] U. Kahrstedt, *Das wirtschaftliche Gesicht Griechenlands in der Kaiserzeit* (Bern, 1954).

[2] Gellius, *Noct. Att.* 16. 13. 9.

[3] Levick, chapter VII. Magie, *RRAM* ii. 1320, n. 32.

[4] Strabo 542 (Heraclea) uses the same language as he does for Sinope, on which see p. 63, n. 1.

Cicero, calling Narbo Martius a *specula populi Romani,* goes on to declare the colony a bulwark against hostile nations. Elsewhere, Cicero alludes to his hearers' ancestors, *qui colonias sic idoneis in locis contra suspicionem periculi collocarunt, ut esse non oppida Italiae, sed propugnacula imperii viderentur.*[1] Appian observed that Sulla settled veterans in Italy ὡς ἕξων φρούρια κατὰ τῆς Ἰταλίας.[2] And the Emperor Claudius once alluded to the reliance of a weary realm on colonies of veteran legionaries dispersed throughout the world.[3] Their function is plain. Once established in colonies, the veterans were organized and drilled in case their services should one day be needed. An inscription from Pisidian Antioch reveals a prefect of the veterans in that colony;[4] in other places a quaestor of veterans and a centurion of veterans are attested.[5] Possibly the drilling of young recruits devolved upon resident veterans: a *praefectus tironibus* is attested in Narbonensian Gaul.[6] The veterans were associated locally in *collegia* whose military character is suggested in a dedication to a knight at Arles from the Collegium Honoris et Virtutis: at Rome the temple of Honos and Virtus was in the immediate vicinity of the temple of Mars before the Porta Capena, and it was from that temple that the equestrian *transvectio* began.[7]

The Augustan colonies in Pisidia have long been regarded as particularly clear examples of garrison colonies, installed because of the threat of the Homonadensian War. These foundations have been connected hitherto with a special emergency, although there has always been some difficulty in explaining why the colonies were not founded until two decades after the death of Amyntas, who had been killed by the Homonadensians. Recent analysis has yielded satisfying results: not only Antioch but also two of the lesser Pisidian colonies were sent out in the mid-20's B.C.[8] Hence the Homonadensian War could

---

[1] Cic. *de Leg. Agr.* ii. 73.   [2] App. *BC* i. 96.   [3] Tac. *Ann.* 11. 24.
[4] *JRS* 14 (1924), 201.
[5] *ILS* 2466 (quaestor veteranorum; Virunum); 2467 (centurio veteranorum; Scardona).   [6] *ILS* 2691.
[7] *AE* 1954. 104 (Arles). For location of the temple at Rome: Livy 29. 11. 13, and on the *transvectio* see P–W 8. 2293. On *collegia veteranorum*: P–W 4. 399–400.
[8] Antioch's foundation *c.* 25 B.C. is fixed by Strabo 577 (colony sent there

not have been an enterprise of nearly so great a magnitude as used to be thought. The garrison colonies represent prophylactic rather than emergency measures. They are not to be too sharply distinguished in function from the Black Sea foundations of Caesar and the Mauretanian foundations of Augustus, nor from Berytus and Heliopolis in Syria. Sherwin-White was unable to discover any military function for the Syrian colonies;[1] yet the Ituraeans were notorious brigands, like the Homonadensians. Augustus' two colonies split the Ituraean territory in two.[2] The military strength of Berytus is nowhere more obvious than in Josephus' report that Quinctilius Varus paused there as governor to pick up fifteen hundred soldiers.[3] Nor should it be forgotten that Berytus was a focus for Near Eastern commerce. Augustus' colony at Alexandria Troas, also an economic centre, completed to the south-west the chain of colonies along the Propontis and Black Sea. Augustus managed to pay off his veterans by garrisoning his empire and encouraging its trade. Whether the eastern Greeks went on speaking Greek or changed over to Latin was doubtless a matter of indifference to him.

Nor can the majority of the colonists in the East have objected to being sent there. Nearly all the legionary colonists had served in that part of the world, and there were good precedents for settling veterans in regions which they knew well. Furthermore, an indeterminate number of them were easterners anyway. Of Caesar's colonists from Rome, many were Greeks returning home, while it is likely that many of the dispossessed Italians from Campania had had Greek ancestors. Finally, in cases where there was no Greek ancestry, an opportunity to become influential local dignitaries in Roman colonies was offered to men who were destined to be nobodies in Italy. The Italian backgrounds of the distinguished colonial families of

---

after Amyntas' death) together with Pliny, *NH* 5. 94, which names Antioch as a *colonia* but none of the other Pisidian colonies. Levick has now demonstrated from numismatic evidence that Cremna (pp. 53–55) and Lystra (pp. 60–61) were also both founded in 25 B.C. The view of Grant, *FITA* 238–44, that Lystra was founded in 43 B.C. has been adequately refuted by Levick.

[1] Sherwin-White, *The Roman Citizenship*, p. 174.

[2] Cf. for a similar analysis A. H. M. Jones, *JRS* 21 (1931), 265 ff. on 'The Urbanization of the Ituraean Principality'.   [3] Jos. *BJ* 2. 67.

the East are in many cases so obscure as to be quite un-identifiable.[1]

Romanization is an unnecessary postulate for eastern coloni-zation of this age. It is chiefly a word which describes what subsequently happened in certain areas of the western em-pire, and what did not happen in the East. For the eastern provinces it could never have constituted premeditated policy. The colonies there were widely scattered, but not without purpose. By a series of strategic deductions men were com-pensated for service, economies were revived, and the empire was garrisoned.

[1] e.g. the Caristanii (*JRS* 3 [1913], 253 ff.) and the Flavonii (*JRS* 48 [1958], 74 ff.) of Pisidian Antioch.

VI

ROMANS AND THE HELLENIC LIFE

EN had been going east from Italy for several generations. The attraction of the Greek world was multiform: opportunities for trade and commerce had
already drawn off Romans and Italians in the second century.
They left their traces on inscriptions at the centres of inter-
national traffic.[1] Greek culture had lured other Romans, men
of family or ambition, to absorb the wisdom of the Greeks at
its sources. Philosophers, rhetoricians, and grammarians were
widely scattered throughout the East, although there were
concentrations of them in cities like Athens and Rhodes. But
commerce and education did not account for all the Romans
who penetrated the Greek East. Some went there as soldiers,
while others found refuge there to live out their lives as political
exiles from Rome. When Mithridates Eupator, the Pontic
king, rose up against the Romans of the East in 88 B.C., there
were more than enough to provide one of history's most
spectacular, calculated slaughters.[2]

Constant intercourse, cultural and diplomatic, between
Rome and the East made the Hellenic way of life known
among the Romans. Provincial governors with their extravagant entourages passed regularly from Italy to the East and
back again. Meanwhile the eastern cities dispatched successions
of literate Greeks to advance their interests at Rome. Certain
professors emigrated from their Greek environments to teach
the barbarians of Italy. And the Roman generals of the late
Republic often provided the city of Rome with cultural gifts
from the East in the form of learned prisoners of war, who
were subsequently freed in order to instruct their conquerors in
the liberal arts.[3] Outside Rome but still in Italy, three cities,

---

[1] See J. Hatzfeld, *Les Trafiquants italiens dans l'orient hellénique* (Paris, 1919).

[2] References are conveniently collected in Greenidge–Clay, *Sources for Roman History 133–70 B.C.*, revised by E. W. Gray (Oxford, 1960), pp. 168–9.

[3] Cf. Chapter I.

founded by Hellenes long ago, preserved their vestigial poli-
ties.[1] A wealthy Roman adolescent could spend a holiday at
Neapolis, speaking Greek and even wearing Greek garments.
Cicero objected to such behaviour, which was obviously in
vogue.[2]

Romans who could afford it had acquired a liking for Greek
art. Sallust claimed that the depraved fondness for *objets d'art*
(as well as heavy drinking) was the direct result of Sulla's
taking an army to the luxurious stews of Asia;[3] but in fact it
had begun long before. In the second century Aemilius Paullus
had commissioned the Athenian Metrodorus to do the paintings for his Macedonian triumph, and Greek artisans or their
works had been imported for the Porticus Metelli.[4] Affluence
and culture among upper-class Romans found expression in
architecture, sculpture, paintings, and mosaics, and there was
no denying the pre-eminence of Greeks in such matters; as
Virgil observed, Rome's task was to rule, while others shaped
objects of beauty.[5]

The first century witnessed a great revival of the old Attic
style in sculpture, precisely because that was what Romans
demanded.[6] Some paid for their works of art; others, like
Verres and Piso, stole them. Neither Antony nor Octavian
was averse to helping himself to objects which pleased the

[1] Tarentum, Rhegium, and Neapolis: Strabo 253. Also pp. 80–84 of this
chapter.

[2] Cic., *pro Rab. Post.* 10. 26–27: Deliciarum causa et voluptatis non modo
notos civis Romanos, sed et nobilis adulescentis et quosdam etiam senatores
summo loco natos non in hortis aut suburbanis suis, sed Neapoli, in celeberrimo
oppido, in tunica pulla saepe vidi, ibidem multi viderunt chlamydatum illum
L. Sullam imperatorem.

[3] Sall. *Cat.* 11. 5–6.

[4] Plin. *NH* 35. 135 (Metrodorus). Vitruv. 3. 2. 5; Plin. *NH* 36. 34–35
(Porticus Metelli).

[5] Virg. *Aen.* vi. 847–8: Excudent alii spirantia mollius aera, / credo equidem,
vivos ducent de marmore vultus . . . : / tu regere imperio populos, Romane,
memento / (hae tibi erunt artes). On Roman interest in the arts, note the salutary warning of R. Meiggs, *Roman Ostia* (1960), p. 431 : 'Few features point the
contrast between the ancient and modern world more sharply than the wealth
of sculpture, painting, and mosaics from Roman sites. The contrast is in part
misleading. Much of the painting should be compared with the work of the internal decorator rather than the original artist; changing tastes have replaced
mosaics by carpets.'

[6] Cf. P. Gardner, *New Chapters in Greek Art* (1926), p. 279.

eye.[1] But thefts had no effect on the lively commerce in art, nor on the regular employment of Greek artists—architects, sculptors, mosaicists—by well-to-do Romans in Italy itself.[2] The sculptor and engraver C. Avianius Evander, whom Antony had brought to Alexandria, went on to Rome to find work; a certain Diogenes of Athens was used to decorate Agrippa's Pantheon.[3] Roman patronage may be held responsible for Greek neo-Atticism—and not only in the fine arts: Dionysius of Halicarnassus hailed the Attic revival in Greek literary style and attributed it to the refined taste of Roman aristocrats.[4]

Variously encountering things Greek, Rome conceived of the Hellene as literate, leisurely, worldly, and somewhat effeminate. The core of a Roman's view of Greek life was *mollitia* and *otium*.[5] This view by no means denied the vast erudition which Greeks brought to the Romans; indeed, erudition was nourished in an atmosphere of luxury and leisure, time to savour experience and then to reflect upon it. The young Marcus Cicero discovered that a Greek centre of learning offered more than purely academic instruction.[6] But it was notably in Asia, as distinct from old Greece, that a loose and immoral life was to be found, rejuvenating and refreshing for a Roman tourist.[7]

[1] On Verres, Cic. *II Verr.* 4 *passim*; for Cicero's private interest in Greek art, not acknowledged in a public speech, cf., for example, *ad Att.* 1. 8. 2. On Piso, Cic. *de Prov. Cons.* 6–7; *pro Sest.* 94: Nisbet, *Comm. on Cic., In Pisonem* (1961), p. 175, suggests there may not be much exaggeration here. On Antony and Octavian, see below Chapter VII, p. 86.

[2] Cf. J. M. C. Toynbee, *Some Notes on Artists in the Roman World* (1951).

[3] Evander: Hor. *Sat.* 1. 3. 91 and Porphyr. Schol. ad loc.; Plin., *NH* 36. 32. Diogenes: Plin., *NH* 36. 38.

[4] Dion. Hal. *de Orat. Ant.* 3.

[5] Prop. i. 6. 31 on *mollis Ionia*. Sallust (*Cat.* 11. 5) says of Sulla's soldiers in Asia: loca amoena, voluptaria facile in otio ferocis militum animos molliverant. Observe Silius, *Pun.* 12. 31–32 on Naples: Nunc molles urbi ritus atque hospita Musis / otia et exemptum curis gravioribus aevum. Also Statius, *Silv.* 3. 5. 85–86: Pax secura locis et desidis otia vitae / et numquam turbata quies somnique peracti. See, p. 76, n. 2, Horace and Ovid on *otiosa Neapolis*.

[6] Cf. Cic. *ad Att.* 14. 16. 3 with *ad Fam.* 16. 21. 2.

[7] Hor., *Odes* 3. 6. 21 ff.: Motus doceri gaudet Ionicos / matura virgo et fingitur artibus / iam nunc et incestos amores / de tenero meditatur ungui. Cic. *pro Flacc.* 2. 5 (the fragment of the Schol. Bob.): Sed si neque Asiae luxuries infirmissimum tempus aetatis.... For old Greece, on the other hand, cf. Cic. ibid. 26. 62–63; *ad Quint. frat.* 1. 1. 16. See also R. Syme, *Proceedings of the Massachusetts Historical Society* 72 (1963), 8.

However, it might not be thought quite right for an impressionable youth. Ionian dances were notorious, as Horace reveals; a fragment of a speech of Cicero warns against *Asiae luxuries* at an *infirmissimum tempus aetatis*.[1] Greek culture could be acquired with less *mollitia* and more *otium*, not to mention reduced expense, in the more easily accessible city of Naples. *Otiosa Neapolis* was Horace's phrase, confirmed by Ovid's remark that the spot was created for leisure.[2]

However, the extent of travel, far and near, depended upon taste and wealth. The Romans liked to have a change; they hankered after a Greek holiday. The passionate Epicurean Lucretius observed in sonorous hexameters the urge to get away, to find new sights and new sensations; it was all self-deception; men were only trying to escape from themselves, and they were doomed to fail in the attempt.[3] A century later the younger Seneca reflected upon mental tranquillity and recalled the words of Lucretius to mark the exodus from Rome. Restless Romans went to the nearest Greek settlements to forget the squalor of their city. A loose and soft existence *à la grecque* was one of the current fashions: *Nunc Campaniam petamus*.[4] Lucretius and Seneca described a genuine malaise, although not every restless Roman was trying to flee from himself. Some people found it expedient or desirable to flee from the Principate. Republican Rome had provided the precedent. When a man turned his back on Rome and his political enemies, he looked to the Greeks to receive him.

---

[1] See above, p. 75. n. 7.

[2] Hor. *Ep.* 1. 5. 43. Ovid, *Met.* 15. 711–12: in otia natam / Parthenopen (= Neapolin, Strabo 246).

[3] Lucretius, *de Rerum Natura*, iii. 1057 ff.: . . . ut nunc plerumque videmus / quid sibi quisque velit nescire et quaerere semper / commutare locum quasi onus deponere possit. Ll. 1068–9: Hoc se quisque modo fugit, quem scilicet, ut fit, / effugere haud potis est. Similarly, Hor. *Odes* 3. 16. 18–20.

[4] Sen. *de Tranquill. Animi* 2. 13: Inde peregrinationes suscipiuntur vagae et litora pererrantur et modo mari se, modo terra experitur semper praesentibus infesta levitas. Nunc Campaniam petamus. Iam delicata fastidio sunt. Inculta videantur: Bruttios et Lucaniae saltus persequamur. Aliquid tamen inter deserta amoeni requiratur, in quo luxuriosi oculi longo locorum horrentium squalore releventur: Tarentum petatur laudatusque portus et hiberna caeli mitioris regio vel antiquae satis opulenta turbae. Iam flectamus cursum ad urbem . . . 14. Aliud ex alio iter suscipitur et spectacula spectaculis mutantur. Ut ait Lucretius: Hoc se quisque modo semper fugit.

Thus had Rutilius Rufus and Marcus Marcellus withdrawn to Mytilene; T. Pomponius Atticus, fleeing from the régime of Cinna, went to Athens and liked it so much that he stayed there for twenty years.[1]

The young Tiberius retired to Rhodes in 6 B.C. Officially but euphemistically a legate of the emperor, he was called 'the exile'.[2] Rhodes had been the home of many another political refugee from Rome in earlier days. Later accounts of the exile of a future emperor were palliated by comparison with the presence of the favoured Agrippa on Mytilene in the fateful year 23 B.C.[3] Tiberius' activities at Rhodes are revealing: the cast-off Roman became Greek. Living modestly in the Rhodian countryside, he occasionally strolled unaccompanied in the gymnasium and mingled with the Greek natives *prope ex aequo*. He was constantly in attendance at the lectures of the local professors of philosophy. As the years passed and Tiberius became more and more of an exile, he took to wearing the Greek cloak and slippers, which constituted his dress for the final two years of his sojourn on Rhodes. He contributed chariots for the races at Olympia and Thespiae.[4] Tiberius' experience of the Greek way of life was the product of bitter necessity; yet he was fond of that life and brought back with him to Rome a living and influential memorial of his Greek tastes, the astrologer Thrasyllus.[5]

Tiberius was perhaps the most celebrated of the Romans who went to reside in the East under the Augustan Principate, but he was not the only one. To be sure, there were numerous governors and officials, but they are irrelevant to this discussion; there was no doubt about their connexions with Rome. Private Romans in the East furnish the greater interest. If they were not traders, their presence there, coupled with their political inactivity, may have some significance. The Greek world had much to offer: education, antiquities, leisure, and

[1] Dio frag. 97. 2 (Rutilius). Cic. *Brut.* 250; Sen. *ad Helv.* 9. 4 (Marcellus). Nepos, *Att.* 2–4 (Atticus).

[2] Suet. *Tib.* 12. 1; 13. 1.   [3] Ibid. 10. 1.

[4] Ibid. 11. 1; 13. 1. *SIG*³ 782 (Olympia); *AE* 1960. 307 (Thespiae).

[5] Suet. *Tib.* 14. 4. Cf. Cichorius, *RS*, p. 396. Thrasyllus married a princess of Commagene: *Hermes* 59 (1924), 477 f. On Tiberius' Greek tastes, cf. Chapter X below, pp. 133–4.

titillations of the most diverse kinds. Athens entertained vast
crowds drawn by the fame of the ceremonies of initiation into
the mysteries.[1] Even the Greek Crinagoras said it was something not to be missed.[2] Augustus himself was an initiate,[3] and
doubtless so too were many Romans whose names have not
been recorded.

The initiation ceremony did not make a man any less of
a Roman. It could not be said that a well-hellenized youth,
who had been sent to the East for his education, would not
subsequently prove his loyalty and devotion to Rome, perhaps
even by service in the very parts where he had been taught.
Education, initiations, Greek tours all merely satisfied the
craving for the Hellenic life that so many Augustan Romans
had.

But ties with the fatherland were sometimes severed. If it
were admitted that the Hellenes provided a desirable complement to the Roman way of life, it was only a short step to the
discovery that the Hellenic life was preferable to the Roman.
There is no evidence as to the numbers which made this discovery; that was, after all, a personal matter. Horace and
Propertius have left traces of renunciations of Rome in the
early decades of the Augustan Peace. Not every one cared to
attend the birth of the restored Republic.[4]

Horace directed one of his epistles to an unidentifiable
friend, Bullatius,[5] who had gone to the East and intended to
remain there. The poet tried to dissuade him by the philosophical commonplace that what Bullatius really wanted could
be found anywhere at all provided that it was accompanied
by peace of mind.[6]

---

[1] Philostr. *Vit. Apoll.* 4. 17; cf. Strabo 719–20 and Dio 54. 9. 9–10 on the
Indian Zamarus, who immolated himself after being initiated.

[2] *Anth. Pal.* xi. 42.

[3] Dio 51. 4. 1. Graindor, *Athènes sous Auguste*, pp. 20–22, is wrong in thinking
that Dio 54. 9. 10 records a *second* initiation of Augustus in 20 B.C.

[4] Some Romans, apparently, were not very eager to witness the death of the
Republic either: a law of Julius Caesar provided that no citizen between the
ages of twenty and forty should be absent from Italy for more than three successive years unless he were serving in the army and no senator's son should go
abroad except in the company of a magistrate (Suet. *Jul.* 42. 1).

[5] Hor. *Ep.* 1. 11.

[6] Ibid. 25–27: Nam si ratio et prudentia curas, / non locus effusi late maris
arbiter aufert, / caelum, non animum mutant, qui trans mare currunt.

Bullatius' sentiments found an echo in the nephew of the consular Volcacius Tullus (consul suffect in 33 B.C.). His uncle took him as a member of his staff when he went out to govern the province of Asia. A friend of the poet Propertius, the proconsul's nephew, as mentioned in a previous chapter, did not return to Rome but lived for many years in Cyzicus.[1] Propertius tried to bring him back by assuring him that there was no need to be ashamed of Rome's past when compared with the traditions of Greece. In the present all great things had been arrogated by Rome; there was no need to go abroad.[2] Tullus was apparently not persuaded. In Cyzicus itself there was another poet who was sympathetic to the feelings of the expatriate: that was Erucius the Cyzicene, a versifier in Greek and the son of another expatriate. The father Erucius had served in the eastern campaigns of Sulla and later married an Athenian woman, with whom he appears to have settled at Cyzicus.[3]

The expatriate class of any nation is full of diversity. Some Romans created for themselves tiny Roman worlds in the midst of the Hellenes, but such people were not numerous: traders perhaps, and certain colonists.[4] Even for a patriotic Roman the Hellenic life was too attractive not to be sampled when there was an opportunity. A sojourn in the East might even extinguish flagging patriotism. That some became voluntary expatriates was not surprising, but it was slightly alarming. Even an opulent man of commerce could forsake Rome for the world in which he made his money. Horace urged Numicius not to be like Ulysses' lotus-eating crew,

cui potior patria fuit interdicta voluptas.[5]

However, at least one Roman philhellene did not abandon his loyalty to Rome though he abandoned the Latin language. Q. Sextius Niger was a learned Roman professor of philosophy who chose to speak and write in the language of the great

---

[1] Prop. i. 6. 19–20 and 34. Despite learned commentaries, the situation is clear. The proconsulship of Volcacius Tullus is epigraphically attested: *CR* 69 (1955), 244. Cf. R. Syme, *Hist.* 11 (1962), 152, citing also the Pergamene orator Volcacius Moschus. Above, Chapter II.   [2] Prop. iii. 22. 17–18.

[3] On Erucius: Cichorius, *RS*, pp. 304–6.

[4] Cf. Hatzfeld, *Trafiquants italiens* and Chapter V above.

[5] Hor., *Ep.* 1. 6. 64.

philosophers of antiquity.[1] Seneca described him as a sharp-witted man with all the virtues of a Roman: *virum acrem, Graecis verbis, Romanis moribus philosophantem*.[2] Not only that, for he was a man of political promise, *ita natus ut rem publicam deberet capessere*. Julius Caesar offered him the latus clavus, but he refused.[3] Sextius knew what could be given and what could be taken away. Small wonder that he turned his energies to philosophy and lectured in Greek in the city of Socrates while Augustus was Princeps at Rome.

The numerous Romans who were not prepared to take the initiative of a Bullatius, a Tullus, or a Sextius nevertheless took ample advantage of those innocuous opportunities for temporary participation in the Hellenic life such as would not provoke a patriotic appeal from any Augustan poet. Naturally the sons of the better Roman families would receive a Greek education; there was no opprobrium attached to that. On the contrary, it brought prestige, so long as it was not prolonged unreasonably. Young Romans could sit at the feet of Greek lecturers in the city itself or perhaps study in Athens under the supervision of their compatriot Sextius. In the Augustan Age the most fashionable Greek city of learning was Marseilles. Despite its location in the West, that outpost of Greek culture could boast political exiles, luxury, leisure, and philosophy no less distinguished than the best of the eastern cities.[4] The Hellenic life was not to be found only in the East.

The three cities in Italy which, according to Strabo, had not lost their Greek character even by his day were Tarentum, Rhegium, and Neapolis.[5] It was no accident, therefore, that they were precisely the cities which had conferred their citizenship upon the Greek Archias in the age of Cicero.[6] Even in the early second century these appear to have been the leading

---

[1] *PIR* S 474.   [2] Sen. *Ep.* 59. 7.
[3] Sen. *Ep.* 98. 13.
[4] Above all, Strabo 181: πάντες γὰρ οἱ χαρίεντες πρὸς τὸ λέγειν τρέπονται καὶ φιλοσοφεῖν, ὥσθ' ἡ πόλις μικρὸν μὲν πρότερον τοῖς βαρβάροις ἀνεῖτο παιδευτήριον, καὶ φιλέλληνας κατεσκεύαζε τοὺς Γαλάτας ὥστε καὶ τὰ συμβόλαια ἑλληνιστὶ γράφειν, ἐν δὲ τῷ παρόντι καὶ τοὺς γνωριμωτάτους Ῥωμαίων πέπεικεν ἀντὶ τῆς εἰς Ἀθήνας ἀποδημίας ἐκεῖσε φοιτᾶν φιλομαθεῖς ὄντας. Milo went into exile there and found the mullets delectable (Dio 40. 54. 3).
[5] Strabo 253.
[6] Cic. *pro Arch.* 3. 5; 5. 10.

Greek cities of the West. Unless Livy is here guilty of anachronism, an orator in the year 193 B.C. could ask, 'How are men of Smyrna and Lampsacus any more Greek than the peoples of Neapolis, Rhegium, and Tarentum?'[1]

Tarentum and Rhegium have left scanty traces of their Greek civilization. Tarentum was obviously a pleasant spot in the late Republic and early Empire. It received a colony of C. Gracchus and was thereafter much better off than before, according to Strabo.[2] City-weary Romans would find Tarentum a peaceful, rural retreat with a relaxing Greek atmosphere. Horace called it *Lacedaemonium Tarentum* in an ode, *imbelle Tarentum* in an epistle.[3] Seneca noted that the man who flees from himself often makes Tarentum his destination.[4] However, its charms soon deteriorated. Veterans were sent there in A.D. 60, and Dio of Prusa was able to remark that Tarentum was among those cities once flourishing but now entirely empty.[5]

A few more Greek inscriptions have survived from Rhegium than from Tarentum, but the evidence is still slight.[6] Rhegium's population was swollen with Roman settlers sent by Octavian after the Sicilian War.[7] Her constitution looks suspiciously Roman, in spite of Greek terms for the various municipal offices. An Hellenic veneer remained, but that was about all. If Rhegium could claim a gymnasiarchy, she had also to admit a quattuorvirate.[8]

Neapolis was different, a city defiantly Greek. After the Social War she was loath to receive the Roman citizenship,[9]

---

[1] Livy 35. 16. 3.   [2] Strabo 281.
[3] Hor. *Odes* 3. 5. 56; *Ep.* 1. 7. 45. Cf. *Odes* 2. 6. 9 ff.
[4] Sen. *de Tranq. Animi* 2. 13; quoted on p. 76, n. 4.
[5] Tac. *Ann.* 14. 27 (veterans in A.D. 60). Dio Prus. *Orat.* 33. 25.
[6] *IG* xiv. 612 ff. (Rhegium), with *IG* xiv. 668 ff. (Tarentum).
[7] Strabo 258–9.
[8] *IG* xiv. 616 (gymnasiarch); *CIL* x. 6 (IIIIvir). The πρύτανις ἐκ τοῦ ἰδίου καὶ ἄρχων πενταετηρικός and his three συμπρυτάνεις (*IG* xiv. 617–19) are surely IIIIviri quinquennales. So Mommsen in *CIL* x, p. 4. It may seem surprising that Heraclea does not rank as a Greek city in Italy in the time of Augustus; many in that city had, with the Neapolitans, preferred not to accept the Roman *civitas* in the Social War (Cic. *pro Balb.* 8. 21). But Strabo is explicit (p. 253): νυνὶ δὲ πλὴν Τάραντος καὶ Ῥηγίου καὶ Νεαπόλεως ἐκβεβαρβαρῶσθαι ἅπαντα (i.e. of Magna Graecia). Heraclea must by now have lost its Greek character.
[9] Cic. *pro Balb.* 8. 21. Cf. preceding note.

lest her Greek heritage be obliterated. She clung to the Greek language with an unparalleled tenacity for that part of the world. A bulk of Greek inscriptions survives, dating well into the Empire.[1] Tacitus labelled Neapolis a *Graeca urbs*.[2] But Neapolis will not have had to struggle very hard to retain her Hellenic individuality, as the city was a favoured centre of Roman recreation. To have romanized the city would have meant the elimination of a delightful resort. Emigration to the East and sacrifice of country brought an *interdicta voluptas*, as Horace informed Numicius.[3] But no harm could come from a vacation in near-by Neapolis *deliciarum causa et voluptatis*.[4] Cicero had complained that Roman citizens, noble youths, and even certain senators (*quosdam etiam senatores*) were given to Greek leisure in Greek costume at Neapolis,[4] but by the time of Caesar Augustus the city seems to have been regarded as an unobjectionable outlet for the desires of a young Tullus or a Bullatius.

Strabo provides a vivid picture of Neapolis in the Augustan era. The Hellenic life was better preserved there than anywhere else in Italy. There were gymnasia, ephebia, and phratries; inscriptions testify to these institutions, as they do to the use of the Greek language generally.[5] The chief Neapolitan magistrate was still called *demarch* in the reign of Hadrian.[6] The city had hot springs and excellent baths, not at all inferior

---

[1] *IG* xiv. 714–828.

[2] Tac. *Ann.* 15. 33. But Naples was a municipium: Cic. *ad Fam.* 13. 30. 1; cf. *ad Att.* 10. 13. 1.   [3] Hor. *Ep.* 1. 6. 64.

[4] Cic. *pro Rab. Post.* 10. 26.

[5] Strabo 246: πλεῖστα δ' ἴχνη τῆς Ἑλληνικῆς ἀγωγῆς ἐνταῦθα σώζεται, γυμνάσιά τε καὶ ἐφηβεῖα καὶ φρατρίαι καὶ ὀνόματα Ἑλληνικὰ καίπερ ὄντων Ῥωμαίων. Also Dio 55. 10. 9, quoted on p. 83, n. 4. Cf., for example, *IG* xiv. 719, 721, 722, 723, 724, 728, 729. No. 719 is a cursus inscription, entirely in Greek, of one M. Opsius Navius Fannianus: he was Xvir stl. iud., trib. leg. V Mac., quaestor Pont. et Bith., aed., praef. frum. dandi ex s. c., praetor. Is he not the praetorian M. Opsius in Tac. *Ann.* 4. 68 and 71?

[6] SHA, *Hadrian* 19. 1. Roman municipal organization appears in imperial Naples, but the old language is nevertheless tenaciously maintained: *IG* xiv. 745 ἄρξαντα [τὴν] τεσσάρων ἀνδρῶν (= IIIIvirum). Observe especially the mixture of Greek and Roman in *CIL* x. 1491: C. Herbacio Maec. Romano, demarchisanti, IIvir. alimentorum quaest. cur. sacrae pecun., cur. II frum. compar., se Vibo fecit qui ob promiss. venat. phetris divisit quina mil. num. On Neapolitan constitutional irregularities, see Mommsen, *CIL* x, p. 172. The Neapolitan λαυκελαρχία is still obscure: *IG* xiv, pp. 191–2.

to those at Baiae and far less crowded.[1] Visitors who came from Rome to experience ἡ ἐν Νεαπόλει διαγωγὴ ἡ Ἑλληνική did so for a diversity of reasons; some sought peace and quiet (ἡσυχία), others in old age or infirmity wanted to live without effort.[2] Cicero once admirably caught the essence of Neapolis when he described it as a city 'itself suited rather for calming men's passions than for rekindling the animosities of men in trouble'.[3] It was to Augustus' advantage to encourage the prosperity of a place like that.

In A.D. 2 Neapolis instituted quinquennial sacred games in honour of the Emperor.[4] Such an institution was nothing new for Augustus; he had himself established the Actia in Greece several decades before.[5] But the Italica Romaea Sebasta Isolympia were the first of their kind to be held on Italian soil, and a century was to pass before they received a rival in Italy.[6] The Neapolis games, both musical and gymnastic, were ranked next to the four great games of Greece and the Actia: this is quite clear from the order in which the achievements of professional athletes have been recorded on stone.[7] Manifestly, athletes were drawn from Greece and Asia to compete at Neapolis. They will have brought a breath of the East Greek world into Greek Italy. The magistrates of Neapolis did their best to publicize their games among the Greeks who

---

[1] Strabo 246: ἔχει δὲ καὶ ἡ Νεάπολις θερμῶν ὑδάτων ἐκβολὰς καὶ κατασκευὰς λουτρῶν οὐ χείρους τῶν ἐν Βαίαις, πολὺ δὲ τῷ πλήθει λειπομένας.

[2] Ibid.: ἐπιτείνουσι δὲ τὴν ἐν Νεαπόλει διαγωγὴν τὴν Ἑλληνικὴν οἱ ἐκ τῆς Ῥώμης ἀναχωροῦντες δεῦρο ἡσυχίας χάριν τῶν ἀπὸ παιδείας ἐργασαμένων ἢ καὶ ἄλλων διὰ γῆρας ἢ ἀσθένειαν ποθούντων ἐν ἀνέσει ζῆν. Cf. the Tarentines, ibid. 281: καθ' ἡσυχίαν ζῶσι.

[3] Cic. pro Sulla 5. 17: Hic contra ita quievit ut eo tempore omni Neapoli fuerit, ubi neque homines fuisse putantur huius adfines suspicionis et locus est ipse non tam ad inflammandos calamitosorum animos quam ad consolandos accommodatus.

[4] Dio (55. 10. 9) says that a sacred contest was voted to Augustus in Naples because its inhabitants, alone of the Campanians, tried to imitate the ways of the Greeks: τὰ τῶν Ἑλλήνων μόνοι τῶν προσχώρων τρόπον τινὰ ἐζήλουν. Dio's date is 2 B.C., but this is an error for A.D. 2: R. M. Geer, 'The Greek Games at Naples', TAPA 66 (1935), 208 ff., esp. 216. [Hence Strabo's notice of the games (246) will have been a later addition: cf. Chapter X, p. 134.]

[5] Dio 51. 1. 2; Strabo 325.

[6] The Eusebeia were established at Puteoli in A.D. 138: Frederiksen in P-W 23. 2. 2052.

[7] Examples in Geer, op. cit., p. 213, n. 24.

attended other games. A notable inscription, discovered at Olympia, reveals the efforts of the Neapolitan council to attract the Olympic spectators to the isolympic Sebasta.[1]

Augustus sympathized with Neapolitan Hellenism.[2] A little of what the Romans fancied did them good. He not only allowed himself to be honoured by the city's Greek games; he himself attended them when they were celebrated in the last year of his life.[3] The Emperor even saw fit to provide for his own Hellenic relaxation on the island of Capri. That island had been the property of the city of Neapolis and was, like Neapolis, itself Greek in character. In the year 29 B.C. the founder of the Actia took Capri for himself. He provided some compensation in the form of Ischia, which passed into the Neapolitan domain.[4] Augustus made no effort to romanize his new island. In A.D. 14 ephebes were still being trained there *ex vetere instituto*.[5] At that time the aged Princeps was a regular spectator of their exercises.[5]

It is remarkable that shortly before his death Caesar Augustus should have spent so much time in the Hellenic centres of Italy, watching the ephebic training at Capri and the contests at Neapolis. The first of the Romans had a craving for the Hellenic life no less than his compatriots. While he lingered at Capri in the fateful year A.D. 14, Augustus did a thing which would have roused the indignation of Cicero. He distributed Greek clothing to Romans and Roman clothing to Greeks, and stipulated that each should wear the other's characteristic dress and speak the other's language.[6] Whether or not this was an act of senility or of policy, it reveals much about Augustus and the Romans of the restored Republic.

[1] *Inschrift. v. Olympia*, no. 56.
[2] Note Velleius' comment (i. 4) on Naples: eximia semper in Romanos fides.
[3] Ibid. ii. 123; Suet. *Aug*. 98. 5; Dio 56. 29. 2.
[4] Strabo 248; Suet. *Aug*. 92. 2; Dio 52. 43. 2.
[5] Suet. *Aug*. 98. 3.
[6] Ibid. Note that Claudius lived like a Greek at Naples: Dio 60. 6. 2.

VII

THE CITIES

THE triumphant Octavian had found the East in unparalleled weakness. The exactions of governors and publicans in the late Republic had been followed by the cruel demands of the tyrannicides and Antony. The kingdom of the Ptolemies was defunct; Asia was bankrupt. Pausanias observed that the fortunes of Greece reached their nadir between the fall of Corinth and the reign of Nero.[1] In the year 45 B.C. Servius Sulpicius sailed from Aegina to Megara and saw desolation on every side.[2] The cities had been drained of money and resources, and food was short. After Actium Octavian attended to his new allies by distributing surplus corn from the war to various destitute cities.[3] But the practical course with which the future Princeps inaugurated his policy for the East was a general remission of debts.[4] The economic strain was relieved, and the Greeks of Asia realized that the victory of Caesar's heir had opened a new era of peace.

The Greek peoples rejoiced to hear that their triumviral patron had been conquered. This was not paradoxical, for their support of Antony had been a matter of necessity; he had been the man of the moment. But Antony's defeat, no less than his victory, would mean an end to privation, and Octavian knew this. While it was fitting for him to display a certain displeasure toward Antonian partisans, they, like the client dynasts, had no compunction about joining his clientela, now that he was master of the world. Therefore, there was little point in stirring up unnecessary trouble. Octavian was officially angry. A rumour went up that he was abolishing the

---

[1] Paus. 7. 17. 1. [2] Cic. ad Fam. 4. 5. 4.
[3] Plut. Ant. 68. 4–5. On the tesserae used in the distributions at Athens: Rostovtzeff, Festschr. f. Hirschfeld (1903), 305–11, and Graindor, Athènes sous Auguste (1927), p. 37, n. 2; p. 118.
[4] Dio Prus. Orat. 31. 66.

rights of city assemblies,[1] but there is no evidence that he ever did so. That can only have been a threat, an appropriate demonstration of wrath.

The conqueror allowed himself to confiscate a few master-works of art. He stole from Greece a statue of Athena by Endoeus and the teeth of the Calydonian Boar, which he exhibited publicly in Rome.[2] Sometimes he offered compensation: one hundred talents of the tribute of Cos were remitted as payment for a painting of Aphrodite Anadyomene, removed from the island and dedicated at Rome to Julius Caesar.[3] Antony had stolen three enormous works of Myron which had stood on a single base on Samos, and one of these was attractive to Augustus, who took it to the Capitol in Rome. As compensation the other two pieces were returned to the Samians.[4] In Egypt Augustus discovered a statue of Ajax which Antony had taken from Rhoeteum; Strabo noted that it was returned.[5] The Emperor was shrewd in that he showed his regard for the East by his restitution of stolen art works, but as a conqueror he was privileged to take what he wanted for himself.

No less than the late Republic, the Augustan Principate reveals great diplomatic activity. The cities presented their cases to the Emperor through their most intelligent and wealthy citizens. The distinguished Potamo of Mytilene, who had twice served as ambassador to Julius Caesar, served again on an embassy to Augustus in 26 B.C.[6] In the years which followed, the interests of that city were to be well cared for at Rome: Potamo's fellow envoy, the poet Crinagoras, remained in the imperial court; and Pompeius Macer, from the family of Pompey's Mytilenean intimate, Theophanes, entered the imperial service, leaving a son to become praetor in A.D. 15.[7] At Miletus C. Julius Apollonius, the son of Caesar's slave, lived long enough to associate himself with the first temple to

---

[1] Dio 51. 2. 1.

[2] Paus. 8. 46. 1 and 4. On art, cf. Chapter VI above, pp. 74–75.

[3] Strabo 657; Pliny, *NH* 35. 91. The painting deteriorated and was replaced by Nero (Pliny, ibid.).

[4] Strabo 637.   [5] Ibid. 595.   [6] *IGR* 4. 33.

[7] On Crinagoras, see Chapter III, pp. 36–37. For Pompeius Macer, *JRS* 51 (1961), 116–17, n. 42.

Augustus in his city.[1] An offspring of that opulent citizen was highly honoured for his diplomatic successes on behalf of Miletus.[2] The family of Iollas of Sardis, active in diplomacy with Romans of the Republic, was represented in embassies to Augustus.[3] Tralles too sent envoys to the Emperor; the city was noted for the number of wealthy men it contained.[4] The leading ambassador, Chaeremon, was the son of the rich Pompeian, Pythodorus, whose daughter became Queen of Pontus.[5] Embassies made their way to Rome from other places of the East, from Cnidos, Chios, Eresos, Cyrene, Alexandria, Athens, Sparta, and Thessaly.[6]

Augustus knew that the strength of Rome in the East depended upon the support of those very men who represented their cities in embassies to his court. Roman nourishment of the upper classes had begun long before, and Augustus continued it. The cities, in the hands of the right persons, were crucial, and could be made to do much of Rome's work, like the client kings outside the provinces. Augustus was obliged to reconcile astute diplomatic support of a certain class in each city with the maintenance of smoothly functioning local constitutions which would permit that class to predominate. The Emperor could not introduce into Greek πόλεις Roman constitutions which the Hellenes would not tolerate. But changes had already taken place in the Republic, and Augustus had rather to provide the economic stability necessary for effective local administration.

The Greek city council was originally a body whose membership changed at frequent and regular intervals. It became clear in the days of the Republic that a council of that kind was incompatible with the predominance of the upper class and

[1] *Milet* i. 2, no. 7; cf. above p. 8, n. 7.

[2] *Milet*, ibid.; also nos. 6 and 15.

[3] *Sardis* vii. 1, no. 8. The man is mentioned on another inscription from Sardis as giving a donation to the city: *Hellenica* 9 (1950), 8. The republican Iollas: *Sardis* vii. 1, no. 27; cf. p. 11 above.

[4] Strabo 649 (wealthy men in Tralles). Agathias 2. 17 (embassy of Chaeremon to Augustus in Spain, on which cf. Appendix III, p. 157).

[5] Cf. preceding note and p. 8, n. 4 above.

[6] Eresos: *IGR* 4. 7. The inscription is too fragmentary to reveal much. The other embassies are discussed below: cf. pp. 88 (Cnidos), 88 (Chios), 88–89 (Cyrene), 90 (Alexandria), 95 (Athens), 92 (Sparta), 104 (Thessaly).

especially of certain wealthy and educated members of it. Not surprisingly, the βουλή was gradually transformed into a permanent body, with life membership. A parallel with the Roman senate is inescapable. By the beginning of the imperial age most Greek cities of Asia had permanent councils.[1] There was no need for Augustus to make changes.

However, the Emperor interfered on occasion for purposes of enlightened amendment or clarification. He defined the limits of asylum in the sacred territory of Artemis at Ephesus;[2] at Cyme he provided for the return of dedications to the deity to whom they were vowed.[3] A delicate judicial case was referred to him from Cnidos, and he did not hesitate to settle the matter despite the free status of the city.[4] In the cities of Bithynia he revised the law of Pompey by lowering the minimum age for admission to local magistracies.[5] At Chios he confirmed certain privileges granted by Sulla: the island was declared free, and Romans there were to be subject to the laws of the Chians.[6] That was an extraordinary judicial arrangement, without parallel anywhere else.

The edicts from Cyrene show the Emperor again busy with amendment and clarification. As was natural, these documents were the result of diplomatic overtures from the Cyrenaeans. In capital and non-capital trials the Greeks of Cyrene were suffering injustice at the hands of jurors who were Roman citizens; Augustus made fresh and fairer provisions.[7] A new system was announced for facilitating provincial prosecutions of rapacious Roman governors. The effectiveness and the

---

[1] See Jones, *GC*, p. 171 and p. 338, n. 29.

[2] Strabo 641.

[3] H. W. Pleket, *Greek Inscriptions in the Rijksmuseum at Leyden* (1958), no. 57, reprinted with alterations by Mrs. K. M. T. Atkinson in *Rev. intern. des droits de l'ant.* 7 (1960), 231 ff.

[4] *SIG*³ 780. Free status was little more than an honorific title: observe Augustus' interference in Athens, Sparta, Thessaly, Cyzicus, Tyre, and Sidon, all of which were free at the beginning of the Principate. These cases are considered in the present and following chapters. At Cnidos a slight formality in deference to its free status is noticeable: Augustus remarks that he instructed his 'friend' Asinius Gallus to investigate the situation. In fact, Gallus was proconsul of Asia.

[5] Pliny, *Ep.* 10. 79. 2. Cf. Dio 54. 7. 5.

[6] *SIG*³ 785, with L. Robert, *REG* 65 (1952), 128.

[7] *Cyrene Edicts*, i and iv: *E–J*², no. 311.

duration of this system are alike dubious, but it appeared, at any rate, to be in the interest of the provincials.[1]

The third edict was an important affirmation of local authority. Pompey, Caesar, Antony, and Octavian had been accustomed to reward their faithful adherents with the Roman citizenship. Evidently certain Cyrenaeans, and undoubtedly citizens of other cities of the Greek East, had claimed exemption from local liturgies by virtue of their citizenship. This was bound to lead to trouble in the cities, inasmuch as the very people who had been honoured with the citizenship will have been in most cases the wealthiest. Therefore their claim to exemption meant a serious financial loss to the local administration. Both Julius Caesar and Augustus perceived the difficulties and enunciated that Roman citizenship did not exempt any native Greek from undertaking local liturgies in his own city. Caesar addressed himself to Mytilene, Augustus to Cyrene.[2]

These pronouncements were designed to correct an abuse. They were clarification, not a change in policy or tradition. Bestowals of the *civitas* had never entailed local *immunitas*. In surviving instances, a grant of ἀνεισφορία is always specifically added to πολιτεία, if it is intended at all.[3] Caesar and Augustus merely pointed out, doubtless to the immense satisfaction of certain city magistrates, that ἀνεισφορία was not to be arrogated where it had not been bestowed. There is no reason to think that Augustus, unlike Caesar, established by the third edict a class of Roman citizens with minor rights, distinct from those who were citizens at birth.[4] The edict explicitly deals with those who have been honoured with the citizenship, and that was because they were the only Roman citizens in Cyrene who mattered.[5]

---

[1] Senatus Consultum Calvisianum : *Cyrene Edict*, v. For the view that the system of extortion trials established in that document neither lasted long nor was very effective, P. A. Brunt, *Hist.* 10 (1961), 199 ff.

[2] *IGR* 4. 33 (col. *b*) ; 45 (Caesar). *Cyrene Edict*, iii (Augustus).

[3] Cf. the *SC de Asclepiade* &c. (Bruns, *Fontes*, no. 41) in which *immunitas* is granted without the *civitas*; in Octavian's edict concerning Seleucus of Rhosus (*E–J*², no. 301) *immunitas* and *civitas* are both explicitly granted.

[4] The class of Roman citizens with minor rights was an invention of Rostovtzeff, *SEHRE*² ii. 559, n. 6.

[5] P. Romanelli, *La Cirenaica romana* (1943), p. 84: 'L'immigrazione diretta di elementi romani dall'Italia è stata certamente finora nulla o quasi nulla.'

In regard to the Greeks in Egypt, Augustus was prepared to alter the existing arrangements, as elsewhere, only to ensure smooth and reliable local administration. Of the four Greek cities in Egypt,[1] Alexandria alone engaged the Emperor's attention. It was a city with a great Hellenistic past and citizens resentful of the Roman yoke; it lacked that quintessential Greek institution, the βουλή, even in a Roman guise. A large admixture of Jews in the population was a potential source of trouble. Although Augustus received Alexandrian envoys, the βουλή was not restored. Augustus could not be sure of the proud Greeks of that city.[2]

Outside the four Greek cities of Egypt it was difficult in so mixed a population to distinguish Greek from non-Greek, but the distinction had to be made for the simple reason that Greeks were superior to Egyptians and were preferred in positions of authority. The problem was solved in A.D. 4/5 by the creation of a new hellenized aristocracy consisting of two groups: those in the *chora* with satisfactory claims to Greek education and origin (who became known as οἱ ἀπὸ γυμνασίου) and the hellenized residents of the metropoleis. Although these persons were less privileged than ordinary Greeks in paying a poll-tax like Egyptians, they were superior to other Egyptians in paying at a reduced rate.[3] The emperors were to make use of this new class of Greek Egyptians in the lower grades of the civil service.[4]

Augustus liked to leave Greek affairs in the hands of Greeks. His plan emerges in detail in old Greece, which was a country

[1] Naucratis, Alexandria, Ptolemais, Paraetonium: see Jones, *CERP*, pp. 302 ff.

[2] H. A. Musurillo, *Acts of the Pagan Martyrs* (1954), pp. 1–2 (Boule Papyrus) and pp. 84–88. *P. Oxyrh.*, xxv (1959), no. 2435 *verso* records an Alexandrian embassy to Augustus in A.D. 13; lines 56–58 imply that the subject of the embassy was the restoration of the βουλή. Augustus, however, need not be held responsible for having abolished it in the first place. It was restored at last by Septimius Severus: Dio 51. 17. 2–3; *SHA, Sept. Sev.* 17. On anti-Roman Greeks at Alexandria, see below, Chapter VIII, p. 105.

[3] The first ἐπίκρισις was inferred by Van Groningen, *Gymnasiarque*, pp. 39–40, to have been in A.D. 4–5; that coincides with the earliest recorded metropolitan exegete in *P. Osl.* 26. (Cf. Jones, *CERP*, p. 475, n. 26.) The arrangements of A.D. 4–5 are described with great lucidity by V. Tcherikover in *Corpus Papyrorum Judaicarum* (1957), i. 59.

[4] Jones, *CERP*, p. 316.

learning how to be a museum; cultivated Romans admired Greece romantically for what she had been.[1] The multiplicity of independent cities, which had once brought glory and disaster, was rapidly disappearing. The descendants of free citizens were becoming the tenants of great estates. To many of the smaller cities nothing remained but their names.[2] Already in the Hellenistic age cities which hoped to survive had sought longevity in alliances and leagues, whereby they might collectively enjoy a greater power and economic stability. Augustus saw at once what his policy should be, here as throughout the East: to provide impetus and direction to what had been happening for some time before.

He encouraged the leagues. In a minor province they were more convenient units than individual cities, and they belonged to the evolution of Roman Greece. It should be emphasized that their development has nothing whatever to do with the imperial cult, which appears in none of the leagues in Greece before the reign of Claudius.[3] A few great cities flourished under imperial patronage, serving as focal points in the country's economy.

In Laconia the League of the Lacaedemonians had been formed in the time of Nabis under the tyranny of Sparta. Augustus liberated the league from Spartan rule, and the twenty-four cities assumed a new name: the League of Free Laconians.[4] It was bound together by a mutual interest in the marble and purple trade.[5] In Sparta Augustus installed his

---

[1] See esp. Cic. *pro Flacc.* 26. 62–63 on the ancient glories of Athens and Sparta in comparison with 'iam fractum prope ac debilitatum Graeciae nomen'. Cf. also above, Chapter VI.

[2] U. Kahrstedt, *Das wirtschaftliche Gesicht Griechenlands in der Kaiserzeit* (1954), *passim.*

[3] The earliest traces of the cult: *Corinth* viii. 2, no. 68; *IG* ii². 3538 (both concerning C. Julius Spartiaticus). On the whole matter of the secular character of the leagues in Greece at the beginning of the Principate, see Larsen, *Representative Government in Greek and Roman History* (1955), pp. 112–13.

[4] Strabo 366 (formation of the league under Nabis); Paus. 3. 21. 6–7 (Augustus' liberation of the league and its twenty-four cities). On pre-Augustan inscriptions (e.g. *IG* v. 1. 1226, 1227) the league is called κοινὸν τῶν Λακεδαιμονίων; *IG* v. 1. 1161, 1167, 1177, 1243 (imperial) give κοινὸν τῶν Ἐλευθερολακώνων. Cf. Bowersock, *JRS* 51 (1961), 116. Kornemann, *P–W* Suppl. 4. 929 is confused, perhaps misled by Paus. 7. 16. 9–10 (asserting falsely that all Greek leagues were dissolved in 146 B.C.).

[5] Kahrstedt, op. cit., p. 203.

over-ambitious partisan, C. Julius Eurycles, and the city was presented with Cythera, Cardamyle, and Thuria as gifts.[1] Some time between 7 and 2 B.C. Eurycles will have attempted to reassert Spartan control over the league cities, without success.[2] But there was no denying that the cities continued to be linked economically to Sparta, which held a complete monopoly over Laconian coinage until the Severan age.[3] An inscription from Gytheum, the arsenal of Sparta, reveals that Eurycles and his son Laco assisted the Free Laconians in some memorable way.[4] Asopus, another member of the league, received oil from Sparta.[5]

The Achaean League had also existed in the late Republic; its headquarters were at Olympia.[6] The participation of Elis demonstrates that the league was not confined merely to the territory of Achaea. The first Princeps maintained the organization he inherited but shifted its centre of gravity. About 14 B.C. Patrae was chosen to be its guardian city: it was admirably located for trade at the western end of the Gulf of Corinth, but it lacked inhabitants and size. Hence the Emperor established a Roman colony on the site and incorporated adjacent Greek villages in a grand synoecism. The earlier colony of Dyme was swallowed up in the new foundation. Augustus went on to extend the territory of Patrae across the Gulf. Calydon and the Aetolian land to the east were absorbed, as well as Naupactus and Oeanthea in Ozolian Locris. The Emperor accorded freedom to his chosen city, the only one in Achaea to which he gave that honour.[7]

---

[1] See Bowersock, op. cit., p. 113 and n. 11.

[2] Ibid., p. 116. It has been suggested to me that the league was still under Spartan domination at this time and was freed as a result of the condemnation of Eurycles. This is unlikely: Augustus would hardly have satisfied the angry family of Brasidas, which brought Eurycles to trial, by depriving Sparta of her league. Note also that Strabo refers without comment (p. 366) to Eleuthero-laconians. This would be surprising if they had become free just before he was writing: the passage was written between 7 and 2 B.C. and cannot be a Tiberian addition (*JRS* 51 [1961], 115). The liberation of the cities must have happened soon after Actium.   [3] See Head, *HN*[2] 433–6.

[4] *AE* 1929. 99, ll. 19–20. Gytheum as a league member: Paus. 3. 21. 7. Strabo 343 and 363 calls the city τὸ τῆς Σπάρτης ἐπίνειον.

[5] *IG* v. 1. 970. Cf. Paus. 3. 21. 7.

[6] *Inschr. v. Olympia*, nos. 328, 333, 367, 401, 415, 420. No. 415 reveals the participation of Elis.

[7] Strabo 387 (veteran colony); Paus. 7. 18. 7 (synoecism of Greek cities);

Patrae was noted for the abundance and charm of its women, most of whom were textile workers. The traffic in flax, especially the transparent Elean *byssos*, had bound the old Achaean League economically together.[1] As Augustus surely planned, these materials made their way to the new city for processing. The finished products could be conveniently dispatched from Patrae and exported all over the Mediterranean world.

Prospering, the Achaean League incorporated other leagues. There had once been an independent Argolid *koinon*, which emerges, late in the reign of Tiberius, as a member of the Achaean League, although it may have joined under Augustus.[2] By the accession of Gaius a huge amalgamation had taken place. The former *koinon* of Boeotians, Euboeans, Locrians, Phocians, and Dorians now belonged to a common organization with members of the Achaean League.[3] The new group styled itself variously: the Achaeans and Panhellenes, more succinctly the Panhellenes, or the Panachaeans. Although Augustus would have approved of the Panhellenes or Panachaeans, it is erroneous to think they were united in his lifetime. The union occurred in his successor's old age.[4]

In north-western Greece Augustus caused another synoecism and founded a free city. Nicopolis arose from the camp of the victorious Octavian as an enduring monument of his conquest of Antony. In the late Republic both the Acarnanians and the Aetolians had organized themselves into leagues; Nicopolis

---

Paus. 7. 17. 5 (Dyme); Paus. 10. 38. 9 (Ozolian Locris, except Amphissa); Paus. 7. 18. 7 (freedom). On all this, U. Kahrstedt, 'Die Territorien von Patrai und Nikopolis in der Kaiserzeit', *Historia* 1 (1950), 549 ff., rejecting Pausanias' Augustan date for Dyme and Locris because Strabo is ignorant of these annexations. This argument has no weight, since Strabo was not writing between 2 B.C. and 14 A.D. On relations between Athens and Patrae, see the new inscription in *Hesp.* 28 (1959), 280, with new fragment in *Hesp.* 29 (1960), 83.

[1] Paus. 7. 21. 14.
[2] *IG* iv². 665 (Epidaurus). On the Argolid κοινόν: *BCH* 33 (1909), 176–7.
[3] *SIG*³, 767 (Athens; 34/33 B.C.). The large κοινόν was confirmed by Gaius: *IG* vii. 2711, l. 29. *SIG*³, 796A used to be mentioned in this context, but Momigliano, *JRS* 34 (1944), 115–16, dates it rightly to Nero instead of Tiberius.
[4] Cf. Gaius' action cited in the preceding note. See also U. Kahrstedt, 'Das Koinon der Achaier', *Symbolae Osloenses*, 28 (1950), 70–75.

replaced them.[1] For practical purposes a synoecism hardly
differed from a league, but it was a striking reminder of
Actium. Nicopolis gathered into its territory such distant
places as Ambracia, Amphilochian Argos, and Alyzia. Anac-
torium was its commercial centre. Almost every Aetolian was
uprooted: those who did not become Nicopolitans fled into
Locris to Amphissa.[2]

Nicopolis was a thoroughly Greek city. Romanization was
far from Augustus' thoughts. The city's coin legends were all
Greek, and so were its inscriptions.[3] The form of its local
government was Greek.[4] Even the games with which Octavian
celebrated his victory were Greek: the Actia, which were
quinquennial, modelled on the Olympics, and supervised by
Greeks.[5] And these games were not something new. They had,
in fact, been held previously;[6] Octavian only gave them new
distinction.

To the east lay two more great cities of Greece, Corinth and
Athens. Corinth was Julius Caesar's Patrae. He resurrected
a dead city at a commercially vital point by establishing
a Roman colony. His obligations to displaced Romans were
fulfilled, and the economy of Greece was given some hope of
revival. Corinth prospered, growing on the fruits of trade and
banking. Undoubtedly it formed a commercial centre for
eastern Achaea; a century and a half after Augustus' death it
was head of the entire Achaean province, the confluence of
trade from Patrae, Athens, and Thessalonica.[7] But Corinth
was not a free city, and therein Augustus' plan was made clear.
He encouraged another city to head the Achaean province.
Caesar's Corinthians had an evil reputation when the Principate was born: the colonists were grave-robbers, and every
Roman of fashion knew about the trade in Necrocorinthia.[8]

[1] Acarnanians and Aetolians: Kornemann, *P–W* Suppl. 4. 921, 923. Nicopolis: Suet. *Aug.* 18; Pliny, *NH* 4. 5; Paus. 10. 38. 4; Strabo 324–5 and 450.

[2] See references in the preceding note, but above all Kahrstedt, *Historia*, 1
(1950), 549–61.

[3] Ibid., 559–60.

[4] Ibid. The Latin inscription from Nicopolis, *AE* 1928. 15, does not confirm
reports of a colony at Actium (Tac. *Ann.* 5. 10; Pliny, *NH* 4. 5): Kahrstedt,
560, denying that there was a colony.

[5] Strabo 325.   [6] Ibid.; *P–W* 1. 1213.

[7] Aristides, *Orat.* 46. 23 Keil.   [8] Strabo 381.

Augustus' poet lamented the shame.[1] Patrae was the Emperor's answer to Corinth.

Athens, that venerable home of antiquities and pedagogues, was not neglected. Recent excavations now permit remarkable detail and precision about Roman Athens. The so-called Market of Caesar and Augustus, begun through the munificence of the Dictator, was brought to completion after a successful embassy to the Princeps.[2] A temple of Rome and Augustus was constructed on the Acropolis, while in the centre of the agora a vast music-hall was built in commemoration of M. Vipsanius Agrippa, then touring the East with proconsular imperium. Roman architects appear to have been sent to Athens to collaborate with the Greeks.[3] Another extraordinary building appeared: a fifth-century temple of Ares was systematically removed from some unknown site and re-erected in the agora under Augustus[4]—not surprisingly, however, since Ares was the Greek counterpart of the Roman Mars, for whom the Emperor had special regard.[5] And with the emphasis accorded to a fifth-century temple can be compared a revival of fifth-century lettering on inscriptions.[6] The influence of Augustus and the efforts of local partisans may be inferred in these matters, and in others.[7]

Like a few cities in Asia Minor, Athens has bequeathed the names of certain of her eminent philo-Romans by virtue of their tenure of sacred and secular magistracies. When the old Pythais was abolished after Actium, a more modest *theoria* to Delphi, the Dodecais, supplanted it. The priest, herald, and

[1] Crinagoras, *Anth. Pal.* ix. 284.

[2] *IG* iii[2]. 3175, on the gateway to the Roman Forum at Athens.

[3] H. A. Thompson, *Hesp.* 19 (1950), 90 ff.

[4] W. B. Dinsmoor, *Hesp.* 9 (1940), 1 ff.; M. H. McAllister, *Hesp.* 28 (1959), 1 ff., especially 48 ff.

[5] Temple of Mars Ultor at Rome: *Res Gestae* 21, Dio 54. 8. 3 and 55. 10. 1–6. At Nicopolis: Suet. *Aug.* 18, *AE* 1928. 15 (ul[tor]).

[6] *IG* ii[2]. 1040 is the best example of Augustan epigraphical archaism; cf. Raubitschek and Jeffery, *Dedications from the Athenian Acropolis* (1949), p. 149.

[7] e.g. the coinage: cf. Chapter VIII below, pp. 105–6. Professor S. Dow has kindly informed me of his view, based on *IG* ii[2]. 1732–3, that there was an Augustan reform of the Athenian courts. The Augustan revival of the Peiraeus, proposed by Day, *An Economic History of Athens under Roman Domination* (1942), pp. 145 ff., rests on the dubious ascription of *IG* ii[2]. 1035 to the reign of Augustus.

exegetes in the five occurrences of the Dodecais under Augustus were the same.[1] These men, in several attested cases, also served as hoplite general or archon.[2] Eucles, for example, was a son of Herod of Marathon and a member of the distinguished and affluent family which subsequently produced the great Herod Atticus. He assumed from his father the position of overseer of the construction of the Market of Caesar and Augustus, and it was he who went on an embassy to the Emperor to secure the necessary funds for finishing it.[3] He was archon, hoplite general, and five times priest of Pythian Apollo.[4]

Of the important Athenians of this period one is particularly memorable and at the same time mystifying. C. Julius Nicanor came to Athens from Hierapolis in Syria and was a man of enormous wealth.[5] He bought the island of Salamis, which the Athenians had sold after the sack of Sulla, and gave it back to Athens.[6] It was presumably for this act of generosity that he was hailed as the 'New Themistocles'.[7] He was also the 'New Homer', clearly a man of culture.[8] A century later Dio of Prusa recalled the extravagant honours accorded to Nicanor, though he did not mention the strange *damnatio* which the memory of that eminent citizen suffered at an unknown date.[9]

[1] Graindor, *Athènes sous Auguste* (1927), pp. 144 ff. Cf. also J. Day, *An Economic History of Athens under Roman Domination* (1942), pp. 174–5.

[2] e.g. Eucles, five times priest of Pythian Apollo, was both hoplite general and archon (Graindor, pp. 142–3); Polycharmus, five times exegete (Graindor, p. 143), was archon and so was his son (Graindor, *Chronol.*, p. 57); Diotimus, son of Diodorus and five times exegete (Graindor, *Athènes*, p. 143), was archon (Graindor, *Chronol.*, p. 30 and *IG* ii². 1096).   [3] *IG* iii². 3175.

[4] See n. 2 above. On Eucles and other eminent Athenians: Day, op. cit., pp. 172–4.

[5] L. Robert reported in *Hellenica*, 8 (1950), 91 that he had made a study of Nicanor; Attic inscriptions of the Augustan period mentioning Julius Nicanor must be divided between two persons, an Alexandrian and a Syrian. The Alexandrian was doubtless the son of the philosopher, Areius of Alexandria: Suet. *Aug.* 89. 1, cf. above, Chapter III. The man who bought the island of Salamis came from Hierapolis in Syria (Steph. Byz. s.v.).

[6] Strabo 394; Dio Prus. *Orat.* 31. 116; Steph. Byz. s.v.

[7] *IG* ii². 3786–9 (statue bases). The view of A. E. Raubitschek in *Hesp.* 23 (1954), 317 ff. is demonstrably untenable: cf. J. and L. Robert, *REG* 68 (1955), 210, n. 79.

[8] See the statue bases in the foregoing note and the inscription considered by Raubitschek in the article cited there.

[9] In *IG* ii². 3786, 3787, and 3789 'New Homer' and 'New Themistocles' have been erased.

The Augustan system of leagues stretched northward. There had been a league of Thessalians since the fourth century. When Macedonia was humbled, the old league was gradually swollen through incorporation of the regions which encompassed it. Thessalian control spread across Dolopia and penetrated through Phthiotic Achaea as far as the southern confines of Aeniania and Malis. In the east the smaller Magnesian League became a part of the greater Thessalian. In the north Perrhaebia passed from Macedonian to Thessalian domination.[1]

Perhaps because of tumult Augustus saw fit to revoke the freedom which Julius Caesar had granted to the Thessalians, but he did not alter the territory of the confederacy.[2] Its political centre was Larissa.[3] An inscription reveals how a Roman governor could lighten his work by referring internal disagreements to the league authorities.[4] It illustrates the recurrent emphasis on local administration in the arrangements of Augustus.

Further north, in Macedonia, the first Princeps accepted the strange political system which had been operating there since 167 B.C. The country had been divided into four parts, a division which lasted at least into the Flavian era.[5] But it was probably Augustus who brought Macedonia into conformity with the rest of Greece: a Macedonian league emerged under the Principate and united the four divisions in a federal state. The political seat was Beroea, which lay inland, but the economic centre was the port of Thessalonica, a free city.[6]

To consolidate the network of leagues and cities in Greece,

---

[1] Paus. 10. 8. 3. Cf. C. Kip, *Thessalische Studien* (1910), pp. 109, 113, and 129.
[2] Grant of freedom from Julius Caesar: App. *BC* 2. 88; Plut., *Caes.* 48. Pliny, however, only lists Pharsalus as free (*NH* 4. 29). On Augustus' action in Thessaly, see Chapter VIII, p. 104 below, and also Appendix III, pp. 160–1. Above all, Bowersock, *Rheinisches Museum*, 108 (1965): 'Zur Geschichte des römischen Thessaliens.'
[3] *IG* ix. 2. 261 = *E–J*², no. 321, line 12: ἐν τῷ ἐνε[στηκότι Θεσσαλῶν τῶν ? ἐν Λα]ρίσῃ συνεδρίῳ.
[4] The document cited in the preceding note concerns a boundary dispute which C. Poppaeus Sabinus referred to the Thessalian League.
[5] Acts xvi. 12; *AE* 1900. 130, altered in *CP* 44 (1949), 89.
[6] J. M. R. Cormack, 'High Priests and Macedoniarchs from Beroea', *JRS* 33 (1943), 39 ff.; for Macedoniarchs in Thessalonica, p. 43. Cf. Larsen, *Representative Government* (1955), p. 221, n. 24, on Thessalonica. It was free: Pliny, *NH* 4. 36.

Augustus revived the old Delphic Amphictyony. The Augustan Amphictyons were thirty in number, of which the three largest members provided eighteen: the free city of Nicopolis, the Thessalian League, and the Macedonian League each sent six delegates.[1] The scheme permitted the maximum consolidation of the Greeks with the minimum threat to Rome. The plan was masterful: all thirty Amphictyons were never to assemble together at any one time. Not all of the three largest members sent delegates to every session. Athens with one delegate, Delphi with two, and Augustus' city of victory with six were the only members of the Amphictyony who could be represented at every meeting. The rest sent delegates in turn at regular intervals.[2] The imperial Amphictyony testifies to Augustus' political acumen.

Outside Greece there were at least two leagues already in existence when Augustus became Princeps, and again he encouraged a natural evolution. Traces of a union of cities in Asia early in the first century B.C. become by the time of Antony an organized *koinon*.[3] This body was swift in devoting itself to worship of the Emperor and belongs, therefore, to a history of the imperial cult. It gave the lead to other provinces; *koina* of a similar kind mushroomed in the East without any directive from the Emperor. Meanwhile, Lycia, not yet a province under Augustus, looked after itself by means of a league of twenty-three cities which had been joined together for over a century.[4] In effect, the league did the work of a client king. The usefulness of leagues for local government was demonstrated once more. And the fact that certain of the eastern *koina* occupied themselves particularly with the cult of the Emperor obviously did not preclude their being useful in the same way as the Greek and Lycian *koina*.

It has often been pointed out that the corporate organization of eastern cities in leagues facilitated the bringing of complaints against Roman rule. Inevitably it did, though not to

---

[1] Paus. 10. 8. 4. Cf. Larsen, 'The Policy of Augustus in Greece', *Acta Classica* (Proc. Class. Ass. South Africa, 1959), 123 ff.   [2] Paus. 10. 8. 4.

[3] Traces in early first century B.C.: *OGIS* 439; *IGR* 4. 188; Cic. *pro Flacc.* 23. 55–56. The *koinon* under Antony (either 42/41 or 33/32): Preisigke, *Sammelbuch*, 4224 = *E–J²*, no. 300. Cf. Brandis, *Hermes* 32 (1897), 512 ff.

[4] Strabo 664–5. Cf. G. Fougères, *de Lyciorum Communi* (1898).

the extent some have imagined.[1] What must always be remembered is that the leagues were things of the East, not
created and introduced by Augustus as policy. He inherited
many, and allowed others to develop.

Augustus' policy was to create a situation in which the
Greek cities would be able to look after themselves as much as
possible. He had, of course, to assure himself that the political
units were workable and that the right kind of provincials
were in control. When he interfered it was to keep the provincial machinery running smoothly. He had begun well with
a remission of debts; he then gave the empire the greatest of
all possible boons—peace. A succession of earthquakes was the
only persistent impediment to recovery, and in response to
appeals the Emperor furnished financial aid. Tralles, Laodicea, Thyatira, and Chios all were stricken early in the
Principate.[2] In 12 B.C. there were widespread tremors. At that
time, the Emperor paid from his own funds the tribute of the
province of Asia.[3]

The cities of the East could discern a gentle revival of prosperity. The textile industry at Patrae was flourishing, trade at
Corinth was good, and Athens was reaping the benefits of
being a centre of Old World culture.[4] Strabo observed that
Ephesus, by virtue of its favourable location for Asian commerce, was growing more prosperous every day.[5] Second only
to Ephesus was Apamea, the former Celaenae, through which
passed merchandise from Italy and Greece.[6] Laodicea on the
Lycus produced excellent wool, and the exceptionally rich
country in the vicinity of Sardis was made to yield despite
frequent earthquakes.[7] Cyzicus grew in size and beauty to
rival the leading cities of Asia.[8] Tyre in Syria did a thriving
business in purple, while the establishment of quinquennial
games at Syrian Antioch marked the beginning of its rise to

---

[1] P. A. Brunt, *Hist.* 10 (1961), 212 ff.

[2] Agathias 2. 17 (Tralles); Suet. *Tib.* 8 (Laodicea, Thyatira, Chios). Cf.
Appendix III below, pp. 157 and 160.

[3] Dio 54. 30. 3.

[4] Above, pp. 93 (Patrae), 94 (Corinth), 95 (Athens). On the revival of
prosperity at Athens, cf. Day, *Economic History of Athens under Roman domination*
(1942), pp. 167–71.

[5] Strabo 641.   [6] Ibid. 577.   [7] Ibid. 578.   [8] Ibid. 575.

greatness in the empire.[1] Cities, old and new, with names like Caesarea, Sebaste, or Sebastopolis blossomed all over the East.[2] New roads were put through.[3]

By nourishing the life of the cities and entrusting a substantial amount of administrative work to them, Augustus continued the republican tradition of personal dependence on provincials of the upper class. By avoiding a policy of centralization, he eased the strain on Rome; the provincials were profitably occupied with institutions familiar to them. As a patron of the Greek way of life, the Emperor maintained indirectly his own personal pre-eminence, as strong in senatorial provinces as it was in his own. Yet it was precisely because so little was innovatory about Augustus' treatment of the Eastern cities that the hostility and opposition which surged up occasionally in the Republic did so again in his own day. There were still many who hated Rome.

[1] Strabo 757 (Tyre). Malalas 9. V95B (0291) on Antioch: cf. G. Downey, *A History of Antioch in Syria* (1961), p. 168. The games were included in the bequest of an Antiochene companion of Augustus.

[2] New foundations under Augustus (page references to Jones, *CERP*): Caesarea, later Caesarea Germanice, in Bithynia (163–4); Sebaste in Asia (72); Caesarea Paneas in Syria (283); perhaps Caesarea Trocetta in Asia (80) and Caesarea of the Proseilemmenitae in Paphlagonia (169). New names for old cities: Caesarea for Tralles (78), Anazarbus (205), and Strato's Tower (273); Sebaste for Pontic Diospolis (170), Paphlagonian Pompeiopolis (169), Elaeussa (207), and Samaria (273); Sebastopolis for Carana (170), Dioscurias (173), Myrrina (398, n. 86), and probably Larba (77). Megalopolis in Polemoniac Pontus may have taken the name Sebasteia under Augustus (171): cf. Anderson, *Anat. Studies pres. to Ramsay* (1923), 8–10.

[3] E. Gren attributes to Augustus the beginnings of the great road system of Asia Minor: *Kleinasien und der Ostbalkan in der wirtschaftlichen Entwicklung der römischen Kaiserzeit* (1941), p. 44. On the Via Sebaste through Pisidia, which belongs somehow in the context of the Homonadensian War, see R. Syme, *Klio* 27 (1934), 135 ff. On northern roads, D. R. Wilson, 'Historical Geography of Bithynia, Paphlagonia, and Pontus' (unpublished Oxford B.Litt. thesis, 1960), chapter IV.

VIII

OPPOSITION AMONG THE GREEKS

IT was hardly a secret that Rome had a policy of encouraging the aristocracies of eastern cities and supporting the establishment of oligarchies. The wealthier provincials had much to gain from the Roman domination; new avenues of favour and advancement were open to them. But it was not surprising that the lower strata of eastern society, which endured Roman rapacity and war without hope of palpable compensation, were the core of discontent and sedition.

In the century before Augustus, the revolt of Aristonicus and the Mithridatic Wars show most vividly the sources of opposition to Rome. The Citizens of the Sun, who rallied round Aristonicus, comprised the dregs of Asia, the destitute and enslaved.[1] Rome had nothing to offer them, no land redistribution nor debt cancellation nor liberation of slaves. A few decades later, however, Mithridates tried to win over discontented Greeks by making precisely those liberal promises which Rome normally withheld.[2]

In Athens there was a democratic revolution. At the end of the second century a series of constitutional changes, favoured by Rome, had led to the supremacy of a small oligarchic faction.[3] Unprecedented things were happening: one man held the archonship for two years in succession, another for three.[4]

---

[1] Strabo 646; Diod. 34. 2. 26.

[2] App. *Mithr.* 48; 62. Cf. Plut. *Sull.* 18. 5. Note also the efforts of Ephesus to recover the loyalty of the lower classes: *SIG*³ 742, on which cf. Oliver, *AJP* 60 (1939), 468 ff. and Rostovtzeff, *SEHHW*, p. 943.

[3] Ferguson, *Hellenistic Athens* (1911), 427–40 is still authoritative, although the view there reproduced from *Klio* 4 (1904), 1–17 that an oligarchic revolution took place at Athens in 103/102 B.C. cannot stand. The rise of the narrow oligarchy and Roman support of it are well documented in Accame, *Il Dominio Romano in Grecia* (1946), 165–9.

[4] Argeios was archon in 98/97 and 97/96 B.C.; Medeios was archon in 91/90, 90/89, and 89/88. Cf. Dinsmoor, *Archons of Athens* (1931), p. 280.

The hoplite general acquired extraordinary powers.[1] By the early eighties the situation was growing intolerable. Struck by the initial successes of Mithridates, the Athenian people saw an opportunity to shake off the tyranny of the pro-Roman oligarchs. Under the leadership of politically minded philosophers and with the support of an officer of Mithridates, the *demos* of Athens—the most unruly part of it, says Pausanias— rose against Rome and declared for the Pontic king.[2] Athens' resistance was strong, but the forces of Sulla were stronger. The siege and sack of 86 B.C. were bitter reminders of Roman omnipotence.

The conflict between partisans and enemies of Rome could thus, as at Athens, erupt in civil strife between the upper and lower classes. But it would be naïve to suppose that the Greek opposition was located exclusively in the lower classes; the matter is more complex.

Plutarch's general analysis of stasis provides guidance in this inquiry. Although by no means all civil disturbances had anti-Roman elements, patterns of social cleavage recur. Stasis, says Plutarch, breaks out in one of three situations: when members of the ruling class dispute with one another, when members of the lower classes are envious of those who rank above them, and when members of the upper classes abuse those who are beneath them.[3] These three possibilities resolve themselves into two: a conflict between factions within the same class (inevitably the upper), and a conflict between the classes themselves. Those who are neither conspicuously aristocratic nor impoverished will, on occasion, attach themselves to one of the two extremes or perhaps remain inert in disputes which do not concern them; sometimes the mass of citizens will unite with one upper-class faction against another.

---

[1] Ferguson, *Klio* 4 (1904), 7–8.

[2] Paus. I. 20. 5: (ὁ Ἀριστίων) ἀνέπεισε δὲ οὐ πάντας, ἀλλ' ὅσον δῆμος ἦν καὶ δήμου τὸ ταραχῶδες. Other evidence for the revolt is conveniently assembled in Greenidge–Clay–Gray[2], *Sources for Roman History* (1960), p. 170. It seems best to distinguish two successive rebel leaders, Athenion and Aristion, even though the former is mentioned only in Poseidonius, *FGH* ii. A. 87. F. 36: see Ferguson, *Hellenistic Athens*, pp. 440–51, and Accame, *Dominio Romano*, pp. 168–71. Observe that Plutarch, in *Praec. rei pub. ger.* 14 (809 E), links together Aristion, Nabis, and Catiline.

[3] Plut. *Praec. rei pub. ger.* 20 (816 B).

Anyhow, Plutarch's observations show the necessity of considering divergent interests not only within individual cities but even within a single class of citizens: it is a mistake to regard provincial cities as units, with a single allegiance or unanimity of interest. Outbreaks of stasis, in which internal dissension becomes visible for a moment, deserve careful attention, especially in the East where the cities were particularly prone to such behaviour. It has already been noted that stasis could arise from conflicting attitudes toward Roman domination; there were naturally other causes too, personal feuds and local economic crises. Plutarch and Dio of Prusa reveal much about riots over issues of that kind. But in the late Republic and early Principate, when the fixity and permanence of Roman rule were not altogether assured, civil strife itself born of incompatible views about Rome ought to be expected. Certain Athenians in 88 B.C. still had hopes that Rome would be crushed.[1]

Under the Pax Augusta eastern cities had their share of stasis, and anti-Roman agitation may have had some part in it. At any rate, in Cyzicus some Roman citizens (perhaps local magnates) were flogged and executed in factious riots; the Emperor, present in the East at the time, deprived the city of its precarious free status for a five-year period.[2] In the following year, when Augustus was in Syria, he found the free cities of Tyre and Sidon confounded by stasis; details are wanting, but the fact that he cancelled the freedom of those two cities suggests that more Roman citizens may have suffered, as at Cyzicus; possibly undesirable factions were in the ascendant.[3] At an unknown date there was also trouble in Cyprus, and

---

[1] The anti-Roman sentiments of the democratic rebels in 88 can be seen in the speech of Athenion apud Poseid., FGH ii. A. 87. F. 36, pp. 245–6; the anarchy, for which the Roman senate is said to have been responsible (p. 246, ll. 15–17), must refer to the oligarchy of the 90's; it cannot correspond with the anarchy on the archon list (IG ii². 1713) for 88/87, since Athenion's speech belongs in early 88. It is worth noting that in Smyrna there was less confidence that Rome would be defeated: rebel issues of gold staters lacked a magistrate's name (Robinson, Num. Chron. 16 [1936], 187 ff.). Aristion did not shrink from having his name on Athenian staters in gold: Greenidge–Clay–Gray², Sources, p. 285. [M. Thompson, The New Style Silver Coinage of Athens (1961), i. 416–24, re-dates the ΒΑΣΙΛΕ ΜΙΘΡΑΔΑΤΗΣ–ΑΡΙΣΤΙΩΝ coins to c. 121 instead of 87/86—wrongly according to D. M. Lewis, CR, N.S., 12 (1962), 290 ff.]   [2] Dio 54. 7. 6.   [3] Ibid.

a certain Paquius Scaeva was dispatched to deal with it on the authority of Augustus and by senatorial decree.[1] More telling was the widespread outbreak of civil commotion throughout the cities of the empire in A.D. 6, when proconsuls were chosen *extra sortem* to cope with the emergency.[2] These troubles were undoubtedly attempts on the part of Rome's enemies to exploit her weakness at the time of the great Pannonian rebellion and an economic crisis in the city. It is clear that the empire at large did not rally to the support of the Principate. The elder Pliny preserves a report that Augustus contemplated suicide.[3]

In Thessaly a man called Petraeus was burned alive, a sensational event which Plutarch recalled a hundred years afterward.[4] The father of this Petraeus was doubtless the loyal Caesarian, L. Cassius Petraeus, who led a Thessalian faction in support of the Dictator against the faction of Hegesaretus.[5] In the year after Caesar's assassination, the elder Petraeus was beheaded.[6] It is not too much to assume that the lurid death of his son was similarly the result of factional rivalry. There was undoubtedly trouble in Thessaly even before Petraeus' death: Augustus presided over an obscure trial of Thessalians, and himself appointed one of the eponymous generals of the Thessalian League.[7] It is difficult to see precisely what sort of discontent provoked the murder of Petraeus and the trial, but it looks as if his enemies were chafing at his leadership of the league. These must have been disappointed aristocrats. The removal of a leading Roman partisan was a serious offence; it was perhaps the reason why the Thessalians were deprived of the freedom which Julius Caesar had granted to them.[8] It was hard to encourage an aristocracy, when the aristocracy was divided within itself.

[1] *ILS* 915.   [2] Dio 55. 28. 2.   [3] Pliny, *NH* 7. 149.

[4] Plut. *Praec. rei pub. ger.* 19 (815 D).

[5] Cf. the full discussion in Bowersock, *Rheinisches Museum*, loc. cit. See also Appendix III below, p. 161. On the name Πετραῖος in Thessaly, cf. L. Robert, *Hellenica* 1 (1940), 121 ff.

[6] Cic. *Phil.* 13. 33. E. W. Gray has suggested (privately) that Brutus may have ordered the execution.

[7] See Appendix III, pp. 160–1.

[8] Caesar's grant: App. *BC* 2. 88; Plut. *Caes.* 48. Not mentioned by the elder Pliny.

Alexandria may have presented to Augustus a dilemma of the same kind. At any rate, the so-called Acts of the Pagan Martyrs presuppose a divided Alexandrian aristocracy under later emperors. Against the violently anti-Roman Isidore and Hermaïscus were balanced the friends of Rome, C. Julius Dionysius, Ti. Claudius Balbillus, and Theon the exegete (evidently murdered by the rival faction).[1] Since the βουλή which the Alexandrian nobility so much desired was as absent under Augustus as it was under his successors down to Septimius Severus, Alexandrian hostility to Rome must have existed from the beginning of the Principate.[2]

Augustan Sparta provided a clear instance of a dissentient aristocracy, one which caused the Emperor no small embarrassment. C. Julius Eurycles, dynast of Sparta and Augustus' own nominee, abused the Emperor's friendship by using ill-got moneys to stir up internal strife in the cities of the province Achaea.[3] In the free city of Sparta his tyranny was especially resented, and he was brought to trial before Augustus, who was compelled to send his friend into banishment.[4] An anecdote in Plutarch reveals that the opposition to Eurycles came from the old Spartan nobility: one of his accusers was a descendant of Brasidas, who invoked at the trial Thucydides' account of his great ancestor.[5] Eurycles' father had been a pirate.[6] An old and overlooked aristocracy was protesting against the new.

Athens, with a long but broken tradition of democracy, could be expected to preserve a lingering hostility to Roman rule. Augustus had his friends in that city, and he had removed certain of the more obviously oligarchic features in the constitution which the Athenians received from Antony; he had even granted the Athenians the exceptional privilege of

---

[1] Cf. H. A. Musurillo, *The Acts of the Pagan Martyrs* (1954), p. 276. Theon the exegete: ibid., p. 19, line 19 (Acta Isidori).

[2] See p. 90 above, n. 2, citing, among other things, the new Oxyrhynchus fragment concerning an Alexandrian embassy to Augustus precisely in A.D. 13.

[3] Jos. *BJ* 1. 531. Cf. Bowersock, *JRS* 51 (1961), 112 ff.

[4] Ibid. Also *AJ* 16. 310; [Plut.] *Reg. et Imp. Apophtheg.* 207 F.

[5] Plut., ibid. The accuser refers to the seventh book of Thucydides: the scholia to that author reveal that in the thirteen-book edition book seven began at the present 4. 78 and ended at 4. 135. D. M. Lewis kindly pointed this out to me.   [6] Plut. *Ant.* 67.

issuing coins without the Emperor's head.[1] But the people cannot have forgotten or forgiven the repeated Roman tampering with their constitution;[2] the revolution of 88 B.C. and the sack of Sulla had not happened so long ago. In Athens, if anywhere, the bitter class struggle of 88 over the matter of fidelity to Rome might have been renewed under Augustus. Certainly, Augustus did not always find the Athenians compliant. When he went to Greece in the winter of 22/21 B.C., a statue of Athena on the Acropolis turned round and spat blood: if Rome's partisans could engineer miracles in 48 B.C., her enemies might have done the same on the occasion of Augustus' visit.[3] The Emperor was angry and did not wish the fact to escape the Athenians' notice; he refused to spend the winter in Athens and resided on Aegina instead.[4] That island and Eretria were released from paying tribute to Athens, and the city was forbidden to sell its citizenship for money.[5] Plutarch says that Augustus' anger was due to misbehaviour of the Athenian *demos*.[6]

Once it is seen that relations between Augustus and Athens were not always so cordial as some have supposed, it becomes easier to credit reports of a revolt at Athens toward the end of Augustus' life. This revolt deserves attention, although it has not yet had much. The literary evidence is uniformly late and Christian, perhaps all derived from Julius Africanus; but he is not an author to be despised.[7] It is true that the late Christian writers would have been only too glad to preserve reports of

[1] Accame, *Dominio Romano*, pp. 178–9. For the coinage: Shear, *Hesp*. 5 (1936), 287–8.

[2] In 86, 44/43, 39/38, and after Actium: Accame, ibid., pp. 171–9. App. *Mithr*. 39 is still a puzzle: it alludes to laws at Athens laid down by Rome in the period before Sulla; Strabo 398 seems to get in the way, although Appian may be referring to Roman support of the oligarchy of the 90's (cf. above, p. 103, n. 1).

[3] Dio 54. 7. 3. On miracles, see above, p. 9.

[4] [Plut.] *Reg. et Imp. Apophtheg.* 207 E. For the date: Bowersock, *CQ*, N.S. 14 (1964) 120 f. Note that Stamires, *Hesp*. 26 (1959), 260 ff., has redated *IG* ii². 1071, in which Augustus' birthday is associated with Apollo, to 21 B.C. (but reckoning on the old dating of Augustus' travels).

[5] Dio 54. 7. 2.

[6] [Plut.], ibid.

[7] Cf. P. Graindor, *Athènes sous Auguste* (Cairo, 1927), p. 42. On Africanus Kroll in *P–W* 10. 116 ff., esp. 117.

rebellion against Rome, but it would be wrong simply to assume that they fabricated them.

Jerome's Eusebius asserts that the Athenians were guilty of *res novae* and that the leaders of the sedition were put to death; a date of A.D. 9/11 is provided. The Armenian version, giving a date of A.D. 13/14, also mentions revolt and punishment. Jerome is less reliable than the Armenian text; Syncellus, writing in Greek, gives a precise date of A.D. 13 and uses the verb στασιάζειν to describe what happened.[1] Orosius says that the doors of Janus, closed in 2 B.C., were opened again twelve years later because of sedition at Athens and commotion among the Dacians.[2] The reference to the doors of Janus provides a date of A.D. 11, which perhaps derives from Jerome inasmuch as the other testimony converges on the year 13; it is reasonable to assume that the doors were opened because of the Dacian disturbance and that the troubles at Athens were subsequent and not simultaneous. Therefore, the revolt can be dated about A.D. 13, possibly just before or just after that year, certainly before Augustus died. The leaders were executed; the affair is described variously as *res novae*, stasis, and *seditio*. These descriptions are perfectly compatible: when an anti-Roman faction gains the upper hand, stasis becomes revolt.

Repercussions can be conjectured. A mysterious legate in Athens about this time may have been sent there specially by the Emperor to deal with the crisis.[3] Certain coins, apparently deriving from dies on which the name of Augustus was erased

---

[1] Euseb. (Helm), p. 170, 396 l, 16; Karst, p. 212.

[2] Oros. 6. 22. 2, repeated by Paul the Deacon in *Misc. Hist.* 7. 25.

[3] According to Ehrenberg's interpretation of *E–J²* 81a: *Studies pres. to D. M. Robinson* (1953), ii. 942. See Bowersock, *HSCP* 68 (1964), 209. In a paper read to the Oxford branch of the Classical Association on 25 May 1961, I invoked R. Scranton, *Hesp.* 12 (1933), in connexion with the Augustan revolt at Athens: Scranton reported archaeological evidence for destruction and siege at several points in the city, and he deduced partly from lamps in building fill a date in the early first century A.D. But Mr. E. Vanderpool, of the American School of Classical Studies in Athens, has written to me that lamps of the type found by Scranton are now believed to be characteristic of the second century A.D., though they may begin as early as A.D. 50: cf. H. S. Robinson, *The Athenian Agora* (1959), 5. p. 49, nos. H21 and H22. Vanderpool also suggests that the 'destruction' noted by Scranton may be due merely to neglect: rotten wood and metal sockets may have survived when the allegedly burnt gateway was finally removed.

or partially erased, imply a time of revolt.[1] And the incorporation of Achaea and Macedonia into the imperial province of
Moesia may have been provoked in part by the Athenian outbreak. In connexion with this move, Tacitus observed that
people in Achaea and Macedonia had been complaining of
burdens;[2] doubtless some of the complaints were made at
Athens.

The kind of Greek opposition which confronted Augustus
did not cease at his death, and it is salutary to compare the
troubles which broke out under his immediate successors. Cyzicus was again inflamed and again deprived of an almost
meaningless freedom: certain Romans had been thrown into
prison.[3] Meanwhile, in Sparta, the son of Eurycles, C. Julius
Laco, was expelled from the tyranny he held there after the
rehabilitation of his father's memory;[4] it is tempting to think
that the old aristocracy resisted once more, for peace came at
last when the Emperor Claudius presented the Roman citizenship to the family of Brasidas.[5] In Lycia there were riots in
which Romans were murdered, and the same thing happened on Rhodes; the result was annexation to Rome in both
cases.[6]

Together with agitation in the provinces must be set the
Greek literary opposition. In the time of Mithridates Eupator
there were Greeks doing for that king what many were doing
for Rome—writing panegyrics for Greek audiences in their
own language. Two Greeks living at the Pontic court, Metrodorus from Scepsis and Aesopus, wrote encomia of Mithridates;
Heracleides of Magnesia and Teucrus of Cyzicus recorded
his exploits, presumably with a favourable bias.[7]

Although of the Greek men of letters who stood against the

---

[1] The suggestion was made by Mrs. Shear in *Hesp.* 5 (1936), 294.

[2] Tac. *Ann.* 1. 76. Tacitus does not here or anywhere else (e.g. in his account
of Piso's tirade against Athens in 18 A.D.) mention a revolt in Athens, but his
silence is inconclusive.

[3] Tac. *Ann.* 4. 36; Suet. *Tib.* 37; Dio 57. 24. 6. The year was A.D. 25.

[4] Tac. *Ann.* 6. 18. Cf. *JRS* 51 (1961), 117.

[5] *JRS* 21 (1931), 205 on Ti. Claudius Brasidas.

[6] Dio 60. 17. 3 (A.D. 43) on Lycia. Cf. Suet. *Claud.* 25; also R. Syme, *Klio*
30 (1937), 228. On Rhodes: Dio 60. 24. 4 (A.D. 44).

[7] Metrodorus: *FGH* ii. B. 184 (note especially Strabo 609). Aesopus: *FGH*
ii. B. 187a. Heracleides: *FGH* ii. B. 187. Teucrus: *FGH* iii. A. 274.

Augustan principate only one can be named, a passage in Livy suggests that neither he nor his nameless sympathizers should be forgotten. In the ninth book of his history Livy took the trouble to compose a long excursus on Alexander the Great.[1] He had often asked himself how Rome would have fared against that great conqueror, had he turned his energies to the West. This was not a purely academic question which Livy imported from the schools of rhetoric: he was trying to combat the subversive views of certain Greeks who were maintaining that Rome would have yielded to Alexander. These Greeks were disposed to denigrate Rome in favour of the Parthians.[2] They had to be answered, and Livy emphasized that Alexander would have been decisively repulsed. Alexander was a mere youth when he died, and he had flaws of character that would have grown worse; he was no match for the solid and ancient might of Rome.[3]

One of the Greeks whom Livy had in mind was Timagenes of Alexandria, *felicitati urbis inimicus*.[4] This man had been captured by Aulus Gabinius in 55 B.C. and brought to Rome, where he was freed.[5] Being a cultivated Greek, he established himself at Rome as a professor of rhetoric and became a member of that artistic circle of Greeks friendly to Antony; Timagenes introduced his patron to the highly influential Alexas of Laodicea.[6] But in time Timagenes, like so many others,

---

[1] Livy 9. 16. 19–19. 17. This excursus is the starting-point for a book by P. Treves: *Il Mito di Alessandro e la Roma d'Augusto* (1953).

[2] Livy 9. 18. 6: Id vero periculum erat, quod levissimi ex Graecis qui Parthorum quoque contra nomen Romanum gloriae favent dictitare solent, ne maiestatem nominis Alexandri, quem ne fama quidem illis notum arbitror fuisse, sustinere non potuerit populus Romanus. Some scholars (e.g. H. Fuchs, *Der geistige Widerstand* [1938], p. 40) have asserted that *levissimi ex Graecis* refers only to one man, such as Timagenes. But there is no reason why this should not be a genuine plural, alluding to writers like Metrodorus (against these Dionysius of Halicarnassus inveighs, *AR* 1. 4) as well as to Timagenes. Cf. Tacitus' outburst against the still unidentified *Graecorum annales, qui sua tantum mirantur* (Tac. *Ann.* 2. 88): 'If Tacitus is hinting at the *Parallel Lives* of Plutarch, his censure is not well-aimed' (R. Syme, *Proc. Mass. Hist. Soc.* 72 [1963], 14).

[3] Livy 9. 18. 1 ff.

[4] Sen., *Ep.* 91. 13.   [5] Suid. s.v. Τιμαγένης.

[6] Ibid.; Seneca's account of Timagenes' early career, *ex captivo cocus, ex coco lecticarius* (*Controv.* 10. 5. 22), can be rejected as slander. On Antony and Alexas: Plut. *Ant.* 72.

transferred his allegiance to the future Augustus.[1] Then there was a quarrel: Augustus broke with Timagenes and banned him from his house.[2] If the Emperor had hoped that he would recount his exploits for the edification of the Greek-speaking world, his hopes were crushed. It was true that Timagenes had written a history of Augustus' *acta*, but after the breach he consigned this work to the flames.[3] His acid tongue was turned against the Principate; he used to say that fires at Rome grieved him for one reason only: he knew that any new buildings would be superior to those that had been destroyed.[4] Timagenes lived out the remainder of his life in the house of another historian, the sober Asinius Pollio, who will have understood his guest's point of view.[5] One day Timagenes choked and died, but the Greeks did not forget him. An historian of Lindos on Rhodes wrote his biography.[6]

Apart from scant quotations from Timagenes, no Augustan text from the Greek opposition has survived.[7] But it is fair to suspect that apocalyptic prophecies of Rome's fall, couched in Greek hexameters, were circulating in the East no less at the beginning of the Principate than they were in the late Republic and again in the reign of Tiberius.[8] Such literature would have found a warm reception among the discontented segments of the Greek population of the Empire. There was much dissatisfaction with imperial control, and redress was difficult, requiring persistent litigation or open rebellion. It is salutary to observe an inscription from Augustan Mantinea

---

[1] Sen. *Controv.* 10. 5. 22: usque in amicitiam Caesaris enixus. No reason to doubt this, and it fits with the rest of Timagenes' activity: he wrote an account of the deeds of Augustus.

[2] Ibid. also Sen., *de Ira* 3. 23. 4–5.   [3] Ibid. 3. 23. 6.

[4] Sen. *Ep.* 91. 13.

[5] Id. *de Ira* 3. 23. 5; Suid. s.v. Πωλίων (if, as seems likely, the consul of 40 B.C. is there confused with Asinius Pollio of Tralles).

[6] Suid. s.v. Εὐαγόρας Λίνδιος.

[7] The attempt of D. Marin to connect Dionysius of Halicarnassus with the Augustan opposition by making him the author of the treatise *De Sublimitate* does not convince: 'L'Opposizione sotto Augusto e la Datazione del Saggio sul Sublime', *Studi in Onore di Calderini e Paribeni* (1956), i. 157 ff. Nor can the views of H. Hill in 'Dionysius of Halicarnassus and the Origins of Rome' (*JRS* 51 [1961], 88 ff.) be accepted: anti-Augustan traces are alleged in the *Roman Antiquities*. Cf. below, p. 131.

[8] On the dating of the Sibylline Oracles, see H. Fuchs, *Der geistige Widerstand* (1938), pp. 30–36. An oracle under Tiberius is recorded in Dio 57. 18. 5.

which describes an envoy to the Roman senate μὴ κομίζων κατηγορίαν ἀν[θυ]πάτων ἀλλ' ἔπαινον,[1] clearly a welcome change. Though many men looked to Rome for prestige, power, and advancement, history occasionally reveals those who protested, for one reason or another and often in vain, against the Roman domination.

---

[1] *SIG*³ 783, ll. 29–30. On trouble in Augustan Arcadia, cf. A. J. Gossage, *PBSA* 49 (1954), 51 ff.: *SIG*³ 800, formerly dated to A.D. 42, is there assigned convincingly to A.D. 1/2.

IX

THE IMPERIAL CULT

THE East had grown accustomed to the worship of men and women. Hellenistic monarchs and rich benefactors had been accorded cults as tokens of gratitude and of political adhesion. There were many forms and titles of honour, and not all of them carried imputations of divinity: a saviour or a founder was a greater man than a simple benefactor, but he might still lack a cult. The highest honour was worship, disclosing little about the religious life of the Hellenic peoples but much about their ways of diplomacy. A benefactor could be encouraged, by appropriate indications of esteem, to provide further benefactions; similarly a prospective benefactor might be secured. It was hardly an accident that benefactors and proxenoi often coincided in the Greek world, nor should it occasion surprise when Roman benefactors emerge as patrons there. Mutual interest buttressed the system of honours, and therefore underlay the worship of benefactors, magistrates, and kings.[1]

Eastern cults were multiform. Some were purely local, the creations of individual cities; others were imposed by a ruling monarch or resulted from a co-operative effort on the part of cities in a province.[2] Cults of local benefactors flourished alongside those of ruling dynasties; both the living and the dead were worshipped. A man who had received a cult in his own lifetime might be honoured for generations to come, provided that there was no offence to later kings or patrons. Titus Flamininus was worshipped three centuries after his death, but

[1] On all this, see Chapter I above, pp. 12–13.
[2] Cf. Wilcken, *Sitzungsberichte d. preuss. Akad.* (Ph.-Hist. Kl.), 1938, 298 ff.; Habicht, *Gottmenschentum und griechische Städte* (1956); Bikerman, *Institutions des Séleucides* (1938), 236 ff. On the cult imposed by Antiochus III, note Welles, *Royal Correspondence of the Hellenistic Period* (1934), no. 36. For cults established co-operatively by provincial cities in the Republic, cf. above, p. 98, n. 3.

the cult of Sulla at Athens lasted only a few years.[1] The worship of a god might be combined conveniently with honours to a man: disrespect did not accrue to either. It had always been possible to celebrate more than one benefactor at once by merely including him on the list of those being remembered; there was nothing to prevent the joint worship of a benefactor and a god, or—as it turned out—a benefactor and a city.[2] For it was as easy and as politically desirable to establish cults of an influential city as of an influential person. So, at Smyrna in 195 B.C. there arose a temple to the Goddess Roma.[3]

In the early stages, the worship of men may have been a spontaneous expression of gratitude; such, perhaps, was the cult of Demetrius the Besieger at Athens.[4] But the motive of political adhesion, doubtless present from the start, became increasingly conspicuous. Apart from worship established by ruling dynasties, the initiative will have come from the politically alert segments of municipal or provincial society and inevitably from those who could afford to pay the expenses of games and priesthoods. Under the Roman protectorate these segments of society coalesced. As the democratic constitutions of the Greek cities were gradually modified in an oligarchic direction, cults of Romans proliferated.[5] The story of Roman influence in the East forms a coherent unity; Rome's partisans acquired greater and more permanent power and were thereby enabled to manipulate the Greek system of honours in the interest of confirmed or prospective patrons. After Sulla's sack of Athens in 86 B.C., the philo-Roman aristocracy against which the mob had rebelled was reinstated; not surprisingly

---

[1] Plut. *Flam.* 16 (Flamininus). *IG* ii². 1039; *SEG* 13. 279 (Sulla), on which cf. Raubitschek, *Studies in Honour of A. C. Johnson* (1951), 29 ff.

[2] Note οἱ ἀλ[λο]ι ἱερεῖς τῶν εὐεργετῶν in the provisions for a priest of Diodorus Pasparus at Pergamum (*IGR* 4. 292, ll. 38–39); also the games at Lete in Macedonia in honour of M. Annius, to be held ὅταν καὶ τοῖς ἄλλοις εὐεργέταις οἱ ἀγῶνες ἐπιτελῶνται (*SIG*³ 700). Εὐεργέσια are mentioned in *IGR* 4. 291. The cult of Mucius Scaevola was conjoined with Σωτήρια: *OGIS* 439; *IGR* 4. 188. The worship of Servilius Isauricus was linked with that of Roma, and the worship of Paullus Fabius Maximus with that of Apollo: see Appendix I.

[3] Tac. *Ann.* 4. 56. Other cults of Roma are listed in Magie, *RRAM* ii. 1613.

[4] Cf. the remarkable hymn to Demetrius in Athenaeus 6. 253.

[5] On the constitutional alterations, see above, pp. 87–88. An amplified list of cults of Roman magistrates is provided in Appendix I.

a cult of Sulla suddenly appeared there.[1] Later, when honours, both divine and secular, were accorded to Julius Caesar throughout the East in 48 B.C., the efforts of Theopompus, a friend from Cnidus, could be traced.[2] Honours, though common, were not voted without the initiative of someone or some group of citizens; at least one eminent Roman, the orator Cicero, was disappointed in a wish for Greek adulation.[3] And it is instructive to recall that while the younger Flaccus was accused by hostile representatives of the lower classes of Asia, the cities of that province had earlier contributed funds for a cult in honour of his father.[4] The friends of the elder Flaccus were presumably the people whom Cicero invoked at the trial, namely the cultivated eastern nobles who supported Rome with their influence and their money.[5] For cults were costly affairs: it was precisely the Roman partisans who could both obtain the honours and underwrite their expenses.

It is worth noticing M. Tullius Cratippus of Pergamum, whose father must have been the philosopher friend of Cicero and counsellor of the orator's son.[6] The elder Cratippus acquired the Roman citizenship at the hands of Julius Caesar, though he took the name and tribe of Cicero himself.[7] Cratippus was an intimate of other great Romans, notably Pompey, the exile Marcellus, and Brutus.[8] An inscription revealed that his son, bearing the nomen of Cicero, was a high priest of Roma and Salus at Pergamum sometime before 29 B.C.[9]

---

[1] See p. 113, n. 1 above.

[2] Raubitschek, *JRS* 44 (1954), 65 ff. Cf. p. 9 above.

[3] Plut. *Cic.* 24. 7. Cf. p. 12 above.

[4] Cic. *pro Flacc.* 55 (pecunia . . . a civitatibus); cf. 56 (pecunia a tota Asia ad honores L. Flacci). Cf. *Hermes* 32 (1897), 512 ff. and above, p. 98, n. 3. Observe that Cicero says the best men of Asia were not at the trial: Sed sunt in illo numero multi boni, docti, pudentes, qui ad hoc iudicium deducti non sunt, multi impudentes, illiterati, leves, quos variis de causis video concitatos (*pro Flacc.* 9).

[5] Ibid. 52: Ubi erant illi Pythodori, Archidemi, Epigoni, ceteri homines apud nos noti, inter suos nobiles, ubi illa magnifica et gloriosa ostentatio civitatis? Spoken with reference to Tralles.

[6] Cic. *Brutus* 250; *de Off.* 1. 1; *ad Fam.* 12. 16, 16. 2, 21. 3. See O'Brien-Moore, *Yale Classical Studies* 8 (1942), 25 ff.

[7] Plut. *Cic.* 24. Cf. *CIL* 3. 399.

[8] Plut. *Pomp.* 75 (Pompey); Cic. *Brut.* 250 (Marcellus); Plut. *Brut.* 24 (Brutus).   [9] *CIL* 3. 399.

Wealth in the family may be inferred from the sacred office he held, the financial burdens of which were never slight; and his Roman connexions also point to affluence.

The late republican cults were thus integrally tied to the diplomatic relations between Rome and the East. They were another manifestation of the system of reciprocal personal support by which Roman rule and the eastern aristocracies simultaneously acquired stability. Augustus was the heir to this polymorphous system, and he took care to preserve it. There was no need for him to institute a new policy for the East. Actium was a sufficient signal to the friends of Rome to acclaim Octavian as their new benefactor, saviour, and patron.[1] They worshipped him not because they were spiritually insensitive but rather because they wanted to establish those diplomatic ties which had worked so well in the Republic. The first Princeps cannot have failed to perceive all this; where cult was concerned, what happened was undoubtedly what he wished, but there was nothing he had to do to make it happen, except to defeat Antony.

The Emperor was not obliged to set up new provincial organizations for the management of his cult. The foundation of *koina* was the work of the Greek peoples: there were several *koina* already in existence before Augustus, and more appeared naturally in the course of time.[2] They were established for various reasons of convenience and economy. Those in old Greece were purely secular and remained so under Augustus.[3] This did not mean that the corporate energy of a province's cities could not sometimes be applied to provincial

[1] See the lists in L. R. Taylor, *The Divinity of the Roman Emperor* (1931), 270 ff. Cf. also K. Latte, *Römische Religionsgeschichte* (1960), 312 ff., rightly finding the origins of the eastern imperial cult in republican worship of Roman magistrates and Dea Roma.

[2] Kornemann, *P–W*, Suppl. 4. 930–5; cf. above, pp. 91–99. Before Augustus there were *koina* at least in Greece, Asia, Lycia, and Cyprus. On this subject, cf. also Sherwin-White, *The Roman Citizenship* (1939), pp. 236–41. It is instructive to recall the old dogma of Hardy (*Studies in Roman History* [1910], p. 248): 'The system of provincial assemblies was introduced by Augustus and was applied by him both in the eastern and western parts of the empire.' This is not even true of the West, where the Three Gauls would appear to be the only case in point; the *concilia* in Narbonensis, Baetica, and Africa are now all known to be Vespasianic.

[3] See above, p. 91, n. 3.

cults; that had occurred under the Republic. The worship of
the upright Q. Mucius Scaevola and of the elder Flaccus in
Asia was evidently a provincial rather than a local matter,
presumably the concern of the *koinon* which is explicitly attested for Asia under Antony.[1] By the time of Claudius even
the *koina* in Greece celebrated the Emperor's divinity.[2] But the
koina were not established for reasons of cult, nor can Augustus
be held responsible for establishing them. The Greeks discovered for themselves that those organizations could be conveniently adapted to cult observances. In 29 B.C., when the
natives of Asia and Bithynia, whom Octavian liked to call
Hellenes, asked permission to dedicate sacred precincts to
him at Nicomedia and Pergamum, he had only to consent.[3]

He must have consented gladly, although Greek zeal had to
be tempered, since formal recognition of excessive eastern
adulation could be suspect among Romans. The Emperor
stipulated that his cult must be shared with that of the Goddess Roma;[4] a joint cult seemed more modest and provided
no difficulty to the Hellenes. Roma was an old goddess in the
East by then and had shared her worship before.[5] About
municipal cults, however, the Emperor was not so particular,
and cults of himself alone flourished unsuppressed in certain
eastern cities.[6]

Resident Romans in the civilized portions of Asia Minor
could not be expected to collaborate with the Hellenes in
a cult of the Princeps and his city, and in the beginning they
did not. This emerges plausibly from an order to the resident
Romans of Ephesus and Nicaea to honour Roma and the
divine Julius in special precincts granted for this purpose.[7]

[1] Cf. below, p. 150. The *koinon* under Antony is mentioned in *E–J*² 300.

[2] *Corinth* viii. 2. no. 68; *IG* ii². 3538.

[3] Dio 51. 20. 7. Dio's verb is ἐπέτρεψε; cf. προσέταξε in respect to the arrangements for Romans in the same passage.

[4] Suet. *Aug.* 52. Cf. Tac. *Ann.* 4. 37: Cum divus Augustus sibi atque urbi
Romae templum apud Pergamum sisti non prohibuisset. . . . On the Augustan
formula for polite refusal, see Charlesworth, *PBSR* 15 (1939), 1 ff.

[5] See the list in Magie, *RRAM* ii. 1613. She had shared her worship with
Servilius Isauricus (Appendix I below). Cf. Cic. *ad Quint. Frat.* 1. 1. 26.

[6] Magie, *RRAM* ii. 1294, n. 52, and the list on 1614.

[7] Dio 51. 20. 6. These Romans were principally businessmen (certainly
not natives in possession of the citizenship): note Dio's words, τοῖς Ῥωμαίοις
τοῖς παρ' αὐτοῖς ἐποικοῦσι. Ephesus and Nicaea were the headquarters of the

But by 3 B.C. when Paphlagonia was incorporated in the Roman *provincia*, the resident Romans in that outpost of empire were required to swear an oath at the altar of Augustus.[1] The Emperor had no illusions about romanizing the East; and if Romans could worship his father, those who lived among Greeks might as well join their neighbours in worshipping him. Like the cults of the late Republic, the imperial cult reflected the influence of the philo-Roman aristocracies of the East. The wealthy friends of Rome once again exhibited their allegiance; their funds paid for the elaborate games in honour of the Emperor, and their names adorned the lists of high priests. Their service in the cult conferred added prestige; the *koina* provided opportunities for them to become provincial, as well as merely local, magnates. Such evidence as there is available would suggest that the high priests of the Asian *koinon* should be identified with the prominent men called Asiarchs.[2] The identification is valuable because Strabo observed of the Asiarchs at Tralles that they were the leading men of the province and very rich.[3] St. Paul met some in Ephesus.[4] Naturally enough, the kind of men on whom Rome relied in eastern diplomacy happened also to be the men who presided over the imperial cult. Rome's eastern partisans were easily recognizable—wealthy, cultivated, often endowed with Roman citizenship; many were rhetors. The high priests were precisely men of this description.

The surviving names of high priests from the time of Augustus are telling: M. Antonius Lepidus, C. Julius Lepidus, C. Julius Xenon, C. Julius M[- - -].[5] The Roman citizenship was

publicans; cf. Hatzfeld, *Trafiquants italiens* (1919), pp. 101–3 and 160 (Ephesus), 134 and 172 (Nicaea).

[1] *ILS* 8781 = *E-J²* 315 (Gangra). Again Roman businessmen: οἱ πραγματευόμενοι παρ' αὐτοῖς Ῥωμαῖοι.

[2] Larsen, *Representative Government in Greek and Roman History* (1955), pp. 118–19 and 222, n. 33, arguing cogently against Magie, *RRAM* ii. 1298–1301. Dig. 27. 1. 6. 14 is nearly decisive: ἔθνους ἱεραρχία, οἷον Ἀσιαρχία, Βιθυναρχία, Καππαδοκαρχία, παρέχει ἀλειτουργησίαν ἀπὸ ἐπιτροπῶν, τοῦτ' ἔστιν ἕως ἂν ἄρχῃ. Most recently on Asiarchs, Sherwin-White, *Roman Society and Roman Law in the New Testament* (1963), pp. 89–90.

[3] Strabo 649.   [4] Acts xix. 31.

[5] *Sardis* vii. 8. no. 10 (Antonius Lepidus); *E-J²* 353 (Julius Lepidus); Keil-von Premerstein, *Denkschr. Wien* 54, ii (1911), 41 f. (Xenon); *E-J²* 98a (Julius M[- - -]).

received from Caesar, Antony, or Augustus. And if one surveys the list of priests who served under later emperors, much more can be seen: repeated instances of rhetors and persons of affluence. There is the sophist Scopelian, for example, and representatives of three generations of the great houses of Ti. Claudius Polemo and Antonius Apollodorus.[1] It is men like these whose families ultimately produce knights and senators.[2] The cult, with its roots deep in the Republic, was another means by which the favourites of Rome could rise to prestige and power, and eventually penetrate the senate of the capital city.

While allowing a natural and desirable evolution in the growth of the cult in the East, the Emperor had nevertheless to be vigilant because of a peculiar fact: the emergence of the imperial cult had meant the reappearance of a dynastic cult. Worship of a dynasty was in no way foreign to the Hellenistic East and had coexisted with municipal and provincial worship of individual benefactors. But the cult of Augustus, which had its origins in non-dynastic cults of Roman magistrates and worship of the Goddess Roma, was now being transformed into worship of the house of Augustus, in short into a cult of a dynasty. Inevitably, highly placed members of Augustus' family travelling in the East received the usual honours, some divine;[3] even the young Tiberius had acquired a cult before his retirement to Rhodes.[4] That was to be expected

---

[1] The evidence is admirably assembled by A. Stein, 'Zur sozialen Stellung der provinzialen Oberpriester', in *Epitymbion H. Swoboda dargebracht* (1927), pp. 303–4.

[2] Ibid., pp. 305–11. Cf. Q. Licinius Silvanus Granianus of Tarraco (*ILS* 2714), priest of Rome and Augustus and procurator Augusti in Hither Spain. His son was consul in A.D. 106.

[3] See the list of honours to, e.g., Agrippa, Julia, Gaius, and Lucius in Taylor, *The Divinity of the Roman Emperor* (1931), 270 ff. Note the societies in honour of Agrippa in Sparta, the Agrippiastae (*IG* v. 1. 374), and in a city of Asia (? Smyrna), οἱ φιλαγρίππαι συμβιωταί (*SEG* 18. 518). In *Hist.* 7 (1958), 474–6, Oliver has suggested plausibly that Agrippa encouraged the Argive *gerousia* (*E–J*² 308) and probably also the one at Ephesus to make them useful for the imperial cult and strengthening of loyalty.

One would like to know more about Livia's dedication of a golden epsilon at Delphi: Plut., *De E Delphico* 385 F.

[4] *SIG*³ 781, ll. 7–8: a priest at Nysa in 1 B.C. The cult must have been established when Tiberius was more in favour, unless the people of Nysa were singularly ill informed about court affairs. Such a *faux pas* is not impossible:

inasmuch as these people were avenues to the great patron himself, the Princeps. But a dynastic cult developing from a tradition of magistrate worship was in serious danger of being obscured by new cults of magistrates from outside the imperial house. And here Augustus had to intercede, lest the worship of the dynasty be stifled at the start.

In A.D. 11 Augustus forbade honours to governors in the provinces both during their term of office and for a sixty-day period afterward; corruption was alleged as a result of negotiating testimonials and eulogies.[1] That was a good reason for Augustus' measure, but it cannot have been the only one. Competition with the imperial house in the receipt of honours had to be controlled. The East was in the habit of voting cults to governors and went on doing so for a time even under Augustus.[2] Cults are attested for M. Vinicius (consul 19 B.C.), Paullus Fabius Maximus (consul 11 B.C.), and C. Marcius Censorinus (consul 8 B.C.), but after Censorinus no cult of a Roman governor in his own province is attested.[3] And curbs were imposed also on the more extravagant secular honours which the Hellenic world had been inclined to bestow upon eminent Romans. The words 'saviour' and 'founder' disappear under Augustus from honorific inscriptions of magistrates sent out from Rome, and they rarely reappear.[4] The title 'benefactor' was allowed; it was sufficiently modest and often literally accurate, but with very few exceptions the only Romans for whom the other epithets were deemed suitable were the Emperor and his family.

The suppression of extravagant honours did not, however, apply to easterners themselves, and this strongly suggests that the suppression was calculated policy where Romans were

cf. *AE* 1959, 24, an inscription from Amisus in honour of Nero, Poppaea, and Britannicus! Poppaea is called Augusta, a title which she received in A.D. 63 (Tac. *Ann.* 15. 23).

[1] Dio 56. 25. 6.

[2] Cf. Tac. *Ann.* 3. 55: Nam etiam tum plebem socios regna colere et coli licitum.

[3] See Appendix I. The author of the new *P–W* article on the consul of 19 (2te Reihe, ix. A. 116) assigns the Vinicius cult to the consul of A.D. 30. This is most unlikely: Robert's attribution should stand (*Rev. Arch.* [1935], ii. 156–8).

[4] The last instances appear to be Sex. Appuleius (*ILS* 8783), Q. Lepidus (*AE* 1950, 250), and C. Censorinus (*SEG* 2. 549).

concerned. At Gytheum the Spartan, C. Julius Eurycles, received a cult in the latter part of the Augustan Principate, and at Thyatira the high priest, C. Julius Xenon, had a cult of his own.[1] By contrast, the city of Cyme under Augustus voted certain honours, including the titles εὐεργέτης and κτίστης, to a private Roman benefactor, L. Vaccius Labeo, who rejected κτίστης as excessive while allowing himself to be called εὐεργέτης.[2]

Particularly interesting are the honours accorded to Greeks in the Roman civil service; these were the local citizens of whom a city was most proud. Early in the Principate, but after Augustus, a cult was established in honour of a prefect of Egypt who had risen to his high office from a priesthood and procuratorship of Asia: the man was Cn. Vergilius Capito, a resident of Miletus.[3] Yet even the worship of an eastern Roman threatened the imperial cult, for his is the last attested cult of a Roman official of any kind other than an Emperor.

But in *dedications* to important easterners the more honorific epithets were allowed to persist. Aspurgus, King of the Bosporus under Augustus and Tiberius, was a saviour and benefactor.[4] Somewhat later those great eastern senators Celsus Polemaeanus and Julius Quadratus were hailed as saviours in their native provinces;[5] if these men did not receive a cult, they still had more than virtually any genuine Roman outside the dynasty.[6]

---

[1] *AE* 1929, 99, ll. 19–20 (Eurycles). For Xenon, see p. 117, n. 5 above.

[2] *IGR* 4. 1302. Cf. Germanicus' rejection of ἐπίφθονοι καὶ ἰσόθεοι ἐκφωνήσεις in *E-J²* 320 (*b*). For the probable derivation of these limited refusals from replies of Augustus himself, cf. Charlesworth, op. cit., pp. 3–6.

[3] *Didyma* ii. 192, no. 278. Cf. L. Robert, *Hellenica* 7 (1949), 206–9.

[4] *IGR* 1. 879.

[5] *Sardis* vii. 1, no. 45 (Celsus). *IGR* 3. 520 and 4. 383 (Quadratus). These and later examples of Roman imperial magistrates as σωτῆρες are collected in Nock, *The Joy of Study: Papers pres. to Grant* (New York, 1951), pp. 142–3. Nock missed L. Calpurnius Proculus (*IGR* 3. 180; Ancyra), probably from Pisidian Antioch (*JRS* 2 [1912], 99): note that a descendant of L. Servenius Cornutus (from Acmonia in Phrygia, *ILS* 8817) is married to a second-century senator called P. Calpurnius Proculus (*PIR²*, C 305).

[6] Exceptions to the rule of restricted honours are very rare: two from Lycia for governors there: Baebius Italicus, κτίστης under Domitian (*ILS* 8818), and Mettius Modestus, σωτήρ under Trajan (*IGR* 3. 523), neither of whom can have been easterners. Two other examples occur much later in the second century:

Provision was thus made to prevent the imperial cult from being choked by a plethora of separate honours. This very caution emphasized the fact that the cult was fundamentally an extension of a diplomatic system which had developed under the Republic. The dynastic element was new in relations between Rome and the East, but, of course, by no means foreign to the Greeks. The imperial cult belongs to that natural evolution which Augustus encouraged in Graeco-Roman affairs. Initiative from Rome was not required, only modification and adjustment.

MAMA 6. 103 (wrongly dated there) from Heracleia Pontica and *ILS* 8830 from Ephesus. Marriages into eastern families may underlie these apparent anomalies. T. Licinius Mucianus, σωτήρ in Galatia *c.* A.D. 177 (*SEG* 6. 14; cf. Magie, *RRAM* ii. 1597), came undoubtedly from Lycia and derived his name from Vespasian's agent, who was once governor of the province Lycia-Pamphylia (*ILS* 8816 with *AE* 1915, 48).

X

GREEK LITERATURE UNDER AUGUSTUS

WHEN the struggle between Octavian and Antony was decided at Actium, no one knew that a monarchy would come into being and put down roots lasting for more than a thousand years. The fall of Alexandria and an end of strife, at least for the moment, closed that gap between East and West which had been opened by the triumviral partition of the empire. Octavian made it easy for the partisans of Antony to transfer their allegiance without undue embarrassment or discomfort, and the republican system of personal ties among Greeks and Romans reasserted itself. In previous decades literate men of the East had used their talents as politicians both in their own cities and as envoys to the great men of Rome; further, they recorded in Greek the exploits of their Roman patrons, devoting themselves to full-scale histories of the Roman protectorate or chronicling the deeds of particular men. Polybius had set the example, and Poseidonius followed it with a continuation of Polybius in fifty-two books. Monographs on great Romans were popular: Pompey was especially fortunate in having both Poseidonius and the Mytilenaean Theophanes to write his career. Poseidonius refused to do as much for Cicero.[1] Some authors required a large perspective: the Sicilian Diodorus, with moderate intelligence and immense industry, related the whole history of the inhabited world down to his own day.[2] Certain of these cultivated Greeks

---

[1] *FGH* ii. B. 188 (Theophanes); Strabo 492 (Poseidonius). Cic. *ad Att.* 2. 1. 2 (Poseidonius' refusal).

[2] The terminal date of Diodorus' history belongs after Caesar's British expeditions, which were certainly included: see 3. 38. 2–3 and 5. 21. 2 and 22. 2. But the expeditions do not themselves provide the terminus, as Schwarz thought (*P–W* 5. 665). Diod. 1. 5. 1 announces a terminal date of 46/45 B.C., and there is no reason to reject this; Diodorus might well have wished to avoid the awkward and fateful year 44. The latest allusion in the surviving parts of

were active politicians and pedagogues in the East; such was Poseidonius, professor, Rhodian prytanis, and ambassador. Others travelled in the suites of the imperatores, as Polybius with Scipio Aemilianus, Antiochus with Lucullus, and Theophanes with Pompey. Still others settled at Rome in the households of generals or as lecturers on rhetoric.

This intercourse between Greeks and Romans not only affected the course of Greek literature and rhetoric; it unified East and West. Gradually and imperceptibly a Graeco-Roman world was emerging. The elder Cato would have been surprised. The war between Antony and Octavian had threatened to destroy this new world, but the victory at Actium allowed it to survive and to flourish. The way was open for philhellenes like Nero and Hadrian, and for Greeks, like Aelius Aristides, who styled themselves Romans.[1] It was not an accident that in 30 B.C. Dionysius of Halicarnassus came to Rome to teach and to write, and that in the following year Strabo also made his way there to assemble his universal history in forty-seven books.[2] The historian and ethnographer Timagenes must already have been there, and within a few years two Mytilenaean littérateurs, Potamo and Crinagoras, were to come to Rome (not for the first time) on an embassy to the Emperor.[3] When Octavian had himself arrived from the East, the learned Athenodorus and Areius were probably to be found in his entourage; his Greek doctor, Artorius Asclepiades, was coming independently but perished in a shipwreck.[4] The flow of Greeks to Rome after Antony's defeat illustrates an important fact: Actium saved Graeco-Roman culture. It brought

---

his work is to Octavian's colony at Tauromenium, best assigned to 36 B.C. (not 21): Vittinghoff, *Römische Kolonisation und Bürgerrechtspolitik* (1952), p. 120, citing O. Cuntz, *Klio* 6 (1906), 467. Diodorus cannot be considered an Augustan author.

[1] On Aristides and his successors, cf. J. Palm, *Rom, Römertum und Imperium in der griechischen Literatur der Kaiserzeit* (Lund, 1959).

[2] Arrival dates are deduced from Dion. Hal. *Ant. Rom.* 1. 7 and Strabo 485. Strabo's history: *FGH* ii. A. 91.

[3] *IGR* 4. 33; 38 (cf. *Anth. Pal.* ix. 559). The envoys sought out Augustus in Spain in 26, and in the following year the senate at Rome issued a decree concerning Mytilene. Crinagoras stayed in Rome.

[4] On Athenodorus and Areius, see above, Chapter III. For Artorius Asclepiades, *PIR²*, A 1183.

an end to that anti-eastern propaganda which the war with Antony had forced upon Octavian.

The greater Greek writers of the Augustan age were Timagenes, Dionysius, Strabo, and Nicolaus of Damascus. There were lesser men like Dionysius' friend at Rome, the rhetor Caecilius,[1] and the poet Parthenius, who also collected erotic tales in Greek for versification in Latin by his friend (and Virgil's), Cornelius Gallus, first prefect of Egypt.[2] And there were other Greek poets, above all the court versifier, Crinagoras, as well as Strabo's friend, the younger Diodorus of Sardis, and Antipater of Thessalonica, the intimate of Piso the Pontifex. Then there was the Roman senator Tuticanus Gallus, who was known to Ovid and whose Greek erotic verses found their way into the Palatine Anthology.[3]

It would be surprising if these men failed to encounter one another at Rome, yet allusions to one another in their works are not common. Parthenius wrote a book entitled *Crinagoras*, but nothing is known of it.[4] Strabo is more communicative than most: he used Timagenes as a source and acknowledges the existence of Dionysius, Nicolaus, and Crinagoras.[5] However, he gives no hint that he knew any of these men personally; and they do not even mention him. But it would perhaps have been superfluous for them to write about one another in works of history or in court poetry. The conviction persists that they will, at least, have met at Rome, since all of them worked there for extended periods with the sole exception of Nicolaus. And even he was in the city on at least three separate occasions.

[1] Dion. Hal. *ad Pomp. Gem.* 3. This man has rightly been identified with Caecilius of Caleacte, as recently by G. P. Goold in *TAPA* 92 (1961), 169. Q. Caecilius Epirota (Suet. *de Gramm.* 16) might also be mentioned: he was a friend of Cornelius Gallus, through whom he could have encountered Parthenius (cf. below, n. 2) and Crinagoras (below, n. 4), also, therefore, Dionysius (see the argument in the text for Dionysius' circle). Another rhetor in Rome about this time and worth noting was the anti-Ciceronian L. Cestius Pius (from Smyrna), who taught in Latin (*PIR*², C 694).

[2] Cf. Parthenius, *Erot.*, *praef.*; also Virg. *Ecl.* 10. On the hitherto neglected importance of Parthenius in the literary history of the late Republic, see now W. V. Clausen, *Greek, Roman and Byzantine Studies* 5 (1964).

[3] *Anth. Pal.* v. 49. The authorship was unravelled by Cichorius, *RS*, pp. 323–5. Cf. Ovid, *Pont.* iv. 12 and 14.   [4] *Etym. Mag.* s.v. ἄρπυς.

[5] Strabo 656 (Dionysius), 719 (Nicolaus), 617 (Crinagoras).

An examination of the lives and works of certain of these Greek authors can uncover a common milieu in which all of them moved. Now, as under the Republic, literate Greeks associated themselves with the Roman aristocracy; Dionysius settled in Rome, Strabo travelled with his patron, and Nicolaus' diplomatic successes were the result of the trust which Augustus placed in him. It was an old and familiar pattern. But it was due precisely to Actium that several Greek writers happened to be in Rome in the early twenties. And others followed later: Nicolaus on his embassies and Antipater of Thessalonica in the company of Piso the Pontifex.

When Alexandria fell, Timagenes was already in Rome. He had been captured by Gabinius and taken there, where he received his freedom and established a school of rhetoric.[1] He became a friend of Antony and introduced him to certain influential easterners of his acquaintance.[2] But as Actium drew near, Timagenes managed to transfer his allegiance to Octavian, and he remained at Rome until that disastrous quarrel with the Emperor which led to a retirement in the house of Asinius Pollio.[3] Timagenes had a sharp tongue and refused to restrain it; he was also a prolific writer. His interest in geography and ethnology left their traces in his history, a work of unknown length, perhaps arranged according to the reigns of certain eastern monarchs and spanning a period from the wars of Alexander's successors at least down to Pompey the Great.[4] The work was outspoken in its criticism of Rome.[5] It is in doubt whether Timagenes carried his history down to 30 B.C. or even further. He had certainly written an account of the deeds of the Princeps; for it was this that he burned after his breach with him, but as it was patently a panegyric deriving from the days of their friendship (and thus was burned), it was probably a work distinct from and earlier than the history.[6]

---

[1] Suid. s.v. Τιμαγένης. Cf. above, pp. 109–10.
[2] Plut. *Ant.* 72 (an introduction to Alexas of Laodicea). Cf. Jos. *AJ* 15. 197; *BJ* 1. 393.   [3] Sen. *de Ira* 3. 23.   [4] *FGH* ii. A. 88. F. 1–12.
[5] Ibid., F. 9 (Plut. *Pomp.* 49, alleging that Theophanes persuaded Ptolemy Auletes to leave Egypt in order to provide Pompey with a pretext for a new command). Strabo (*apud* Jos. *AJ* 15. 9) on Antony's execution of Antigonus the Jew may also derive from Timagenes.
[6] Sen. *Controv.* 10. 5. 22; Sen. *de Ira* 3. 23.

Much of his history must have been available by 29 B.C., when Strabo came to Rome and used the work of Timagenes in preparing his outline of universal history. Strabo's history in forty-seven books, of which all but four were devoted to the period after Polybius,[1] was probably not begun before he reached Rome; the Triumvirate was not an auspicious age in which to inaugurate such a history. Yet the forty-seven books were written hastily and finished by the mid-twenties.[2] Hence, Timagenes' history was largely ready when Strabo arrived.

It could be asked why Timagenes wrote history at all, but a better question would be why he should not. Cultivated Greeks, especially professors, regularly did that sort of thing. Besides, Timagenes had two novelties to offer: though a friend of great Romans, he refused to write a panegyric of Rome, and—more remarkably—he chronicled his material by the reigns of kings. The kings of Egypt might have provided a structure for his account; after all, he came from Alexandria, and extant fragments of the work conveniently arrange themselves into a period embracing the foundation and collapse of the kingdom of the Ptolemies. His view of Roman intervention in Egypt in the age of Pompey was not at all sympathetic.[3]

Strabo, already perhaps contemplating his *Geography*, may have seen Timagenes at Rome in the forties. Strabo must have been there then, for he observes that he saw that living monument, Servilius Isauricus, before his death at an advanced age in 44 B.C. and heard the grammarian Tyrannio, who had been in Rome for two decades; Strabo himself cannot have been over twenty years old when he was there.[4] Timagenes will have been lecturing, and writing his *History*. When Strabo returned to the city from the East in 29, it was natural for him

---

[1] Strabo 515. For Timagenes as Strabo's source: *FGH* ii. A. 91. F. 10, 11, 12, and (?) 18.

[2] *P–W* 2te Reihe, 4. 90 (Honigmann, opting for completion by 25 B.C.). The work was called ὑπομνήματα: this was Cicero's word for the outline he sent to Poseidonius for more elaborate treatment (*ad Att.* 2. 1. 2).

[3] See Plut. *Pomp.* 49, mentioned above, p. 125, n. 5.

[4] Strabo 568 (Isauricus, on whose death see Dio 45. 16. 1). Strabo 548 (Tyrannio, captured by Lucullus and brought to Rome [Suid. s.v.] and alive in 46 [Cic. *ad Att.* 12. 2. 2.]). Strabo was born about 64: *P–W* 2te Reihe, 4. 76–77.

to turn to a history. It could be brought triumphantly down to Octavian's capture of Alexandria, a good moment for beginning to write and a good subject with which to terminate.[1] Timagenes' work was to hand for ready reference; and in retelling the events which Poseidonius had related in his continuation of Polybius, Strabo introduced something new. His grandparents had been partisans of the Pontic king.

Strabo came from Amaseia in Pontus, where his ancestors were clearly wealthy and influential. A great-great-grandfather was a distinguished general in the service of Mithridates Euergetes, and the general's nephew was priest of Comana.[2] His grandfather had served under Eupator in the war against Rome; but when Lucullus was in the East and the king ordered two of Strabo's cousins to be executed, his grandparent rebelled and secured fifteen forts for Lucullus.[3] However, a partisan of Lucullus fared badly under Pompey, for promises given were never fulfilled. Strabo, who had been born about 64, went with his family to Nysa, where he studied under the rhetorician Aristodemus.[4] He must then have proceeded to Rome. How long he stayed there is unknown, perhaps into the middle thirties: he saw in Rome a Sicilian pirate torn apart by the beasts, and that could have happened only after the close of the Sicilian War.[5] Strabo claimed to have travelled widely, from the Euxine to Ethiopia, from Armenia to Etruria;[6] his journeys cannot all be dated, and they were not perhaps so very extensive. One obvious place, Athens, he appears never to have visited. Parts of the East he will have seen in his childhood, and Egypt he explored later with a prefect.[7] So much is certain. Possibly he travelled during the Triumvirate,

---

[1] R. Syme, in *HSCP* 64 (1959), 65, assumes that Strabo's history ended with the fall of Alexandria, not 27 B.C.

[2] Strabo 477 and 557 (Dorylaus the general), and again 557 on Dorylaus the priest.   [3] Strabo 557–8.

[4] On Strabo's birth date, see p. 126, n. 5 above. For Aristodemus of Nysa: Strabo 650; also L. Robert, *Hellenica* 1 (1940), 148 (on Aristodemus' doctrine that Homer was a Roman).

[5] Strabo 273.

[6] Ibid. 117, but he confesses considerable and necessary reliance on the reports of others.

[7] e.g. ibid. 816. L. Waddy, *AJA* 67 (1963) 29 ff., thinks Strabo did visit Athens, but evidence is still lacking.

inasmuch as he was making his way westward across the Aegean in 29.[1]

With so distinguished a background and a career not wanting in interesting vicissitudes, Strabo composed his *History*; he then devoted himself entirely to the *Geography*, a work not unlike the *History* in purpose, and designed to complement it.[2] Both were written to be useful to men of affairs in high office; his philosophical works—history and geography ranked as such—were essentially political, and he took care to stress that by πολιτικός he did not mean any uneducated member of a πόλις but precisely the cultured and superior men who managed the affairs of state.[3] These were the Roman aristocrats. Thus the writings of Strabo take their place in that honoured tradition of Greek compositions for the education and laudation of Roman patrons. Strabo's Roman patron cannot be missed, nor should he be underestimated: he was Aelius Gallus, second prefect of Egypt, who took Strabo with him on service there, even on his abortive campaign into Arabia Felix. It is fair to infer a close relationship with Strabo from their travels together in Egypt;[4] the pattern of Greek adviser and Roman imperator was familiar.

Now Aelius Gallus was, in all probability, the man who adopted Sejanus.[5] The natural father of Sejanus became a prefect of Egypt early under Tiberius, and his name was Seius Strabo.[6] The suspicion arises, therefore, that the geographer may have acquired his name from the father of Sejanus.[7] The

---

[1] Strabo 485.

[2] Ibid. 13 : Διόπερ ἡμεῖς πεποιηκότες ὑπομνήματα ἱστορικὰ χρήσιμα, ὡς ὑπολαμβάνομεν, εἰς ἠθικὴν καὶ πολιτικὴν φιλοσοφίαν, ἔγνωμεν προσθεῖναι καὶ τήνδε τὴν σύνταξιν· ὁμοειδὴς γὰρ καὶ αὕτη, καὶ πρὸς τοὺς αὐτοὺς ἄνδρας, καὶ μάλιστα τοὺς ἐν ταῖς ὑπεροχαῖς.

[3] See the passage quoted in the preceding note. Also (ibid.) : κἀκεῖ δὲ πολιτικὸν λέγομεν οὐχὶ τὸν παντάπασιν ἀπαίδευτον . . . .

[4] Aelius Gallus: *PIR*², A 179.

[5] So Borghesi conjectured from the Aelius Gallus who is a partisan of Sejanus in Tac. *Ann.* 5. 8 : *recte fortasse*, *PIR*², A 255, though the *Fasti Ost.* for A.D. 31 show that this Gallus cannot have been a son of Sejanus. The reconstruction of F. Adams in *AJP* 76 (1955), 70 ff., accepted by R. Sealey in *Phoenix* 15 (1961), 102–3, will not do: it makes Sejanus' consular brothers simultaneously his uncles—not impossible but unlikely. Borghesi still seems right about L. Aelius Sejanus.   [6] *PIR*, S 246.

[7] An alternative explanation of Strabo's name (*P–W* 2te Reihe, 4. 79–80) is suggested by the fact that he saw the old Servilius Isauricus (Strabo 568) ; and

cognomen Strabo had appeared occasionally in the Republic, but it was not normally inherited in a family. The situation was different with the house of Seius Strabo, whose grandson also bore the cognomen.[1] It is not excessive to suppose that the geographer received the citizenship from his patron, Aelius Gallus, but took his cognomen from the family of his patron's adopted son. Thus his name will have been Aelius Strabo. The taking of names from two families has such triumviral parallels as Antonius Lepidus and Julius Lepidus, each recalling by nomen and cognomen two of the three triumvirs; and, furthermore, the borrowed cognomen of Aelius Strabo should be compared with the name of a close kinsman of Sejanus, presumably his brother: L. Seius Tubero, consul in A.D. 18.[2]

Tubero was the cognomen of a great patrician branch of the Aelii,[3] which is well represented in the reign of Augustus. The historian and jurisconsult, Q. Aelius Tubero, had two sons, one consul in 11 B.C. and the other in A.D. 4.[4] It seems hardly accidental that in this period the protégé of an Aelius bears the cognomen of a Seius and that a Seius bears the cognomen of an Aelius—this in addition to the clear evidence of an adoption in the name L. Aelius Sejanus. The relation between the Aelii Tuberones and Aelius Gallus is beyond detection, but the two branches were connected somehow. The geographer moved in a circle that included a Roman historian, future consuls, and Sejanus; moreover, Sejanus was a great-nephew of Maecenas.[5]

there is evidence for a Servilius Strabo in the vicinity of Nysa in 51 B.C. (Cic. *ad Fam.* 13. 64. 1; cf. Jos. *AJ* 14. 239). But Strabo's remark that he saw Isauricus carries little weight: after all, a man of Strabo's age might easily have missed seeing a great man of the previous generation, and therefore it was worth recording that he had, in fact, seen him.

[1] One can recall from the late Republic C. Julius Caesar Strabo, Cn. Pompeius Strabo, and P. Servilius Strabo (cf. preceding note). But Sejanus had a son named Strabo: *Fasti Ost.* for A.D. 31. Badian, *Hist.* 12 (1963), 142, n. 18, is therefore not quite accurate when he asserts that the cognomen Strabo did not pass to descendants.

[2] For Antonius Lepidus and Julius Lepidus, see above, p. 117, n. 5. On Sejanus' consular brothers: Vell. 2. 127. 3. Against identifying Seius Tubero with one of them: F. Adams, *AJP* 76 (1955), 70 ff. (unconvincing: cf. above, p. 128, n. 5).   [3] On the Aelii: Val. Max. 4. 4. 8.

[4] On the identification of historian, jurisconsult, and father of two consuls: *P–W* 1. 537–8 and *PIR²*, A 274. Fragments of Tubero's histories appear in H. Peter, *Historicorum Romanorum Reliquiae* (1870), i. 311–15.

[5] *ILS* 8996 (Volsinii). Cf. R. Syme, *The Roman Revolution* (1939), p. 358.

Dionysius of Halicarnassus should be added to this select company. He was under the patronage of no less a person than Q. Tubero the historian, who was the recipient of a treatise on Thucydides;[1] appropriately enough, for it would appear that he tried to introduce Thucydidean overtones into his own history.[2] There were eastern connexions in his family, notably a father who was legate in Asia under Q. Cicero and an ancestor farther back to whom the philosopher Panaetius had dedicated several essays.[3] Dionysius was as clear as Strabo about his position among the aristocrats of Rome: in the preface to his *Roman Antiquities* he stated explicitly that he wrote for the benefit of those who were descendants of Rome's greatest families. He wished to provide noble Romans of the present with instructive examples of ancient Roman virtue in the past.[4] And furthermore Dionysius credited the Roman nobility of his own day with the recent revival of Attic style in

---

[1] Dion. Hal. *de Thucyd.* 1 and 55; *ad Amm.* ii. 1. Cf. *Ant. Rom.* 1. 80 on Tubero: δεινὸς ἀνὴρ καὶ περὶ τὴν συναγωγὴν τῆς ἱστορίας ἐπιμελής. A descendant of Dionysius of Halicarnassus bore the name Aelius Dionysius (*PIR²*, A 169); as he was a grammarian active under Hadrian, it is possible that he received his gentilicium from that emperor. But it is no less possible that he inherited it from the Augustan historian.

[2] Dion. Hal. *de Thucyd.* 25, addressed to Tubero: 'I wish to describe the style of Thucydides in all its aspects that need discussion, for the special benefit of would-be imitators of that writer.' Cf. ibid. 55: 'I could have written more to your liking but not more truthfully.' Dionysius was not an admirer of Thucydides' style. *PIR²*, D 102, claiming the historian's son as the addressee of Dionysius, must be rejected; *PIR²*, A 274 gets the matter right, as did W. R. Roberts in *CR* 14 (1900), 441 (although he thought that the historian was identical with the consul of 11 [*sic*]). There are a number of Thucydidean reminiscences in Livy (e.g. i. 49. 2, 58. 5, 59. 9; iii. 20. 5, 27. 6, 71. 1, 71. 3; iv. 57. 4, &c.): Livy was himself not fond of Thucydides' style (Sen. *Controv.* 9. 1. 14), but Q. Tubero was one of his sources (cf. Livy 4. 23. 1).

[3] The legate was L. Aelius Tubero (Cic. *pro Planc.* 100), who also wrote history if the first letter to Quintus be considered genuine (*ad Quint. Frat.* 1. 1. 10, in which a forger might have confused Q. Tubero with L. Tubero). On Q. Aelius Tubero, the friend of Panaetius and perhaps a tribune of the plebs (Cic. *Brut.* 117): Cic. *de Fin.* 4. 23; *Tusc.* 4. 4.

[4] Dion. Hal. *Ant. Rom.* 1. 6. 4. It should be said here that two of Dionysius' friends who might be Romans, Ammaeus and Pompeius Geminus, cannot be identified. And Geminus may be a Greek: cf. Richards, *CQ* 32 (1938), 133 f. However, Richards's notion, revived by Goold, *TAPA* 92 (1961), 172, that Geminus is the author of the *de Sublimitate* has little to recommend it. Goold's attempt to prove that the *de Subl.* must precede Manilius is unconvincing.

Greek; Romans of breeding and culture had good judgement, an opinion held also by Strabo.[1]

There can be no doubt that Dionysius' history of early Rome was, like the history and geography of Strabo, designed in the first instance for upper-class Roman readers; patrons' names have already suggested that the audiences at which both writers aimed were virtually the same. Dionysius liked to observe in his history symptoms of decline in the modern Roman world when compared with earlier ages;[2] yet he was hardly the first to notice this falling-off in Roman virtues. Polybius, Panaetius, and Poseidonius had done the same. The theme of decline is no indication of hostility toward Rome nor of concern with a Greek public; on the contrary, the theme is expounded precisely to show the need for a resurgent rule of the old aristocracy.[3] The decline was attributed to the growing influence of new and pernicious elements in society. Dionysius, no less than his predecessors, was philo-Roman; the notion of decline served to encourage and to flatter the very class of Romans to which he adhered.

Yet an author who wrote in Greek cannot have neglected his Greek readers. It was useful to Dionysius to explain his Roman sympathies by proving in his history that Rome was, in fact, a Greek city in origin, indeed that nearly everything great about Rome derived from Greece.[4] Dionysius' perpetuation of the old contrast between barbarians and Hellenes does not show him in an anti-Roman mood:[5] just the opposite, for Romans were to be numbered among the Hellenes. Dionysius

---

[1] Dion. Hal. *de Orat. Ant.* 3. Cf. Strabo 13: οὐδὲ γὰρ ἂν οὔτε ψέγειν δύναιτο καλῶς οὔτ' ἐπαινεῖν, οὐδὲ κρίνειν ὅσα μνήμης ἄξια τῶν γεγονότων, ὅτῳ μηδὲν ἐμέλησεν ἀρετῆς καὶ φρονήσεως καὶ τῶν εἰς ταῦτα λόγων.

[2] Dion. Hal. *Ant. Rom.* 4. 24; 10. 17. 6.

[3] Cf. Palm, *Rom. Römertum und Imperium*, p. 13.

[4] On Dionysius' Greek audience, note *Ant. Rom.* 16. 4. 1. On the Greek origins of Rome and the Romans, especially *Ant. Rom.* 1. 89. 1–2. Cf. Palm, op. cit., pp. 13–16. It was not new to claim Rome as a Greek city: Gabba, *Rivista Storica Italiana* 71 (1959), 365–9.

[5] See Hill, *JRS* 51 (1961), 89 with n. 7, but his interpretation of Dionysius as an opposition writer cannot stand. See above, p. 110, n. 7. Nor, on the other hand, can the view of Gabba stand, op. cit., p. 365, that Dionysius is combating the anti-Roman history of Timagenes: *Ant. Rom.* 1. 4. 2 is an objection only to historians like Metrodorus, who lived in the courts of barbarian kings. This point was rightly stressed by Jacoby, *FGH* ii. C. 224.

gave expression to the fusion of cultures which characterized the Graeco-Roman world. Strabo viewed the situation somewhat differently when he used the word ἐκβεβαρβαρῶσθαι to describe the de-hellenization of Magna Graecia.[1] The twofold nature of the Roman empire is admirably exemplified in these writers, whose works in the Greek language were designed for both Romans and Greeks, though above all for the ruling class of Romans. It is instructive to notice Metilius Rufus, a pupil of Dionysius and the son of a close friend of his: Metilius was proconsul of Achaea under Augustus and possibly a legate of Galatia.[2]

Strabo returned to Italy after his sojourn in Alexandria and probably spent the remainder of his life, which was to be a long one, in the vicinity of Rome, perhaps at Naples.[3] Dionysius was in Rome at least until 7 B.C., when his history was at last complete.[4] So both men would have had an opportunity of meeting the excellent Greek poet, Antipater of Thessalonica, who returned from the East in the company of Piso the Pontifex about 11 B.C.[5] Piso came from a cultivated family with a taste for Greek literature; his father, the consul of 58 B.C., had been the patron of Philodemus of Gadara.[6] Antipater wrote occasional verse about places and objects he had seen or journeys he had made; he may have accompanied

---

[1] Strabo 253. Cf. Athen. 14. 632 A for another instance of this verb with the same sense.

[2] Dion. Hal. de Comp. Verb. 1: ὦ 'Ροῦφε Μετίλιε πατρὸς ἀγαθοῦ κἀμοὶ τιμιωτάτου φίλων. [μετιλιε FP: μελιτιε MV.] The identification with the proconsul attested in IG iii². 4152 and 4238 was made by Groag, Reichsbeamten von Achaia (1939), p. 14. The name Metilius appears also on the Sebasteion at Ancyra, perhaps indicating a Galatian governor of that name: E–J² 109, l. 20. (Cf. R. K. Sherk, The Legates of Galatia [1951], 26 ff.). Goold, op. cit., unaccountably perpetuates the false reading 'Melitius'.

An interesting discrepancy between Dionysius (Ant. Rom. 3. 29. 7) and Livy (1. 30. 2), pointed out to me by Mr. R. M. Ogilvie, is now understandable: the list of Alban principes whom Tullus Hostilius made senators is the same in both authors (apart from an obvious MSS. corruption in Livy) with one exception—Dionysius names the Metilii and Livy does not.

[3] Strabo lingered for some time in Alexandria (101 ἡμεῖς ἐπιδημοῦντες τῇ Ἀλεξανδρείᾳ πολὺν χρόνον). On his peculiar knowledge of Naples and its environs: P–W 2te Reihe, 4. 84–85.

[4] Dion. Hal. Ant. Rom. 1. 7.

[5] Cichorius, RS, p. 327.

[6] See above, p. 3 with n. 6.

the Pontifex during a proconsulship of Asia.[1] A poem that is plausibly assigned to Antipater, concerning the removal of animals from Africa for exhibition in Rome, is a metrical version of a passage in Strabo written before 19 B.C.[2] This is not without interest, because Strabo derived his information about Africa, as he expressly states, from a Cn. Piso, clearly the man who fought against Julius Caesar in Africa and was consul in 23 B.C.[3] Hence, the milieu of Strabo embraced Pisones and, therefore, the poet of Piso the Pontifex.

There were other Greek poets, also writers of occasional verse. The court poet, Crinagoras of Mytilene, commemorated such events of the Augustan age as Marcellus' return from Spain or the marriage of Juba II to Cleopatra.[4] Strabo notes the origin of the poet,[5] though he does not admit to personal acquaintance; yet he must have seen Crinagoras at Rome. The younger Diodorus of Sardis, however, was the geographer's acknowledged friend; this man was a son of the great Diodorus Zonas and an historian as well as a poet. He lived in Rome under Augustus, where Strabo will have known him. Only a few poems survive: one celebrates the young Tiberius and another his brother Drusus.[6]

The Roman circle of Greek writers and their patrons has a particularly remarkable feature: the preponderance of persons who subsequently emerge among the intimate adherents of the Emperor Tiberius. A review of names and facts will suffice to make this plain: Seius Strabo, Sejanus, Seius Tubero, and Piso the Pontifex, all known to have been Tiberius' trusted friends;[7] an Aelius Gallus, manifestly descended from the prefect, appears later as a partisan of Sejanus; Diodorus of Sardis

---

[1] Cichorius, *RS*, p. 328. The Asian proconsulship is deemed plausible by R. Syme, *JRS* 50 (1960), 17.

[2] *Anth. Pal.* vii. 626; Strabo 131. Cf. Cichorius, *RS*, pp. 332–4.

[3] Strabo 130, a passage which knows nothing of Balbus' march to the land of the Garamantes, for which he triumphed in 19 B.C. On Cn. Piso, cf. Tac. *Ann.* 2. 43 and the *Bell. Afr.* 3. 1; 18. 1.

[4] *Anth. Pal.* vi. 161; ix. 235. See above, Chapter III, pp. 36–37.

[5] Strabo 617.

[6] *Anth. Pal.* ix. 219 (to Tiberius) and 405 (to Drusus). Cf. Cichorius, *RS*, pp. 298–302.

[7] These men are well known. Cf. Tac. *Ann.* 4. 29, calling Seius Tubero an *intimus amicus* of Tiberius, and *Ann.* 6. 11 on Piso's twenty-year prefecture of the city.

is remembered largely for his poems to Tiberius and his brother; and a son of Q. Aelius Tubero the historian held the consulship precisely in the year of Tiberius' adoption by Augustus.[1] Parthenius, author of the *Crinagoras*, is known to have been one of Tiberius' favourite authors.[2] Cumulatively, the evidence is compelling. It has been noticed earlier that Tiberius was something of a philhellene; during his sojourn on Rhodes he lived like a Greek and competed at Olympia and Thespiae.[3] It was then that he took to himself the astrologer Thrasyllus and added the poet Apollonides of Nicaea to his literary acquaintances.[4] Perhaps it will, therefore, come as no surprise to find him in a circle of Greeks and philhellenes at Rome. Strabo ceased to work on his geography about 3/2 B.C., but soon after the accession of Tiberius he began his labours again, making additions and corrections.[5] There is no need to wonder why the accession moved him to new activity in his old age.

Nicolaus the Damascene was the only great Augustan author of works in Greek who did not spend a substantial part of his life in Rome. Three times he visited the city and perhaps met such men as Strabo, Dionysius, or Crinagoras, though surviving fragments of his books give no hint of this. Nicolaus was an influential diplomat and a voluminous writer. He belonged to the grand tradition of internationally minded Greek philosophers. His parents were wealthy and cultivated citizens of Syrian Damascus; his father, Antipater, had held numerous magistracies in his own city and served repeatedly on embassies.[6] Nicolaus, born about the same time as Strabo, received

---

[1] The younger Aelius Gallus: Tac. *Ann.* 5. 8. See p. 133, n. 6 above on Diodorus. Sex. Aelius Catus, son of Q. Aelius Tubero, was consul in A.D. 4.

[2] Suet. *Tib.* 70. 2; cf. p. 124, n. 4 above.

[3] Suet. *Tib.* 13. 1; *SIG*³ 782 (Olympia); *AE* 1960. 307 (Thespiae). Cf. Chapter VI above.

[4] Suet. *Tib.* 14. 4 (Thrasyllus). On Apollonides, see *Anth. Pal.* ix. 287 (on Tiberius), with which cf. Cichorius, *RS*, p. 335 (establishing Apollonides' provenance as Nicaea, not Smyrna).

[5] On the composition of the Geography, see Anderson, *Anat. Studies pres. to Ramsay* (1923), 1 ff., revising E. Pais, *Ancient Italy* (Chicago, 1908), 379 ff. The latest allusion in Strabo (828) is to the death of Juba II, probably in A.D. 23: Anderson, op. cit., p. 1.

[6] Suid. s.v. Ἀντίπατρος. Antipater was at some time in Rome for a rhetorical competition: Suid. s.v. Ποτάμων; cf. Cichorius, *Rom und Mytilene* (1888), p. 63.

a full and formal Greek education, culminating in those philosophical studies whose virtues he explained to King Herod of Judaea.[1] For Nicolaus became the intimate counsellor and agent of the Jewish king. The date of his admission to Herod's inmost circle is unknown, but during the Triumvirate he was tutor of the offspring of Antony and Cleopatra.[2] As Herod was a partisan of Antony, it is likely that even in the thirties Nicolaus had taken his place at the side of the king.

Herod transferred his allegiance to the future Princeps in 30 B.C., and so must Nicolaus have done. Although he disappears from history for a time, it is recorded that in 20 B.C. Nicolaus saw at Antioch a human freak which envoys from India were bearing to Augustus.[3] In 14 he is discovered travelling with Herod along the coast of Asia Minor and negotiating successfully with Greeks on behalf of the Jews.[4] In the years between 30 and 14 the philosopher may have encouraged the king in that ardent philhellenism which marked his reign.[5] And perhaps he assisted in domestic crises as well as affairs of state; such, at least, was his role subsequently.

Herod was the father of children by two women, one of common origin and one a princess; the rivalry between Antipater, the commoner's son, and the two sons of Mariamne the princess produced a long series of upheavals in the royal household. Nicolaus opposed Antipater, and he journeyed with Herod to Rome in 12 B.C. to assist in ordering the domestic troubles of the king before the Emperor himself; and again in 5 B.C. before Quinctilius Varus, the governor of Syria, Nicolaus exposed the treachery of Antipater, who had by then scored a temporary victory through terrifying his father into executing the sons of Mariamne.[6] But Antipater was disinherited before Herod died, and Archelaus was named the successor. It

---

[1] Suid. s.v. Νικόλαος Δαμασκηνός; *FGH* ii. A. 90. F. 135.

[2] *FGH* ii. A. 90. T. 2.

[3] Strabo 719; cf. Dio 54. 9. 8. The freak was a boy without arms, a living herm, which Strabo (ibid.) says that he also saw (presumably at Rome, cf. Suet. *Aug.* 43. 4).

[4] *FGH* ii. A. 90. F. 134; Jos., *AJ* 12. 125 ff. and 16. 27 ff.

[5] Cf. above, Chapter IV, p. 55.

[6] *FGH*. ii. A. 90. F. 135; cf. *BJ* 1. 452 ff., *AJ* 16. 90 ff. (12 B.C.). *FGH*, ibid., F. 136, 5–7; Jos., *BJ* 1. 629 ff., *AJ* 17. 99 ff. (5 B.C.). The executions: Jos. *BJ* 1. 551.

required the supreme diplomatic arts of the Damascene to secure that succession. Openly opposing the Jews who contested Archelaus' title to rule, Nicolaus travelled again to Rome and convinced Augustus of the wisdom of Herod's final choice.[1]

As an intermediary with Rome, Nicolaus carried on the tradition he inherited from his father. It is clear that Augustus had a high regard for him, not only from the embassies already mentioned but also from another and crucial one which took place in 8 B.C. when the king had invaded Arabia. After the Emperor in anger terminated his friendship with Herod as the result of the charges of open aggression which Syllaeus the Arab had levelled against him, Nicolaus was dispatched to Rome, where he succeeded in reconciling Augustus with Herod, and, further, in securing the disgrace and execution of Syllaeus himself.[2] That was no small achievement.

If Nicolaus had never written a word, he would have been an important Augustan figure; but his writings were vast, including a biography of the early career of the Princeps, a collection of ethnological data, a universal history in a hundred and forty-four books, and an autobiography.[3] Nicolaus' life of Augustus is an especially precious document, evidently derived, in large part, from the Princeps' own autobiography.[4] The extant fragments conclude with Octavian's journey to Campania to win over the soldiers of Caesar. At what point Nicolaus' work terminated is a matter for conjecture. Augustus' autobiography extended to the Cantabrian War and

---

[1] *FGH* ii. A. 90. F. 136, 8–11; Jos., *BJ* 2. 14 ff., *AJ* 17. 219 ff.

[2] *FGH* ii. A. 90. F. 136, 1; Jos., *BJ* 1. 574 ff., *AJ* 16. 299 ff. See above, Chapter IV, p. 56.

[3] *FGH* ii. A. 90. Suidas' eighty books for the history (T. 1) cannot be right: cf. T. 11. See the recent work of B. Z. Wacholder, *Nicolaus of Damascus* (Berkeley, 1962).

[4] Cf. Blumenthal, *Wiener Studien* 35 (1913), 123 ff.; Jacoby, *FGH* ii. C, pp. 264–5; *P–W* 17. 402–3 (Laqueur). The excursus on the murder of Caesar (*FGH* ii. A. 90, *Vita Augusti*, 58–106) has been thought to come from an entirely different source because the role of the Caesarians on 16 March 44 B.C. in § 49 is contradicted by that in § 103: cf. *P–W*, ibid. This need not be so, as the first item merely records the *report* given to Octavian when he landed in Italy. It is notable that the excursus assumes widespread popular support for Caesar's monarchy.

accordingly cannot have been completed before 25 B.C.[1] As Nicolaus' biography must have been written in the late twenties,[2] it followed swiftly on the completion of Augustus' own account. The speed with which Nicolaus applied himself to the task is significant: surely it had something to do with Augustus' presence in the East, as far as Syria, between 22 and 19 B.C. Nicolaus was acting as Augustus' literary agent among the Greeks; it may be presumed that when Octavian conferred with Herod on the island of Rhodes in 30 B.C. he met Nicolaus for the first time and was impressed.[3]

Nicolaus told Herod on their journey to Rome in 12 that history was instructive for kings and men of state; it was useful.[4] So, turning to Ephorus and also the recent work of Timagenes, Nicolaus set about the composition of a universal history.[5] If Nicolaus' work was begun as a digest for the edification of Herod, it gradually became something far more. The story was apparently carried down to the king's death in 4 B.C., and Nicolaus made use of the memoirs of Herod himself.[6] The latter part of the history was a vindication and panegyric of Herod's reign, and—to some extent—of Nicolaus' life in his service.

But the universal history was not enough. Adopting a Roman habit, Nicolaus wrote an autobiography.[7] Here, as in his other works, he had a Greek public principally in mind; and in this he differed from his contemporary Greek historians. He had

---

[1] Suet. *Aug.* 85. 1. The Cantabrian War probably ended in 26 B.C., so that the autobiography may have been composed during Augustus' illness in 25: R. Syme, *AJP* 55 (1934), 306, n. 39, and *HSCP* 64 (1959), 65. Schulten, *Los Cántabros y Astures y su guerra con Roma* (1943), p. 123, dates the end of the autobiography to 19 B.C.—surely wrongly: cf. Schmitthenner, *Hist.* 11 (1962), 64, n. 55.

[2] Jacoby, *FGH* ii. C, p. 263. Laqueur's arguments against this are unconvincing: *P–W* 17. 405–6. Most recently, B. Z. Wacholder, in his *Nicolaus of Damascus* (1962), pp. 25–26, has reaffirmed a date in the late twenties for the *vita*.

[3] Jos., *BJ* 1. 387–92; *AJ* 15. 187–93.

[4] *FGH* ii. A. 90. F. 135.

[5] Cf. Jacoby, *FGH* ii. C, p. 233.

[6] Jos. *AJ* 15. 174 on the ὑπομνήματα. See *AJ* 16. 183–6 on bias and panegyric in Nicolaus' account of Herod's reign.

[7] See Jacoby, *FGH* ii. C, pp. 288–9, recalling the autobiographies of Rutilius Rufus, Catulus, Sulla, and Augustus.

now to justify and to explain his life. With his worldly success and immense influence, he was neither pretentious nor pushing in high social circles. For ambitious Greeks this was hard to comprehend. Nicolaus had to explain why it was better to spend on good causes the money which his wealthy friends had given him, rather than hoard it for himself; he had to answer charges of consorting with common people at Rome instead of systematically cultivating the rich and mighty (he had, of course, no need to do that); and he was accused of being humane and friendly toward his slaves.[1] The apology of Nicolaus is a revelation: his detractors found modesty and humanity incompatible with power.

The Augustan empire could exhibit still other Greek authors with some share of power, but their contributions to literature are not easily appreciated owing to the paucity of surviving fragments. In the court of the Emperor, Athenodorus of Tarsus and Theodorus of Gadara had literary pretensions. Each composed monographs on his *patria*; Theodorus also devoted himself to rhetorical and historical studies.[2] And there were the geographical advisers of the young Gaius Caesar, Isidore of Charax and the scholarly King Juba II of Mauretania. Both men undertook to describe certain regions of the East for the instruction of the prince before his fatal journey.[3]

That, however, was but a small part of the labours of Juba: he composed a history of Rome in the Greek language and earned for himself the remarkable distinction of being more adept than any other king in the writing of history.[4] In addition, he made a comparative study of cultures, which he published in a work entitled *Similarities*; his artistic interests were

[1] *FGH* ii. A. 90. F. 138 and 139.
[2] *FGH* iii. C. 746 (Athenodorus, on whom cf. above, pp. 32, 39). *FGH* iii. C. 850 (Theodorus, on whom above, p. 35). On minor writers in Rome at this time and before: a convenient register is still provided by Hillscher, 'Hominum literatorum Graecorum ante Tiberii mortem in urbe Roma commoratorum historia critica', *Jahrb. für klass. Phil.* Supplementband 18 (1892), 355–440.
[3] Pliny, *NH* 6. 141 (Isidore of Charax and Juba II). H. Peter, *Die geschichtliche Litteratur über die römische Kaiserzeit* (1897), i. 417, claimed Tiberius as the recipient of Isidore's observations on the East. But Pliny implies that both Isidore and Juba wrote for the same person: *ad eundem Gaium Caesarem*.
[4] Plut. *Sert.* 9. 8.

reflected in his treatise on painting and his history of the theatre.[1] Mauretania had a learned and prolific monarch.

It could never be said that the reign of Augustus was deficient in Greek literature; the bulk of it was actually enormous. Lacking were imagination and genius; creativity—in drama, mime, fiction, elegy, pastoral, or epic—was utterly absent. There were historical works in abundance, and occasional verse to celebrate persons and events; there were also the products of the schools, treatises on rhetoric and literary criticism. The authors themselves, not without interest, are all distinguished by their dependence upon men of state. The Emperor, who is reported to have liked Greek literature (especially the Old Comedy), nevertheless looked in his reading chiefly for precepts and examples to instruct his household, his generals, and his governors.[2] The collapse of the Republic and the organization of the Principate left no room for the exercise of the Greek imagination. Diplomacy and the consolidation of the Graeco-Roman world were too consuming an occupation. Even an anonymous papyrus scrap of Augustan Greek poetry betrays the political obsession of the age: the verses celebrate the victory at Actium and a ship 'heavy laden with a cargo of good order and prosperity's great riches'.[3]

---

[1] *FGH* iii. A. 275. F. 13–14 (Similarities), 15–19 (Theatrical History), 20–21 (Painting).

[2] Suet. *Aug.* 89. 1–2.

[3] D. L. Page, *Greek Literary Papyri* (1942), i. 470, no. 113.

XI

NOVUS STATUS

AUGUSTUS proclaimed his hope that the foundations of the new régime would survive unshaken after his death,[1] and in recognizing the Graeco-Roman character of his empire, he provided a guarantee of its survival. The split between East and West, threatening under Antony, was postponed for three centuries. The wisdom and the shrewdness of Augustus were to perpetuate the patterns of diplomacy which had so effectively held together the empire of the late Republic.[2] Maintaining and strengthening the links between Rome and the aristocracies of the East, the Emperor could entrust much to their care, just as kingdoms, large and small, were left to client dynasts. Augustus' policy towards the Greek-speaking peoples allowed the evolution in Graeco-Roman affairs to continue, not only in his own lifetime but long after he was dead.

Certain of the later emperors, by their own ardent philhellenism, gave new strength to the Greek elements in the empire. Such were Gaius, Nero, and Hadrian. But quite apart from the extravagances of these men, the mutual dependence of Greeks and Romans was destined anyhow to become increasingly pronounced. Tiberius, the heir of Augustus, had already appeared as a philhellene at Rome and on Rhodes, and during his reign he gathered round him a company

---

[1] Suet. *Aug.* 28. 2. His hope: mansura in vestigio suo fundamenta rei publicae quae iecero. Suetonius observed: Fecitque ipse se compotem voti nisus omni modo, ne quem novi status paeniteret.

[2] Evidence is still accumulating to substantiate this interpretation. Professor Louis Robert has seen an inscription in Mysia, 'honorant le proconsul Cornélius Scipion (sous Auguste) et émanant de gens importants dont la patrie est indiquée': *L'Annuaire du Collège de France* 61 (1961–2), 312–13. Cf. *IGR* 4. 1211 (a letter of Scipio; Thyatira) and Grant, *FITA*, p. 387 (Augustan coin of Pitane, with Scipio's name and head).

of Greeks including poets, grammarians, and the astrologer Thrasyllus.[1] Meanwhile, Antonia, the widow of the elder Drusus, was also patronizing Greek men of culture.[2] It was natural that, when Philip of Thessalonica assembled a garland of Greek verse in the reign of Gaius,[3] he drew from the works of poets at the imperial court under Augustus and Tiberius as under Gaius himself. All three emperors were patrons of Greek *literati*. The enchanting poet Mesomedes owed his position in the court of Hadrian no more to the undoubted Hellenic tastes of that Emperor than to a tradition that began with Crinagoras.[4]

Under Augustus Athenodorus of Tarsus had been invested with imperium and dispatched on a special mission; the family of Theophanes of Mytilene could boast a knight and a senator. These were indications of what was to come. The equestrian order under Claudius included a doctor from the island of Cos and an eminent Hellene whose career was to end with the prefecture of Egypt.[5] A new senator from the East emerged, M. Calpurnius Rufus of Attaleia, and before long there appeared yet another, connected with the Attalids and the royal house of Galatia.[6] The floodgates were open; down to the reign of Commodus origins in Asia Minor can be

---

[1] Cf. Suet. *Tib.* 70. 2–3; Tiberius was the recipient of numerous commentaries by learned men on his favourite Greek poets (whom he liked to imitate), Euphorion, Rhianus, and Parthenius. On Thrasyllus, see especially Cichorius, *RS*, pp. 390–8, 'Der Astrologe Thrasyllos und sein Haus'.

[2] Notably Thallus and Honestus: see Cichorius, *RS*, pp. 356–8 and 362–5.

[3] On the dating of the Garland of Philip, see Cichorius, *RS*, pp. 341–55.

[4] Mesomedes: *PIR*, M 362. The hymns have been included in E. Heitsch, *Die griechischen Dichterfragmente der römischen Kaiserzeit* (1961), pp. 22–32.

[5] Augustan Greeks: Chapter III above. *SIG*[3] 804 (C. Stertinius Xenophon of Cos: cf. *IGR* 4. 1053). On the complex evidence for T. Claudius Balbillus: H. Musurillo, *The Acts of the Pagan Martyrs* (1954), 130–1, and most recently H. G. Pflaum, *Les Carrières procuratoriennes équestres* (1960), 34–41. Cichorius maintained that Balbillus was the son of Thrasyllus the astrologer: *RS*, pp. 393–8.

[6] M. Calpurnius M. f. Rufus: An inscription from Attaleia published in *Türk Tarih Beleten* 11 (1947), 94, no. 10 = 22 (1958) 26, no. 11 = *SEG* 17. 568 shows that he was a legatus pro praetore under Claudius, presumably in Lycia-Pamphylia (cf. R. Syme, *JRS* 48 [1958], 3, n. 29). He probably came from a family of Italian settlers. L. Servenius Cornutus from Phrygian Acmonia: *MAMA* 6. 254 and 262 (= *ILS* 8817). Note also M. Plancius Varus, from Perge in Pamphylia: *Anadolu* 2 (1955), 61. Also probably from a family of Italian settlers.

established for sixty-nine senators.[1] That was the remarkable but nevertheless predictable outcome of Augustus' organization of the empire. Statistics, however, always demand qualification.

The hellenizing of the senate has received much attention from modern scholars; the evidence was pressed too far and made the basis of exaggerated generalization. Now warnings have been issued: a large number of so-called oriental senators came from Roman colonies or places with Italian settlements, and many lack any characteristically Greek names.[2] This is certainly true, but caution must not be overdone. There is no need to abandon collective terms such as oriental or easterner, nor is it legitimate, by way of reaction, to deny a gradual hellenizing of the senate or indeed of the imperial civil service generally. It was to be expected that the most acceptable easterners, to begin with at least, were likely to be men with Italian ancestry; but such men, being expatriate and hellenized Italians, are notable on that account. Further, there were marriages into native families of the upper class, creating an amalgam of Italian and local Greek. L. Servenius Cornutus had mixed blood of this kind.[3] Finally, quite enough undisputed Greeks made their way into the senate to support a view of continuing consolidation between East and West. Q. Pompeius Macer under Augustus was one of them, and three more entered the senate under Vespasian.[4] It has been rightly noticed that statistics about genuinely Greek senators are initially suspect, inasmuch as many of those enumerated were not the first senators in their families: thus Ti. Julius Aquila Polemaeanus (consul suffect in 110), was a son of Ti. Julius Celsus Polemaeanus (consul suffect in 92), who had been adlected to aedilician rank under Vespasian, and

---

[1] Cf. most recently Habicht, *Istanbuler Mitteilungen* 9/10 (1959/60), 122. There is a reference in Plutarch to the desire of Greeks to penetrate the Roman senate in *de Tranq. Anim.* 470 C.

[2] Habicht, op. cit., pp. 122–3. Cf. L. Robert, *Hellenica* 9 (1950), 51, n. 3.

[3] See p. 141, n. 6 above; also Habicht, op. cit., pp. 124–5.

[4] On Macer, see above, p. 41, n. 7. The three Vespasianic senators: Habicht, op. cit., p. 123, n. 44. They were C. Antius A. Julius Quadratus (*suff.* 94, II ord. 105), Ti. Julius Celsus Polemaeanus (*suff.* 92), and King Julius Alexander (*cos.* under Trajan). A fourth eastern senator under Vespasian, C. Caristanius Fronto (*suff.* 90), clearly belongs to a family of Italians settled in Pisidian Antioch (cf. above, p. 72, n. 1).

M. Pompeius Macrinus Theophanes (reaching the consulship undoubtedly under Trajan) was clearly descended from Pompeius Macer.[1] But the very fact that Greek senators tended to belong to certain favoured families only illustrates more vividly those Graeco-Roman relations which Augustus had inherited and encouraged. Balance and circumspection are required in interpreting the evidence for oriental senators. It would be wrong to minimize their importance precisely for those reasons which make them most interesting: they came from hellenized Italian families, Greeks of the upper class, and mixtures of both.

Some were descendants of kings, an inevitable result of the annexation of client kingdoms. The dynasts of Augustus had been given the citizenship and encouraged to intermarry. When their kingdoms were ripe for annexation, the faithful ruling houses were stripped of power and honour. Compensation was bound to follow. Thus King Julius Alexander was a Trajanic consular tracing his descent from the Herods of Judaea, and C. Julius Antiochus Epiphanes Philopappus (consul suffect in 109) represented the royal house of Commagene.[2] C. Julius Severus (consul suffect c. 138) claimed ancestors among the Attalids and Galatian princes, while a consul suffect of 148, M. Antonius Zeno, came from the dynasty of Pontus.[3] A member of the Spartan family of Eurycles and Laco appeared in the senate under Trajan and Hadrian.[4]

In the Republic and in the time of Augustus the cultivated men of the East were regularly political leaders in their own cities and repositories of wealth. This potent union of education, affluence, and political power had been exploited by Rome; Augustus, like the imperatores, had depended upon it, and it grew ever more important in the two centuries after the first Princeps' death. In this matter, as in so many others, continuous evolution is discernible. The house of Polemo of Pontus provides a particularly instructive example: deriving from

---

[1] Habicht, op. cit., p. 124, n. 45. Pflaum, in *Germania* 37 (1959), 152, has put Macrinus' consulship into the period 120/22, without adequate reason.

[2] On King Alexander, cf. Groag, *P–W* 10. 151–2; he may have derived more immediately from a minor dynasty in Rough Cilicia. For Philopappus, cf. *OGIS* 405.

[3] C. Julius Severus: *OGIS* 544. For M. Antonius Zeno, *PIR²*, A 883.

[4] C. Julius Eurycles Heraclanus: cf. *JRS* 51 (1961), 118.

Laodicea, the family began its history with the rich and pro-Roman Zeno, whose son, the rhetor Polemo, became king of Pontus. Offspring of the rhetor entered two other royal houses in the East; and a Polemo from the Thracian branch was educated at Rome, where he composed Greek verses which found their way into the Garland of Philip in the Palatine Anthology. This literate prince himself became King of Pontus under Gaius.[1] A few generations later the family brought forth one of the great sophists of the second century, M. Antonius Polemo, a man of political no less than intellectual distinction; according to Philostratus, he conversed with cities as his inferiors, emperors as not his superiors, and the gods as his equals. In the grand tradition he settled factional disputes at Smyrna, served on the city's embassies to emperors, and administered the political affairs of Laodicea when he visited his relatives there.[2] Not surprisingly, another member of the family attained the consulship under Antoninus Pius.[3] So with remarkable consistency did the house of Polemo span the centuries from Republic to high Empire.

There were others who illustrate the persistence of money and political power among men of culture. Scopelian, like his ancestors, was a high priest of Asia and a person of wealth.[4] In accord with a familiar pattern, he served repeatedly on embassies to the Emperor and had a singular record of success; sometimes he represented the city of Smyrna, but on his most memorable embassy he spoke before Domitian on behalf of all Asia in protest against that Emperor's edict on the vines.[5] Lollianus of Ephesus might also be mentioned: both rhetorician and hoplite general at Athens, he was famed for quelling a bread-riot.[6] The Athenian sophist Herod Atticus was another of the affluent and cultivated men who dominated the city's political life. Indeed, the family of this man, like that of

---

[1] On republican and Augustan members of this house, see above, pp. 51, 53–54. For the versifier and king: Cichorius, *RS*, pp. 358–9; see also the stemma below, p. 154.

[2] Philostr. *Vit. Soph.* i. 535 (Polemo's conversation); 531 (Smyrna); ibid. (embassies); 532 (Laodicea).

[3] M. Antonius Zeno, *suff.* 148: see above, p. 143, n. 3.

[4] Philostr. *Vit. Soph.* i. 515.

[5] Ibid. 520. Cf. Suet. *Dom.* 7. 2 and 14. 2 on the vine edict.

[6] Philostr. *Vit. Soph.* i. 526.

Polemo, can be traced to the late Republic, when Herod of Marathon interceded with Julius Caesar, and to the Augustan age, when Eucles served on an embassy to the first Princeps.[1] Herod Atticus himself was ordinary consul in 143. Again and again continuity and an old pattern are apparent. The process is concisely exemplified in an Athenian inscription from the third century in honour of Q. Statius Themistocles, keybearer of Asclepius: he is hailed as φιλοσόφων καὶ ὑπατικῶν καὶ Ἀσ[ι]αρχῶν ἔκγονον καὶ ἀπόγονον.[2]

Lucian once described a dream in which two women lectured to him about his future career; one was Sculpture, the other Education, and he followed the counsel of the latter. He knew what he was talking about when he gave the following text to Education: 'You will be honoured and lauded, you will be held in great esteem for the highest qualities and admired by men pre-eminent in lineage and in wealth, you will wear clothing such as this'—she pointed to her own, which was very splendid—'and you will be deemed worthy of office and precedence.'[3]

Lucian understood the Graeco-Roman world. He knew how even a charlatan like the frightful Alexander of Abonuteichus could reach heights of influence and power by virtue of his forceful personality and the fact that a consular was his son-in-law.[4] Nor was the desire of Romans for Greek culture and luxury a secret to the satirist of Samosata, who related in horrifying detail the life of a hired Greek philosopher in the house of a great Roman.[5] The custom of keeping Greek men of learning in one's entourage was rooted in the Republic and explained the presence of Greeks in the imperial court; Lucian

---

[1] On Herod, cf. especially Philostr., *Vit. Soph.* ii. 545–66, and other references in *PIR*², C 802; also P. Graindor, *Un Milliardaire antique* (Cairo, 1930). For Herod of Marathon and Eucles, *IG* iii². 3175. The republican Herod was eponymous archon of Athens in 60/59 B.C.: Dinsmoor, *Archons of Athens* (1931), p. 280.

[2] *IG* iii². 3704, with Oliver in *Hesp.* Suppl. 7 (1949), 247.

[3] Lucian, *Somnium* 11.

[4] Id., *Alex.*, especially 27 (encouraging Severianus' disastrous invasion of Armenia in A.D. 161), 48 (influence in the court of Marcus), and 57 (because of his son-in-law, P. Mummius Sisenna Rutilianus [suff. 146], Alexander was so powerful that the governor of Bithynia had to admit he could not punish him even if he were found guilty after trial). Cf. *PIR*², A 506.

[5] Lucian, *de mercede conductis potentium familiaribus.*

took a cynical view of the motives of a Roman patron: 'People will think him a devoted student of Greek culture and in general a person of taste in literary matters.'[1]

This habit of acquiring an Hellenic veneer elicited fulminations from Juvenal; even the Italian rustic, he complained, had taken to wearing Greek slippers.[2] The Hellenic life still held its fascination. The Emperor Hadrian furnished conspicuous proof of this: well endowed with Greek culture, he had imbibed *Atheniensium studia*—singing, dancing, medicine, geometry, and the fine arts.[3] Many called him *Graeculus*, and in taste and talent he was not far different from the genuine *Graeculus esuriens* satirized by Juvenal in Hadrian's own day.[4]

But if a Greek Lucian could lampoon the relations between Greeks and Romans, he had also to accept them. His remarks on hired Greek philosophers were so outspoken as to threaten his career; he was quick to offer an apology when he took up a post in Egypt and received his salary from the imperial fiscus.[5] And Lucian was not the only eminent author who served Rome. New inscriptions have filled out the biography of the historian and consular, A. Claudius Charax, a native of Pergamum and governor of Sicily and Cilicia.[6] Nor should Cassius Dio and Asinius Quadratus be neglected, both historians and men of state.[7] Such persons belonged to a tradition that reached back to Polybius and evolved by way of Strabo, Dionysius of Halicarnassus, and Plutarch, all of whom had been well connected at Rome.[8] The Greek literary renaissance

---

[1] Lucian, *de mercede conductis potentium familiaribus*, 25.

[2] Juv. iii. 58 ff. Mr. R. Meiggs pointed out to me that the Greeks to whom Juvenal is referring are not inferior freedmen or worse but precisely those Greeks with whom Lucian is dealing in *de merc. cond.*, intellectuals in the houses of the rich. For hellenizing rustics, cf. Juv. iii. 67: Rusticus ille tuus sumit trechedipna, Quirine.

[3] *Epit. de Caes.* 14. 2.

[4] Ibid.; Juv. iii. 78. On Juvenal's time of writing: R. Syme, *Tacitus*, ii. 776.

[5] Lucian, *Apol.*, esp. 12–13.

[6] Habicht, *Istanbuler Mitteilungen* 9/10 (1959/60), 109 ff.

[7] For Cassius Dio, see *A Study of Cassius Dio* (1964) by F. G. B. Millar. Asinius Quadratus: *FGH* ii. A. 97, with *SIG*³ 887 (Olympia).

[8] Augustan writers: Chapter X above. On Plutarch's friends at Rome, see particularly Ziegler, *P–W* 21. 1. 687–94. Plutarch enunciated explicitly the well-known fact that easterners needed influential Roman friends: *Praec. r. pub. ger.* 18 (814 C).

of the second century owed much to long-term Roman support. Even under Augustus Dionysius had observed that the Roman nobility was responsible for the revival of the Attic style; so, too, Roman tastes had stimulated the Attic revival in sculpture and doubtless the deliberate archaizing in Athenian epigraphy.[1]

For about a century wealthy, aristocratic, and cultivated easterners of one kind or another who entered the service of Rome were employed principally among the Greek-speaking peoples.[2] This was essentially just a variant of the old system of entrusting as far as possible local affairs to natives, and kingdoms to client dynasts. The East was the obvious place for eastern knights and senators. It was not until the revolt of Avidius Cassius in A.D. 175 that the dangers of this arrangement were suddenly appreciated; Cassius was a Syrian by birth, and it was in Syria that he rose against Rome.[3] In 176 it became illegal for a man to govern his native province.[4]

The revolt of Cassius was an ominous sign of trouble in the Graeco-Roman world in that it uncovered a fundamental weakness in the imperial structure. There were other revolts and outbreaks, but they were not so serious. The old traditions were not going to break up from lower-class discontent nor from incessant stasis in various forms. Greek opposition to Rome had been making itself felt sporadically ever since Romans had been in contact with the East, but it had never been calamitous. It was apparent under Augustus, and riots and threats under his successors show that it did not die out.[5]

---

[1] Atticism in literature and sculpture: above, pp. 95, 130–1. Dionysius' observation appears in *de Orat. Ant.* 3. Fifth-century lettering in Athenian inscriptions of the early Principate: Raubitschek and Jeffery, *Dedications from the Athenian Acropolis* (1949), p. 149.

[2] See Walton, *JRS* 19 (1929), 38 ff., 'Oriental Senators in the Service of Rome'; Lambrechts, *Ant. Class.* 5 (1936), 105 ff. Also R. Syme in *Proc. Mass. Hist. Soc.* 72 (1963), 1 ff. Cf. the advice of Apollonius of Tyana to Vespasian in Philostr. *Vit. Apoll.* 5. 36: τούτων γὰρ τοὺς μὲν προσφόρους τοῖς ἔθνεσιν, ἃ διέλαχον, φημὶ δεῖν πέμπειν, ὡς ὁ κλῆρος, ἑλληνίζοντας μὲν Ἑλληνικῶν ἄρχειν, ῥωμαΐζοντας δὲ ὁμογλώττων καὶ ξυμφώνων.

[3] On Avidius Cassius, *PIR²*, A 1402.

[4] Dio 72. 31. 1.

[5] Cf. above, Chapter VIII. There was a revolt in Achaea under Antoninus Pius: *SHA* Pius 5. 5; Lucian, *Peregr.* 19; *AE* 1929, 21. On labour disputes and strikes in the second century, cf. Buckler, *Anat. Studies pres. to Ramsay* (1923),

Yet the consolidation process went on. Nor did the ever-present rash of stasis in the East impede the tightening of bonds with the West. Most of the civil disturbances of the second century broke out either in trivial contests for honours or as a result of economic crises. Plutarch rebuked the peoples of the East for their disputes,[1] but he saw no danger to the fabric of relations between Greeks and Romans. That seemed quite secure; Plutarch, like Dio of Prusa, told the Greeks that in fact they were too submissive to Rome.[2]

However, the system which Augustus had fostered was ultimately seen to have carried in itself the germs of its own decay, and the revolt of Cassius was but one symptom of many. Local financial burdens were becoming more and more intolerable, and eastern aristocrats were growing reluctant to undertake them;[3] furthermore, the new positions of honour which were opening up at Rome and were the natural reward for good service in the provinces effectively reduced the prestige of holding merely local offices. Thus began in the eastern cities that δρασμὸς ἀπὸ τῆς βουλῆς of which Libanius complained so

27 ff.; and on class struggles as reflected in the works of Lucian, Baldwin in *CQ* 55 (1961), 199 ff. Aelius Aristides, *Orat.* 26 Keil (to Rome), 65–66, claimed that the lower classes rejoiced in Roman rule; an upper-class Greek might like to have thought that, or at least to have said it in public. But the Roman oration of Aristides cannot be pressed as an historical document; it is a literary piece with many antecedents. Cf. Oliver, *The Ruling Power* (1953), p. 892: 'The historical and political judgments of Aristides are very superficial.' Rostovtzeff had a different opinion: *SEHRE²* i. 131.

[1] Plut. *Praec. rei p. ger.* Plutarch dedicated this treatise probably to a certain Menemachus of Sardis, who had been banished (*de Exilio* 600 A); and he observed continuing strife in that city (*Praec.* 825 c: opposition between Pardalas and Tyrrhenus). Cf. also the hortatory addresses of Dio of Prusa and Aelius Aristides on the theme of ὁμόνοια.

[2] Plut. *Praec. rei p. ger.* 814 E; Dio Prus. *Orat.* 31. 111; cf. 36. 17 on a Borysthenite who flattered the Romans by being clean-shaven among his bearded countrymen.

[3] The earliest indication of reluctance may be in Pliny, *Ep.* 10. 113: eos qui inviti fiunt decuriones. Mr. Sherwin-White has suggested that *inviti* is a corruption of *invitati*, and his emendation has taken its place in the Oxford text of Pliny by Sir Roger Mynors. There is no good *historical* reason for altering the text here (admittedly corrupt elsewhere): the introduction of special privileges for decurions under Hadrian (*Dig.* 48. 19. 15; p. 149, n. 2 below) makes it plausible that there was already some reluctance under Trajan. For examples of expenses borne by local magistrates in the second century, see the citations in Rostovtzeff, *SEHRE²* ii. 599–602; also W. Liebenam, *Städteverwaltung im römischen Kaiserreiche* (Leipzig, 1900), 164 ff.

bitterly in the fourth century.[1] As early as the reign of the philhellene Hadrian legislation was introduced offering special privileges to decurions.[2] This was the start of a legal distinction between *honestiores* and *humiliores*, which gathered strength as local magistracies became increasingly less attractive.[3] However, the new legislation in itself reveals the tenacity of the old system of relations between East and West; it had been successful for so long that every effort was made to perpetuate it.

The Empire finally split in two. Augustus, at a pivotal point in Roman history, had long ago forestalled that calamity by encouraging a union of Rome and the East which had begun under the Republic. The result was an extraordinary continuity from the second century B.C. to the third century A.D., and the first Princeps deserves no small share of the credit. That continuity underlies the Greek renaissance of the second century and helps to explain the growth and consolidation of empire: τὸ Ῥωμαῖον εἶναι ἐποιήσατε οὐ πόλεως ἀλλὰ γένους ὄνομα κοινοῦ τινος.[4] Augustus would not have been altogether surprised to see the role of the Greek-speaking peoples under Hadrian and the Antonines.

---

[1] Liban. *Orat.* 48. 23; cf. also, for example, 43. 3 ff. or 45. 5.

[2] *Dig.* 48. 19. 15: Decurions were not to suffer capital punishment except for murdering a parent. Note special privileges granted in A.D. 119 to *splendidiores*, among whom were probably certain *peregrini* such as decurions: *Coll.* 13. 3; *Dig.* 47. 21. 2.

[3] See *Dig.* 48. 5. 38. 8 and 48. 8. 1. 5 (Antoninus Pius). For the whole development, Cardascia, *Rev. hist. de droit français et étranger* 28 (1950), 305 ff. and 461 ff., 'L'Apparition dans le droit des classes d'honestiores et d'humiliores'.

[4] Aristides, *Orat.* 26. 63 Keil.

APPENDIX I

CULTS OF ROMAN MAGISTRATES
IN THE EAST

Seyrig's list in *Rev. Arch.* 29 (1929), 95, n. 4, has long needed to be revised and supplemented. K. Latte, *Römische Religionsgeschichte* (1960), 313, n. 2, still relies on it. For the Empire, in the list below, only magistrates not directly connected by blood with the imperial house are included. On these cults, cf. Chapter IX above.

M. Claudius Marcellus
  Cic. *Verr.* 2. 2. 51.

T. Quinctius Flamininus
  Plut. *Tit. Flam.* 16. *AE* 1929.
  99. Cf. Polyb. 18. 46. 12.

M.' Aquillius
  IGR 4. 292, 1. 39; 293, 1. 24.

M. Annius
  *SIG*3 700.

Q. Mucius Scaevola
  IGR 4. 188; 291. *OGIS* 439.
  Cic. *Verr.* 2. 2. 51.

L. Valerius Flaccus
  Cic., *pro Flacc.* 55.

L. Cornelius Sulla
  IG ii². 1039, 1. 57. *SEG* 13.
  279.

L. Licinius Lucullus
  Plut. *Luc.* 23.

C. Verres
  Cic. *Verr.* 2. 2. 52, 114, 154;
  4. 24.

Cn. Pompeius Magnus
  BCH 8 (1884), 148; 34 (1910),
  401. Dio 69. 11. 1. *Anth.
  Pal.* ix. 402.

Ap. Claudius Pulcher
  Cic. *ad Fam.* 3. 7. 2; 9. 1.

Q. Tullius Cicero
  Cic. *ad Quint. Frat.* 1. 1. 26
  (refused).

M. Tullius Cicero
  Cic. *ad Att.* 5. 21. 7 (refused).

P. Servilius Isauricus
  Ephesos i. 49, n. 3; iii. 149.
  Ath. Mitt. 32 (1907) 254.
  Jahrb. Öster. Inst. 18
  (1915), 282.

C. Julius Caesar
  IGR 4. 28.

M. Junius Silanus
  IG xii. 9. 916. Cf. *SIG*3 767.
  Cf. also J. Hatzfeld, *Les
  Trafiquants italiens* (Paris,
  1919), p. 71, n. 1.

Cn. Domitius Calvinus
  IGR 3. 108.

M. Vipsanius Agrippa
  *SIG*3 1065. Dio 54. 24. 7.

Paullus Fabius Maximus
  IGR 4. 244.

L. Munatius Plancus
  BCH 12 (1888), 15, n. 4.

M. Vinicius
  Rev. Arch. (1935) ii. 156–8.

C. Marcius Censorinus
  SEG 2. 549.

Cn. Vergilius Capito
  Hellenica 7 (1949), 209.
  Didyma ii, p. 192, n. 278.

APPENDIX II

TRIUMVIRAL THRACIAN KINGS

THE client dynasty of Thrace is shrouded in obscurity. Augustus supported many of the great eastern kings raised up by Antony. A man who knew the East well would not have neglected Thrace; hence probability counsels an Antonian dynasty there, accepted and sustained by Antony's conqueror.

Dessau's discussion of the confusing evidence for the Thracian client kings is still fundamental (*EE* ix. 696 ff.). Much of what follows is indebted directly to it, but the problems can profitably be considered again. Since Dessau wrote, some additional inscriptions have turned up; they serve to augment, rather than to alter, his conclusions.

Among the supporters of Pompey in 48 B.C. were a certain Cotys *ex Thracia* and his son Sadalas (Caesar, *BC* 3. 4. 3). A Cotys had been king of Thrace in 57 (Cic. *Pis.* 34. 84): presumably the later Pompeian. His son Sadalas will be the man of that name whom Caesar pardoned after Pharsalus (Dio 41. 63. 1). Now in 42 a certain Thracian Sadalas is reported to have died without progeny (ἄπαις, Dio 47. 25. 1). About the same time in the same part of the world a lady named Polemocratia suffered the death of her husband; she entrusted her young son to Brutus, who turned him over to the care of the Cyzicenes (App. *BC* 4. 75). At Bizye, *arx regum Thraciae* (Pliny, *NH* 4. 47), an inscription appeared on which a King Cotys honoured his parents, who happened to be King Sadalas and Queen Polemocratia (*EE* ix. 698). Appian does not disclose the name of the husband who died about 42, but inasmuch as his wife's name was Polemocratia and as Dio reveals the death of a Sadalas then, the husband of Appian's Polemocratia was surely the Sadalas of Dio and the Bizye inscription. Dio states that he left no children; evidently the historian was not aware of the small child who was immediately given over to Brutus and the Cyzicenes. The Bizye inscription reveals that the child's name was Cotys. If Polemocratia's husband was the son of the Pompeian Cotys, as he must be, then her son carried—not surprisingly—the name of his grandfather. He evidently became a king.

So much for Thracian kings in Thrace, i.e. Odrysians centred in

Bizye. There was also a line of Thracian princes in Macedonia, near Philippi. Fighting for Pompey in 48 was a Rhescuporis from Macedonia (Caesar, *BC* 3. 4. 3); Appian (*BC* 4. 87) notices that there were Thracians named Rhescuporis and Rhescus, belonging to the Sapaean house, near Philippi. Two inscriptions reveal the existence of a King Cotys who was the son of a King Rhescuporis: *EE* ix. 700, no. 2 (Athens) and *PBSA* 12 (1905/6), 178 (Bizye). Both documents reveal that the Sapaeans reached the throne, and the provenance of the latter shows that they were acknowledged, probably established, at Bizye, home of the Odrysians. Another inscription from Athens furnishes the name of King Rhescuporis' father, namely Cotys (significantly *not* called King): *EE* ix. 700, no. 1.

Thus after 42 there were a Sapaean King Rhescuporis, a Sapaean King Cotys, and an Odrysian King Cotys. Before Actium Antony numbered among his partisans a certain Sadalas (Plut. *Ant.* 61) and a Rhoemetalces who deserted to Octavian (Plut. *Mor.* 207 A). Rhoemetalces will have been a Sapaean, for his brother was a Rhescuporis (Dio 55. 30. 6) and his son is expressly designated Sapaean by Strabo (556). Sadalas being strictly an Odrysian name, Antony had, it would appear, conciliated both the Odrysians and the Sapaeans. The sequence of kings from both houses after 42 confirms this.

Antony's client dynasty appears to have been created through a marriage. The Augustan Rhoemetalces is described by Dio (54. 20. 3) as uncle and guardian of Cotys' children. This Cotys must either be the offspring of Sadalas and Polemocratia or of Rhescuporis. The fact that Dio does not call Rhoemetalces the brother of Cotys suggests in itself that he was the brother of Cotys' wife. If Cotys were his blood brother, their joint father would have been Rhescuporis, for Sadalas, being an Odrysian, would be ruled out. As it happens, two inscriptions reveal that Rhoemetalces' father was a King Cotys: *PBSA* 12 (1905/6), 175 (Bizye), correctly interpreted in *EE* ix. 696 and *AE* 1957. 98 (Hisarläk). Both texts exhibit the genealogy of Rhoemetalces' homonymous nephew, son of his known brother. Therefore Cotys, father of Rhoemetalces and clearly a Sapaean, will be the son of Rhescuporis. The other Cotys, whose children have Rhoemetalces as their uncle, can only be the son of Sadalas and an Odrysian, married to the Sapaean sister of Rhoemetalces.

When the Odrysian Cotys died is unknown, but it must have occurred before Lollius' governorship of Macedonia in 19 or 18

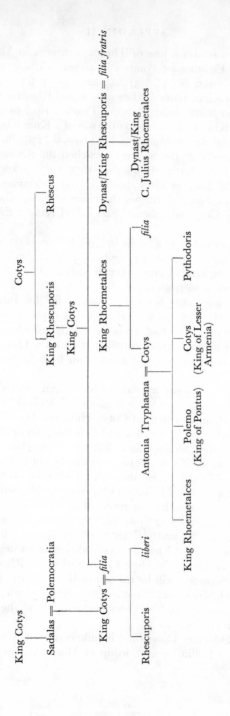

(Dio 54. 20. 3). His death could have provided a suitable occasion for an Odrysian attempt to remove the upstart Sapaeans. In 29 B.C. M. Licinius Crassus had conciliated the Odrysians at the expense of their enemies, the Bessi (Dio 51. 25. 5), and Octavian had some hereditary ties with them (his father had crushed the Bessi, Suet. *Aug.* 3. 2). But the Odrysians cannot have been altogether pleased with the appointment of Rhoemetalces as guardian of Cotys' children. The mysterious campaign of Marcus Primus against the Odrysians *c.* 23 (Dio 54. 3. 1) ought to be connected with the death of Cotys. It is important that none of the Thracian kings of the Principate is called Sadalas.

The evidence thus encourages the view that Augustus adopted Antony's arrangements in Thrace. When a breach appeared in the Antonian union of Odrysian and Sapaean lines, Augustus gave his support to the house of the Sapaean Rhoemetalces. It was a Rhoemetalces, perhaps this one, who had deserted to the right side before Actium.

Opposite is a revised version of Dessau's stemma, consistent with the foregoing discussion.

Conspectus of epigraphical evidence relevant to the stemma on page 154

EE ii. 252 = *EE* ix. 698 (Bizye). King Cotys honours his parents, who are King Sadalas and Queen Polemocratia.

EE ii. 253, n. 4 = *EE* ix. 700, no. 2 = *CIA* iii. 553 (Athens). King Cotys is son of King Rhescuporis. Set up by Antignotus.

EE ii. 253, n. 6 = *EE* ix. 700, no. 1 = *CIA* iii. 552 (Athens). King Rhescuporis is son of Cotys (*not* called King). Set up by Antignotus.

EE ix. 700 = *PBSA* 12 (1905/6), 178 (Bizye). King Cotys is son of King Rhescuporis. Set up by Ῥωμαῖοι οἱ πρώτως κατακληθέντες εἰς κῆνσον.

EE ix. 696 = *PBSA* 12 (1905/6), 175 (Bizye). Rhoemetalces, δυνάστης of Thracians, is υἱωνός of King Cotys, θυγατριδοῦς of King Rhoemetalces, and son of δυνάστης Rhescuporis.

AE 1957. 98 = *Bull. de l'Inst. Arch. Bulg.* 19 (1955), 169 = 183 (Hisarläk). Identical genealogy with the foregoing, except that Rhoemetalces is no longer δυνάστης but βασιλεύοντος. However, βασιλεύοντος is cut over an erasure of the still distinguishable words ὑπὲρ ὑγίας δυνάστου.

AE 1912. 213 = *Ath. Mitt.* 36 (1911), 287 = 37 (1912) 180 (Byzantium). King Rhoemetalces. Dated A.D. 1/2.

AE 1933. 84 = *BCH* 56 (1932), 203 (Philippi). King C. Julius Rhoemetalces is son of King Rhescuporis.

AE 1937. 168 = *Thracica* 6 (1935), 305 (vicinity of Neapolis). King Rhoemetalces is son of Cotys (*not* King).

APPENDIX III

SUETONIUS, *TIBERIUS* 8:
THE TRIALS OF ARCHELAUS, TRALLIANS
AND THESSALIANS

Suetonius, *Tiberius* 8: Civilium officiorum rudimentis regem
Archelaum Trallianos et Thessalos, varia quosque de causa,
Augusto cognoscente defendit

AT some point the young Tiberius defended the King of Cappadocia, some Trallians, and Thessalians on various charges in the
court of the Emperor. It would be constitutionally disquieting
should the trials have occurred between 27 and 23 B.C., although
that is the period to which they are normally assigned. If there were
a clear indication of such a date, constitutional niceties would have
no weight. But such an indication is lacking; evidence can be adduced in support of a later date, and some details about the trials
can be recovered.

Prevalent opinions must first be cleared away. Gelzer (*P–W* 10.
480) suggested that the trials occurred in Spain, where Tiberius
had joined Augustus in fighting the Cantabrian War. He gave no
reasons for this view, but they can be inferred from the location of
the notice in Suetonius' biography. Chapter VIII appears at first
sight to record events of the 20's: the trials, pleas for assistance from
three eastern cities stricken in an earthquake, the prosecution of
Caepio the conspirator, Tiberius' *cura annonae*, and his investigation
of the Italian *ergastula*. The earthquake, which crippled Laodicea,
Thyatira, and Chios, can be dated to 26 (Euseb. *Chron. Hier.* p. 164
Helm); Tralles was also affected (ibid. and Strabo 579) and sent
an embassy to Augustus in Spain to ask for help (Agathias 2. 17).
It might have seemed that because Suetonius mentioned the trials
before the pleas for assistance they were temporally anterior. And
they could not have occurred before Augustus went to Spain, since
Tiberius would have been too young. But it should be noticed that
despite the fact that Tralles sent its appeal to Spain the pleas for the
stricken cities were, in fact, heard in the senate at Rome (Suet.
Tib. 8), therefore after Tiberius' return from Spain—in 24 at the
earliest. The trials cannot be left in Spain.

Suetonius' reliability in matters of chronology is difficult to
assess: he prefers to group his material together, often carelessly by

topics (cf. *Aug.* 9), but he knows how to indicate temporal relations when he wants to: observe *post hoc*, *exin*, and *inde* in chapter 9 on Tiberius' military career. Chapter 8 contains the words *inter haec* (i.e. the trials, pleas, and prosecution of Caepio) in respect to Tiberius' administration of the grain supply and an investigation of the Italian *ergastula*. The date of his *cura annonae* is assigned (Vell. 11. 94. 3) to his quaestorship, which occurred in 23 B.C. (Dio 53. 28. 4), but Velleius says that he was nineteen years old at the time. Since Tiberius became nineteen some time *in* the year 23 B.C. and a severe shortage of grain is recorded for 22 B.C. (Dio 54. 1. 2–3), Tiberius' *cura annonae* is unlikely to have come at the beginning of 23 and probably *did* come nearer the end of it. The date of his investigation of the *ergastula* is indeterminate.

Accordingly two items, one of which can be dated to late 23, fall chronologically among certain events which include the trials. Of these events, the plea for the stricken cities cannot be before 24; the prosecution of Caepio cannot be before 23, and it may belong to 22, the year in which Dio (54. 3. 4) puts it. (On the still controversial question of the year of the Caepio–Murena conspiracy, cf. Balsdon, *Gnomon* 33 [1961], 395.) Now if the trials are to be dated to the mid or early 20's, it would produce the odd result that Suetonius described something from late 23 as falling *inter* a set of events of which the latest belongs itself to 23 or at best (on the alternative dating of the prosecution of Caepio) to 22, while the next latest belongs to 24 at the earliest. In view of the date of Tiberius' *cura annonae*, Suetonius' *inter haec* must mean that at least one or more of the preceding events in his chapter occurred *after* 23. It is probable —on this approach—that the prosecution of Caepio is such a later event. There is also a case to be made for a date later than 23 for the trials, and the case seems worth making.

The Date of the Trial of Archelaus: Dio (57. 17. 3–4) alludes to this event under the year A.D. 17. His words are: 'Tiberius' anger was aroused against Archelaus, the King of Cappadocia, because this prince, after having once grovelled before him (πρότερόν οἱ ὑπο-πεπτωκώς) in order to gain his assistance as advocate when accused by his subjects in the time of Augustus, had afterwards (μετὰ τοῦτο) slighted him on the occasion of his visit to Rhodes, yet had paid court to Gaius when the latter went to Asia.' This passage confirms what was clear anyway from Suetonius: the trial took place at least before Tiberius' retirement to Rhodes.

Further on in the same passage (Dio 57. 17. 5) reference is made to insanity alleged against Archelaus, as a result of which Augustus was obliged at some unknown date to impose an ἐπίτροπος (Latin *procurator*) over the king's realm. There is no connexion made or implied between the imposition of this official and the trial of Archelaus, and there is thus no justification for assuming that this action was the outcome of the trial. It is best to assume that it came later and that the trial was terminated by an acquittal; that is what one would expect from a royal defence, and it appears to underlie Tiberius' vexation with Archelaus' ingratitude.

Dio does not reveal *when* the king grovelled before Tiberius. The occasion can be surmised. When Tiberius went to Armenia in 20 B.C. to install Tigranes II on the throne, Archelaus, the King of Cappadocia, went with him (Jos. *AJ* 15. 105). It was perhaps on that mission that Archelaus debased himself before Tiberius in search of legal aid. It was in 20 B.C. (Dio 54. 9. 2) that Augustus presented Archelaus with Rough Cilicia and Lesser Armenia, and this indication of imperial favour may have piqued the opposition to the king at home.

If this date for Tiberius' support of Archelaus is accepted, the subsequent history of the two men falls into place. For M. Titius was governor of Syria when the Parthian king handed over his sons as hostages to the Romans (Strabo 748): that happened in 10/9 B.C. (Livy, *Ep.* 141, which must refer to the hostages and the declaration of *pax*, inasmuch as the standards were recovered in 20 B.C.); Archelaus and Titius were on bad terms, but Herod of Judaea succeeded in reconciling the two men while Titius was still governor of Syria (Jos. *AJ* 16. 270). This reconciliation will have been the time of Archelaus' desertion of Tiberius. Titius cannot have been a friend of Tiberius, in view of the harsh treatment he receives at the hands of Tiberius' panegyrist, Velleius (2. 79. 6). Archelaus was an enemy of Titius while he was a friend of Tiberius, and an enemy of Tiberius after he had contracted a friendship with Titius. A network of intrigue is exposed by which a king whom Tiberius had once defended was made to slight him on Rhodes.

Archelaus, then, could have appealed to Tiberius in 20 B.C. Presumably the trial before Augustus took place in Rome, as the itineraries of the Emperor and his stepson in the East were not the same. In 16 B.C. Tiberius went with Augustus to Gaul (Dio 54. 19. 6). Therefore the trial will have occurred between 19 and 16, most probably *c.* 18 B.C.

This argument has provided a possible date for one of the trials. If Archelaus took advantage of Tiberius' presence in the East to seek his aid in court, others such as the Trallians and the

Thessalians did as well. Tiberius was accessible to embassies from such peoples: he exhibited his virtues to several provinces of the East on his way to Armenia (Vell. 2. 94. 2), and on his return he paused at Rhodes (Suet. *Tib.* 11).

Tralles: Apart from the earthquake, evidence for Augustan Tralles is slight. Magie (*RRAM* ii. 1332) connected Tiberius' defence of the Trallians with the appeal of Tralles after the earthquake of 26. This supposition may be quickly dismissed. A plea for a shattered city can hardly be the same as a defence in court: the one took place in the senate, the other at a *cognitio* of Augustus.

The city had been head of a conventus district in the late Republic: Cic. *pro Flacc.* 29, 71; Jos. *AJ* 14. 245; *Milet*, ii. Bouleuterion no. 3. It lost this status under Augustus; it appears in Pliny (*NH* 5. 120) in the conventus of Ephesus under the name of Caesarea. The date and circumstances of the loss of the conventus headship and the acquisition of the name Caesarea cannot be discovered; Pliny's sources for the East are too various to furnish any secure dating (cf. Jones, *CERP*, App. I). Therefore, the issues at the trial of the Trallians, in which Tiberius was involved, cannot be discovered. Factional rivalries are most likely. (Cf. Chapter VIII above, pp. 102–8.)

But Tiberius' activities on behalf of Tralles may be reflected in an inscription from near-by Nysa, the ancestral seat of the eminent Trallian house of Chaeremon (cf. p. 8 above). This document (*SIG*3 781) attests a priest of Tiberius in Nysa at precisely the period of his exile on Rhodes. The cult was undoubtedly established at an earlier and happier time. Could Tiberius have successfully defended the family of Chaeremon and Pythodorus against another Trallian faction? Whatever the cause, the request for his services in the court of Augustus fits best into the context of his mission to Armenia.

Thessaly: As in the case of Tralles, miscellaneous scraps of information have survived. The freedom granted to the Thessalians by Caesar (App. *BC* 2. 88; Plut. *Caes.* 48) is thought to have been revoked by Augustus, because their freedom is not mentioned by Pliny. There is no good reason to connect a loss of freedom with the reference in Suetonius, any more than there is any excuse for bringing in coin legends (Head, *HN*2 312), Augustus' enlargement of the league (Paus. 10. 8. 3), or his titulary generalship of it in 27/26 B.C. (*IG* ix. 2. 415*b*; *Arch. Eph.* 1917, 149).

However, certain items might be relevant. Two Thessalian manumission lists of Augustan date mention ὁ ἐνιαυτὸς ὁ ἐπὶ στρατηγοῦ Σωσάνδρου κατὰ τὸ Καίσαρος κρῖμα (*IG* ix. 2. 1042, ll. 21–22;

21–22; *JHS* 33 (1913), 323, ll. 3–5). The κρῖμα to which this phrase alludes must be a judgement in a trial, a court decision; it cannot be the same thing as an edict (ἐπίκριμα) or a rescript (διάταγμα). The only known trial involving Thessaly in which Augustus was the judge is the one recorded in Suet. *Tib.* 8, *Augusto cognoscente*. It is clear from the inscriptions that the Emperor's decision included an extraordinary appointment of an eponymous general of the Thessalian League for that year.

Contention of rival factions for the supreme magistracy may be suspected. There were certainly rival factions within the league in the days of Caesar and Pompey (Caes. *BC* 3. 35. 2). And sometime in the reign of Augustus a man called Petraeus was burned alive by the Thessalians (Plut. *Praec. rei pub. ger.* 19, 815 D). The leader of the Caesarian faction in the civil-war period was also a Petraeus (Caes. *BC* loc. cit.); he received the citizenship (Cic. *Phil.* 13. 33), probably from Caesar's proconsul, L. Cassius Longinus (cf. the L. Cassius Petraeus in *SIG*³ 825). The Caesarian Petraeus was struck down with an axe in 43 B.C. (Cic. *Phil.* loc. cit.). Hence the man who was burned alive was probably his son. (On the Cassii Petraei of Hypata, cf. Bowersock, *Rheinisches Museum* 108 [1965].) Nothing further is known of the Pompeian, Hegesaretus (Caes., *BC* loc. cit.), but the violent end of the younger Petraeus at the hands of his own countrymen suggests that the opposing faction was still vigorous.

The trial of the Thessalians and the Emperor's appointment of Sosandrus cannot, however, have been the outcome of the tumults in which Petraeus was burned; one of the inscriptions reveals that Petraeus held his second generalship *after* the extraordinary tenure of Sosandrus (*IG* ix. 2. 1042, ll. 27–28). Therefore, the burning of Petraeus cannot come before the trial, as Jones thought (*GC* 324, n. 63), if the κρῖμα is to be associated with it. And surely it must.

Nevertheless, factional disturbances will have led to the trial and the imperial appointment of a league general. As in the case of the two foregoing trials, Tiberius was probably approached by Thessalian envoys during his mission to Armenia. The words τὸ Καίσαρος κρῖμα need not cause any trouble. Augustus is elsewhere called Caesar on a contemporary document (*OGIS* 458, ll. 5, 37, 60).

In conclusion, Tiberius' defence of easterners at the court of Augustus may belong soon after his return from the East in 19 B.C. If Archelaus' appeal to Tiberius for help came in 20 B.C., the appeals of the Trallians and the Thessalians could have reached him either on his way out to Armenia or on his way back.

BIBLIOGRAPHY

THIS list contains only books and articles which have been cited in the foregoing pages. Editions and collections of ancient evidence (literary, epigraphic, and numismatic) have been omitted, and so have all articles in standard works of reference (e.g. *P–W*). Also omitted are the valuable epigraphic bulletins of J. and L. Robert in *REG* and the reports in *Hellenica* of courses given in Paris by Professor Robert. Three unpublished theses are listed separately at the end.

ACCAME, S., *Il dominio romano in Grecia della guerra acaïca ad Augusto* (Rome, 1946).

ADAMS, F., 'The Consular Brothers of Sejanus', *AJP* 76 (1955), 70 ff.

AKARCA, A., *Les Monnaies grecques de Mylasa* (Paris, 1959).

ANDERSON, J. G. C., 'Some Questions bearing on the Date and Place of Composition of Strabo's *Geography*', *Anatolian Studies presented to Sir W. M. Ramsay* (Manchester, 1923), 1 ff.

ATKINSON, K. M. T. (Mrs.), *Ancient Sparta* (Manchester, 1949). Published under the name K. M. T. Chrimes.

—— 'Governors of the Province Asia in the Reign of Augustus', *Hist.* 7 (1958), 300 ff.

—— 'Constitutional and Legal Aspects of the Trials of M. Primus and Varro Murena', *Hist.* 9 (1960), 440 ff.

—— '*Restitutio in Integrum* and *Iussum Augusti Caesaris* in an Inscription at Leyden', *Revue internationale des droits de l'antiquité* 7 (1960), 227 ff.

BADIAN, E., *Foreign Clientelae* (Oxford, 1958).

BALDWIN, B., 'Lucian as a Social Satirist', *CQ* 55 (1961), 199 ff.

BAYNES, N. H., 'The Hellenistic Civilization and East Rome', *Byzantine Studies* (London, 1955), 1 ff.

BIKERMAN, E., *Institutions des Séleucides* (Paris, 1938).

BIRLEY, E. B., 'A Note on the Title *Gemina*', *JRS* 18 (1928), 56 ff.

BLUMENTHAL, F., 'Die Autobiographie des Augustus', *Wiener Studien* 35 (1913), 113 ff.; 36 (1914), 84 ff.

BOWERSOCK, G. W., 'Eurycles of Sparta', *JRS* 51 (1961), 112 ff.

—— 'C. Marcius Censorinus, Legatus Caesaris', *HSCP* 68 (1964), 207 ff.

—— 'Augustus on Aegina', *CQ* n.s. 14 (1964), 120 f.

—— 'A Correction in Strabo', *CR* n.s. 14 (1964), 12 f.

—— '*Anth. Pal.* vii. 638 (Crinagoras)', *Hermes* 92 (1964), 255 f.

—— 'Zur Geschichte des römischen Thessaliens', *Rheinisches Museum* 108 (1965).

BOX, H., 'Roman Citizenship in Laconia', *JRS* 21 (1931), 200 ff.; 22 (1932), 165 ff.

BRANDIS, C. G., 'Ein Schreiben des Triumvir Marcus Antonius an den Landtag Asiens', *Hermes* 32 (1897), 509 ff.

BROUGHTON, T. R. S., 'Roman Landholding in Asia Minor', *TAPA* 65 (1934), 207 ff.

—— 'Some Non-colonial Coloni of Augustus', *TAPA* 66 (1935), 2 ff.

—— Review of Jones, *CERP, AJP* 62 (1941), 104 ff.

—— 'New Evidence on Temple-Estates in Asia Minor', *Studies in Roman Economic and Social History in Honour of A. C. Johnson* (Princeton, 1951), 236 ff.

—— *The Magistrates of the Roman Republic* (New York, 1951–2), 2 vols.

BRUNT, P. A., 'Charges of Provincial Maladministration under the Early Principate', *Hist.* 10 (1961), 189 ff.

BUCHHEIM, H., *Die Orientpolitik des Triumvirn M. Antonius* (Heidelberg, 1960).

BUCKLER, W. H., 'Labour Disputes in the Province of Asia', *Anatolian Studies presented to Sir W. M. Ramsay* (Manchester, 1923), 27 ff.

CALDER, W. M., 'Colonia Caesareia Antiocheia', *JRS* 2 (1912), 79 ff.

CARDASCIA, G., 'L'apparition dans le droit des classes d'honestiores et d'humiliores', *Revue historique de droit français et étranger* 28 (1950), 305 ff., 461 ff.

CHAPOT, V., *La Province romaine proconsulaire d'Asie* (Paris, 1904).

CHARLESWORTH, M. P., 'Some Observations on Ruler Cult', *Harvard Theological Review* 28 (1935), 8 ff.

—— 'The Refusal of Divine Honours', *PBSR* 15 (1939), 1 ff.

CHEESMAN, G. L., 'The Family of the Caristanii at Antioch in Pisidia', *JRS* 3 (1913), 253 ff.

CICHORIUS, C., *Rom und Mytilene* (Leipzig, 1888).

—— *Römische Studien* (Berlin, 1922).

CORMACK, J. M. R., 'High Priests and Macedoniarchs from Beroea', *JRS* 33 (1943), 39 ff.

DAUX, G., *Delphes au IIe et au Ier siècle* (Paris, 1936).

DAY, J., *An Economic History of Athens under Roman Domination* (New York, 1942).

DESSAU, H., 'Reges Thraciae qui fuerint imperante Augusto', *EE* 9 (1913), 696 ff.

DINSMOOR, W. B., *The Archons of Athens in the Hellenistic Age* (Cambridge, Mass., 1931).

—— 'The Temple of Ares at Athens', *Hesp.* 9 (1940), 1 ff.

DOWNEY, G., *A History of Antioch in Syria* (Princeton, 1961).

DUNANT, C., and POUILLOUX, J., *Recherches sur l'histoire et les cultes de Thasos* (Paris, 1957), vol. ii.

EHRENBERG, V., 'Legatus Augusti et Tiberii', *Studies presented to D. M. Robinson* (St. Louis, 1953), 938 ff.

FERGUSON W. S., 'The Oligarchic Revolution at Athens of the Year 103/2 B.C.', *Klio* 4 (1904), 1 ff.

—— *Hellenistic Athens* (London, 1911).

FOUGÈRES, G., *De Lyciorum Communi* (Paris, 1898).

FUCHS, H., *Der geistige Widerstand gegen Rom* (Berlin, 1938).

GABBA, E., 'Storici greci dell'impero romano da Augusto ai Severi', *Rivista storica italiana* 71 (1959), 361 ff.

GARDNER, P., *New Chapters in Greek Art* (Oxford, 1926).

GEER, R. M., 'The Greek Games at Naples', *TAPA* 66 (1935), 208 ff.

GOODFELLOW, C. E., *Roman Citizenship* (Diss. Bryn Mawr, 1935).

GOOLD, G. P., 'A Greek Professorial Circle at Rome', *TAPA* 92 (1961), 168 ff.

GOSSAGE, A. J., 'The Date of *IG* v. 2. 516 (*SIG*³ 800)', *PBSA* 49 (1954), 51 ff.

GRAINDOR, P., *Chronologie des archontes athéniens sous l'empire* (Brussels, 1922).

—— *Athènes sous Auguste* (Cairo, 1927).

—— *Un Milliardaire antique: Hérode Atticus et sa famille* (Cairo, 1930).

GRANT, M., *From Imperium to Auctoritas* (Cambridge, 1946).

—— 'A Capricorn on Hadrian's Coinage', *Emerita* 20 (1952), 1 ff.

GRAY, E. W., Review of Magie, *RRAM*, *JRS* 42 (1952), 121 ff.

—— Review of Buchheim, *Orientpolitik*, *CR*, N.S., 12 (1962), 280 ff.

GREN, E., *Kleinasien und der Ostbalkan in der wirtschaftlichen Entwicklung der römischen Kaiserzeit* (Uppsala, 1941).

GRIMAL, P., 'Auguste et Athénodore', *REA* 47 (1945), 261 ff.; 48 (1946), 62 ff.

GROAG, E., *Die römischen Reichsbeamten von Achaia bis auf Diokletian* (Vienna, 1939).

GRONINGEN VAN, B. A., *Le Gymnasiarque des métropoles de l'Égypte romaine* (Groningen, 1924).

GSELL, S., *Histoire ancienne de l'Afrique du Nord* (Paris, 1928), vol. viii.

HABICHT, C., *Gottmenschentum und griechische Städte* (Munich, 1956).

—— 'Zwei neue Inschriften aus Pergamon', *Istanbuler Mitteilungen* 9/10 (1959/60), 109 ff.

HAHN, L., *Rom und Romanismus im griechisch-römischen Osten* (Leipzig, 1906).

HARDY, E. G., 'Provincial Concilia from Augustus to Diocletian', *Studies in Roman History* [*First Series*] (London, 1910), 235 ff.

HATZFELD, J., *Les Trafiquants italiens dans l'Orient hellénique* (Paris, 1919).

HEPDING, H., 'Mithradates von Pergamon', *Ath. Mitt.* 34 (1909), 329 ff.

—— 'Der Kult der Euergetai', *Klio* 20 (1926), 490 f.

HERZOG, R., 'Nikias und Xenophon von Kos', *Historische Zeitschrift* 125 (1922), 189 ff.

HILL, H., 'Dionysius of Halicarnassus and the Origins of Rome', *JRS* 51 (1961), 88 ff.

HILLSCHER, A., 'Hominum literatorum Graecorum ante Tiberii mortem in urbe Roma commoratorum historia critica', *Jahrb. f. klass. Philol.* Suppl. 18 (1892), 355 ff.

HIRSCHFELD, G., 'Gaius Julius Theopompus', *JHS* 7 (1886), 286 ff.

—— *Die kaiserlichen Verwaltungsbeamten bis auf Diokletian* (Second Edition: Berlin, 1905).

HONIGMANN, E., 'Zu *CIG* 4730', *Hermes* 59 (1924), 477 ff.

JARDÉ, A., 'Un traité entre Cnide et Rome', *Mélanges Cagnat* (Paris, 1912), 51 ff.

JOHN, W., 'Zu den Familienverhältnissen des P. Quinctilius Varus', *Hermes* 86 (1958), 251 ff.

JONES, A. H. M., 'The Urbanisation of the Ituraean Principality', *JRS* 21 (1931), 265 ff.

—— *The Cities of the Eastern Roman Provinces* (Oxford, 1937).

—— *The Greek City* (Oxford, 1940).

—— 'The Proconsulship of Volcacius Tullus', *CR* 69 (1955), 244 ff.

KAHRSTEDT, U., 'Zwei Probleme im kaiserzeitlichen Griechenland: 1. Reliquae civitates in Achaia, 2. Das Koinon der Achaier', *Symbolae Osloenses* 28 (1950), 66 ff.

—— 'Die Territorien von Patrai und Nikopolis in der Kaiserzeit', *Hist.* 1 (1950), 549 ff.

—— *Das wirtschaftliche Gesicht Griechenlands in der Kaiserzeit* (Bern, 1954).

KIP, C., *Thessalische Studien* (Hanover, 1910).

KORNEMANN, E., *Neue Dokumente zum lakonischen Kaiserkult* (Breslau, 1929).

LAMBRECHTS, P., 'Trajan et le recrutement du Sénat', *Ant. Class.* 5 (1936), 105 ff.

LARSEN, J. A. O., *Representative Government in Greek and Roman History* (Berkeley, 1955).

—— 'The Policy of Augustus in Greece', *Acta Classica* (Proc. South African Class. Assoc.) 1 (1958), 123 ff.

LATTE, K., *Römische Religionsgeschichte* (Munich, 1960).

LEVICK, B. M., 'Two Pisidian Colonial Families', *JRS* 48 (1958), 74 ff.

LEWIS, D. M., Review of Thompson, *New Style Coinage*, *CR*, N.S., 12 (1962), 290 ff.

MAGIE, D., 'The Mission of Agrippa to the Orient in 23 B.C.', *CP* 3 (1908), 145 ff.

—— *Roman Rule in Asia Minor* (Princeton, 1950), 2 vols.

MAHAFFY, J. P., *The Greek World under Roman Sway* (London, 1890).

MANSEL, A. MÜFID, 'Fouilles de Sidé et de Pergé', *Anadolu* 2 (1955), 58 ff.

MARIN, D., 'L'opposizione sotto Augusto e la datazione del Saggio sul Sublime', *Studi in onore di A. Calderini e R. Paribeni* (Milan, 1956), i. 157 ff.

McALLISTER, M. H., 'The Temple of Ares at Athens', *Hesp.* 28 (1959), 1 ff.

MEIGGS, R., *Roman Ostia* (Oxford, 1960).

MEYER, P. M., 'Διοίκησις und ἴδιος λόγος', *Festschrift für Hirschfeld* (Berlin, 1903), 157 ff.

MILLAR, F., *A Study of Cassius Dio* (Oxford, 1964).

MOMIGLIANO, A., Review of *CAH* x, *JRS* 34 (1944), 109 ff.

MÜNZER, F., *Römische Adelsparteien und Adelsfamilien* (Stuttgart, 1920).

MUSURILLO, H. A., *The Acts of the Pagan Martyrs* (Oxford, 1954).

NISBET, R. G. M., *Commentary on Cicero's In Pisonem* (Oxford, 1961).

Nock, A. D., 'Soter and Euergetes', *The Joy of Study: Papers presented to F. C. Grant* (New York, 1951), 127 ff.

O'Brien-Moore, A., 'M. Tullius Cratippus, Priest of Rome', *Yale Classical Studies* 8 (1942), 25 ff.

Oliver, J. H., 'On the Ephesian Debtor Law of 85 b.c.', *AJP* 60 (1939), 468 ff.

—— 'Two Athenian Poets', *Hesp.* Suppl. 8 (1949), 243 ff.

—— *The Ruling Power: A Study of the Roman Empire in the Second Century after Christ through the Roman Oration of Aelius Aristides* (Philadelphia, 1953).

—— 'Gerousiae and Augustales', *Hist.* 7 (1958), 472 ff.

Pais, E., 'The Time and Place in which Strabo composed his Historical Geography', *Ancient Italy* (Chicago, 1908), 379 ff.

Palm, J., *Rom, Römertum und Imperium in der griechischen Literatur der Kaiserzeit* (Lund, 1959).

Peter, H., *Die geschichtliche Literatur über die römische Kaiserzeit* (Leipzig, 1897), 2 vols.

Pflaum, H. G., 'La chronologie de la carrière de M. Pompeius Macrinus Theophanes', *Germania* 37 (1959), 150 ff.

Pippidi, D. M., 'Das Datum des Ehrendekrets für Aristagoras', *Epigraphische Beiträge zur Geschichte Histrias* (1962) 89 ff.

Ramsay, W. M., 'Pisidian Antioch', *JRS* 6 (1916), 83 ff.

—— 'Studies in the Roman Province Galatia', *JRS* 12 (1922), 176 ff.

Raubitschek, A. E., 'Sylleia', *Studies in Roman Economic and Social History in Honour of A. C. Johnson* (Princeton, 1951), 49 ff.

—— 'Two Notes on the Fasti of Achaia', *Studies presented to D. M. Robinson* (St. Louis, 1953), 330 ff.

—— 'The New Homer', *Hesp.* 23 (1954), 317 ff.

—— 'Epigraphical Notes on Julius Caesar', *JRS* 44 (1954), 65 ff.

Raubitschek, A. E., and Jeffery, L. H., *Dedications from the Athenian Acropolis* (Cambridge, Mass., 1949).

Richards, G. C., 'The Authorship of the Περὶ "Υψους', *CQ* 32 (1938), 133 ff.

Robert, L., 'Rapport sommaire sur un second voyage en Carie', *Rev. Arch.* 6 (1935), 152 ff.

—— *Études anatoliennes* (Paris, 1937).

—— 'ΠΕΤΡΑΙΟΣ, Onomastique et Géographie', *Hellenica* 1 (1940), 121 ff.

—— 'La bibliothèque de Nysa de Carie', *Hellenica* 1 (1940), 144 ff.

—— 'Le culte de Caligula à Milet et la province d'Asie', *Hellenica* 7 (1949), 206 ff.

—— 'Épigraphie et antiquités grecques', *L'Annuaire du Collège de France* 61 (1961/2), 309 ff.

Roberts, W. R., 'The Literary Circle of Dionysius of Halicarnassus', *CR* 14 (1900), 439 ff.

—— *Dionysius of Halicarnassus: Three Literary Letters* (Cambridge, 1901).

Robinson, E. S. G., 'British Museum Acquisitions 1933-4', *Numismatic Chronicle* 16 (1936), 169 ff.

ROMANELLI, P., *La Cirenaïca Romana* (Verbania, 1943).

ROSTOVTZEFF, M., 'Augustus und Athen', *Festschrift für Hirschfeld* (Berlin, 1903), 303 ff.

—— 'Caesar and the South of Russia', *JRS* 7 (1917), 27 ff.

—— *The Social and Economic History of the Hellenistic World* (Oxford, 1941), 3 vols.

—— *The Social and Economic History of the Roman Empire*, Second Edition, ed. P. M. Fraser (Oxford, 1957), 2 vols.

SCHMITTHENNER, W., 'Augustus' spanischer Feldzug und der Kampf um den Prinzipat', *Hist.* 11 (1962), 29 ff.

SCHULTEN, A., *Los cántabros y astures y su guerra con Roma* (Madrid, 1943).

SEALEY, R., 'The Political Attachments of L. Aelius Sejanus', *Phoenix* 15 (1961), 97 ff.

SEGRÈ, M., 'Giulio Cesare e la χώρα pergamena', *Athenaeum* 16 (1938), 119 ff.

SHEAR, J. P., 'Athenian Imperial Coinage', *Hesp.* 5 (1936), 285 ff.

SHERK, R. K., *The Legates of Galatia from Augustus to Diocletian* (Baltimore, 1951).

—— 'Caesar and Mytilene', *Greek, Roman, and Byzantine Studies* 4 (1963), 146 ff.

SHERWIN-WHITE, A. N., *The Roman Citizenship* (Oxford, 1939).

—— *Roman Society and Roman Law in the New Testament* (Oxford, 1963).

STEIN, A., 'Zur sozialen Stellung der provinzialen Oberpriester', *Epitymbion Heinrich Swoboda dargebracht* (Reichenberg, 1927), 300 ff.

SYME, R., 'Galatia and Pamphylia under Augustus', *Klio* 27 (1934), 122 ff.

—— 'The Spanish War of Augustus', *AJP* 55 (1934), 293 ff.

—— 'Pamphylia from Augustus to Vespasian', *Klio* 30 (1937), 227 ff.

—— 'Observations on the Province of Cilicia', *Anatolian Studies presented to W. H. Buckler* (Manchester, 1939), 299 ff.

—— *The Roman Revolution* (Oxford, 1939).

—— Review of Gordon, *Potitus Valerius Messalla*, *JRS* 45 (1955), 155 ff.

—— Review of Broughton, *MRR*, *CP* 50 (1955), 127 ff.

—— *Tacitus* (Oxford, 1958), 2 vols.

—— 'Livy and Augustus', *HSCP* 64 (1959), 27 ff.

—— 'Piso Frugi and Crassus Frugi', *JRS* 50 (1960), 12 ff.

—— 'Who was Vedius Pollio?' *JRS* 51 (1961), 23 ff.

—— 'Missing Persons III', *Hist.* 11 (1962), 146 ff.

—— 'The Greeks under Roman Rule', *Proc. Massachusetts Historical Society* 72 (1963), 1 ff.

TAYLOR, L. R., *The Divinity of the Roman Emperor* (Connecticut, 1931).

—— 'M. Titius and the Syrian Command', *JRS* 26 (1936), 161 ff.

TCHERIKOVER, V. A., Introduction to the *Corpus Papyrorum Judaicarum* (Cambridge, Mass., 1957), vol. i.

THIELING, W., *Der Hellenismus in Kleinafrika* (Leipzig, 1911).

THOMPSON, H. A., 'The Odeion in the Athenian Agora', *Hesp.* 19 (1950), 31 ff.

THOMPSON, M., *The New Style Silver Coinage of Athens* (New York, 1961), 2 vols.

TOYNBEE, J. M. C., *Some Notes on Artists in the Roman World*, Collection Latomus 6 (Brussels, 1951).

TREVES, P., *Il mito di Alessandro e la Roma d'Augusto* (Milan–Naples, 1953).

VANDERPOOL, E., 'An Athenian Monument to Theodorus of Gadara', *AJP* 80 (1959), 366 ff.

VITTINGHOFF, F., *Römische Kolonisation und Bürgerrechtspolitik unter Caesar und Augustus* (Mainz, 1952).

WACHOLDER, B. Z., *Nicolaus of Damascus* (Berkeley, 1962).

WADDY, L., 'Did Strabo Visit Athens?' *AJA* 67 (1963), 296 ff.

WALTON, C. S., 'Oriental Senators in the Service of Rome', *JRS* 19 (1929), 38 ff.

WILCKEN, U., 'Zur Entstehung des hellenistischen Königskultes', *Sitzungsberichte der preussischen Akademie*, Phil.-hist. Klasse 28 (1938), 298 ff.

WILHELM, A., 'Proxenie und Euergesie', *Attische Urkunden* 5 (1942), 11 ff.

UNPUBLISHED

LEVICK, B. M., 'Roman Colonies in Southern Asia Minor, with special reference to Antioch-towards-Pisidia' (Oxford Univ. D.Phil. thesis, 1958).

MANN, J. C., 'The Settlement of Veterans in the Roman Empire' (London Univ. Ph.D. thesis, 1956).

WILSON, D. R., 'A Historical Geography of Bithynia, Paphlagonia, and Pontus' (Oxford Univ. B.Litt. thesis, 1960).

INDEX

THE following index covers the material in the text and notes, but not in the appendixes. However, the contents of those are clear from their titles, and cross-references in the notes will guide the reader to whatever may be relevant there.